To Shelby

Deny Geurink

3/21/14

LAND OF THE BEAR

SIBERIAN CAMPFIRES

by
Denny Geurink

Œ

Strategic Book Publishing and Rights Co.

Strategic Book Publishing and Rights Co.
12620 FM 1960, Suite A4-507
Houston TX 77065
www.sbpra.com

ISBN: 978-1-62857-888-1

Design: Dedicated Book Services (www.netdbs.com)

Illustrator: A. N. Hitarman

DEDICATION

This book is dedicated to all the men and women who were brave enough to accompany me on my journeys to the far ends of Russia over the past two decades. It's their spirit of adventure and penchant for exploration that made these trips—and, in turn—this book possible. It is also dedicated to the hardworking outfitters, guides, interpreters, and cooks who helped make our wilderness camps warm and comfortable in many inhospitable places.

CONTENTS

ACKNOWLEDGEMENTS

Putting together a book like this is an enormous project and takes the help of many people to make it happen. First, I'd like to thank my friend and outfitter, Dmitri Sikorski, who assisted me with a lot of the historical data about the former Soviet Union, and later Russia, which appears in this book. Dmitri also contributed a number of great photos and added his recollections and perspective from those early years in Russia.

I want to thank Bob Coker for allowing me to use the story he wrote about the harrowing trip he took to Russia on his own back in 1996. It reveals what can sometimes happen if you deal directly with the Russians.

I also want to thank Tom Huggler, Tom Thompson, Noel Hilty, and my wife Connie for sharing their stories with me and letting me use them in this book.

I'm grateful to all the hunters who provided me with photos from their trips like Jim McDivitt, Terry Geurink, David Moore, Ken Horm, Michael Silin, Michael Shutt and . . . . others.

I want to thank Connie for all her help with typing, editing, and research. Also to my daughter Kelli for her help in editing.

And, most of all, I'd like to thank the many hunters, friends, and family who encouraged me to write this book. Every time I told them a story about what happened on a trip they would say: *"You've got to be kidding me! That's incredible! Denny, you need to write a book!"* So I did. Here it is. Hope you enjoy it.

FOREWARD

ONE OF THE FEW things I remember about the Soviet Union from my childhood days is Nikita Khrushchev pounding his shoe on the table at a United Nations General Assembly meeting back in 1960. I don't remember exactly why he was beating the table, but I do remember the former Soviet leader as being a real charmer. He's the same guy who told the world that his country would bury ours! Not exactly an open invitation to Americans to stop by for a visit. Throw in the fear of Russia generated on our side of the pond when President Reagan referred to the Soviet Union as the "Evil Empire" and you can imagine my reaction to an invitation I received in August of 1991 to come over and do a story featuring an exploratory safari to the Land of the Bear.

So began one of the most exciting chapters in my life. This country boy from Allendale, Michigan, was about to have his world changed forever! That pioneering visit took place between the coup and the collapse. It was still the Soviet Union when we arrived in Moscow back in 1991 and I was one of the first Americans to get up-close-and-personal with this vast, secretive country. This was a mysterious land that Americans had only heard scary stories about; a nation and a people who were deemed to be our mortal enemies. About all we knew of the Soviet Union at that time is that it was a forbidden land located in the frozen north.

During the ensuing years since that first historic trip, I've had a chance to explore new lands, learn new customs and traditions, and study a culture very few people knew anything about. Along the way I've had the opportunity to meet many wonderful people, including a number of dignitaries such as the President of Kalmykia, the Vice President of Crimea, the ministers of various conservation and forestry departments, and even a colonel in the Russian army.

I've also had the opportunity to meet everyday people from all walks of life such as guides, cooks, hotel clerks, taxi drivers, teachers, professors, outfitters, and interpreters. And I've had the great privilege of sharing many a wilderness campfire with the Eveny people, an Inuit-like population inhabiting the vast wild regions of Siberia.

I learned a lot about what the Soviet Union was like before the collapse from my new Russian friends. I'll never forget when one of them told me that his wife would get up at 6 A.M. to stand in line at the store, which opened at 8 A.M., to buy bread. We heard a lot about the bread shortages in the Soviet Union back then but this put it in perspective.

Over the past 22 years, I have also had the opportunity to share a campfire with many wonderful people from the United States and Canada as well. Among them, some very prominent people such as Apollo 9 astronaut Jim McDivitt and his friend Earl O'Loughlin, a four-star Air Force general who flew spy plane missions over the Soviet Union during the Cold War. Jim and Earl had so much fun that they took two trips with me.

After returning from my 1991 journey, I wrote a number of stories for various newspapers and magazines, including *Field & Stream*. Many of my friends and colleagues from all around the country interviewed me for stories they wanted to write for their newspapers and magazines. As far as we knew at that time, I was the first outdoor writer ever invited to the Soviet Union. Because of this there was a lot of interest in what I did, what I thought, and how easy—or difficult—the trip was, etc. It was a special time in history. The world as we knew it was changing forever. Even the Berlin Wall came tumbling down!

Stories of my historical trip were highlighted all over the United States by my colleagues in articles written for the *Denver Post*, the *Chicago Tribune*, the *Detroit News*, the *Cleveland Plains Dealer*, the *Grand Rapids Press*, etc. Those many stories spawned a huge interest in Russia; so much interest that my phone began ringing off the hook! I

x   Denny Geurink

received over 400 calls in one week! My wife finally took the phone off the hook so we could get some sleep.

"Denny, if you ever go back, I'd love to go with you," was what I often heard. I did want to go back because I thoroughly enjoyed myself and genuinely liked the Russian people. Well, after a few more trips, and with the interest still growing, I decided that maybe there might be some money to be made from this burgeoning desire to visit Russia. I contacted the outfitter who set up my original trip, Dmitri Sikorski, and asked him if he wanted to get into the tourism business. The rest, as they say, is history. I started a company called Denny Geurink's Outdoor Adventures and began taking people to Russia on a regular basis.

During the past 22 years, I have made over 50 trips to Russia. I've taken hundreds of clients with me, many of them more than once. (One has been there nine times!) Most of these trips have been over a month long; some have been almost three months long. (For me, not my clients; I stayed in Russia while my clients shuttled in and out.) That means I've spent an awful lot of time in small trapper's cabins and tents in the middle of Siberia, miles away from civilization, showers, electricity, and flush toilets.

This book is about these many journeys to the Land of the Bear. It's not a book just about hunting or fishing; it's as much about the people, the food, the land, the impressions, the adventure, and the excitement of trekking through the Siberian wilderness. Many of the stories were written shortly after they happened so they give you my impressions of what was going on at that particular time in history.

A number of stories were written with the help of friends and clients who give you an insight into what their impressions were when they visited this wild land. And some of the stories in this book come from the Russian people themselves. They reveal the harsh reality of living in this vast wilderness region called Siberia. One of the most touching is about a teenage girl who calls her mother on a cell phone to say good bye even as she is being killed and eaten by a bear.

So pull up a log and snuggle in close to the warmth of a Siberian campfire. And, as one of my Eveny guides once told me: "Listen to what the flames tell you about the great adventures that lurk in the wilderness all around you!"

CHAPTER 1

JOURNEY TO THE EVIL EMPIRE

WHAT'S THE WILDEST, MOST outrageous type of adventure you can imagine? I mean really wild! Can you top "road hunting" from a Russian army tank in Siberia? How about stalking red stag with the KGB on a Soviet naval base just a few miles from where Gorbachev was placed under house arrest a few months earlier? How about sharing vodka toasts with the Vice President of Crimea? Give up? Well, that's what I did just a few months ago. No fooling! If you have trouble believing it . . . just think how I felt while it was happening!

It all started in August, 1991 with a call from Bob Knoop, a booking agent out of Dearborn, Michigan. He wanted to know if I was interested in joining him and a few other guys on a trip in September to the Soviet Union to do some big game hunting. At first I thought he was pulling my leg. "Sure. And then you can come along with me on an exploratory trip to the moon in October," I said, chuckling.

"No, I'm serious," Knoop said.

"You're not pulling my leg?" I replied. "A hunting trip to the Soviet Union?"

"Yes," Knoop answered. He sounded serious. "Are you interested?"

Does Mike Tyson like beauty pageants!

Upon further questioning, I found out that Knoop was working with the Russians to set up this trip via a company called CMI International, Incorporated. The folks at CMI had been collaborating with the Russian government on some mining project when the subject of big game hunting came up. Seems the Russians were interested in getting into the tourism business. It was the era of Glasnost and Perestroika, and Gorbachev was reaching out to the outside world. They wanted to set up an exploratory big game hunt and have an American writer come over for a visit, to show him what they had to offer.

Knoop had been reading my stuff at *Field & Stream,* where I was working as a regional editor, and thought I'd be a good fit; thus the call. The clincher for me was when Knoop said the trip wasn't going to cost me anything! They were going to give me the trip for free in hopes of generating some publicity for this new hunting frontier. Free is right in my price range!

Preparations for the big trip were running along smoothly until August 19, 1991 when my wife came into the bedroom at 7 A.M. and said: "Denny, you better get up and turn on the TV. I just heard on the radio that there was a coup in Russia."

"A COUP!" I groaned, vaulting from the bed. "I get a chance to go to Russia and they decide to have a coup! You've got to be kidding me!"

Unfortunately she wasn't kidding. The early news reports were saying that Gorbachev was "too ill" to continue in his post as president of the Soviet Union. A group of new leaders was taking over.

It wasn't long before the real truth came out. The Communist Party hierarchy didn't like the direction Gorbachev was taking the country. All this talk of Glasnost and Perestroika . . . and exploratory hunting trips . . . wasn't sitting well with them. In reality, Gorbachev had been placed under house arrest in a resort area near the Black Sea. As it turns out, he wasn't ill at all. But I was!

Ironically, when we inquired about the status of our trip, we were told we were still welcome, despite the change in power. But we weren't feeling all that welcome anymore. We certainly didn't want to jump into the middle of some sort of political crisis. If Mr. Glasnost wasn't going to be around, we weren't interested.

Needless to say, we felt a whole lot better about the situation several days later when the coup flopped. The hunt was back on! Unfortunately, all the instability knocked our departure date back to September 27. This would mean that the brown bears we had hoped to hunt might already be denned up by the time we got to camp sometime in October. And the wild boar would be more difficult to hunt with all the crops out of the fields but we would still have moose, red stag, roe deer, and plenty of birds to chase. Plus, plans allowed for a day in Moscow and Leningrad (now St. Petersburg). That was good enough for me. Let's go!

The big day finally arrived. After a short connecting flight from Grand Rapids, Michigan, to New York, we found ourselves aboard a giant 747 heading for Moscow. It was my first trip overseas. We were about half way across the Atlantic before reality began to sink in. I was on my way to Russia! Holy cow!

Making the trip with me, along with Knoop, were Ed Stone, a booking agent from Grand Rapids, Michigan, and Terry Geurink, a cousin from Wyoming, Michigan. I had worked out an arrangement with CMI to get Terry along on this trip so he could help me out with taking photos and video to document this historic trip.

We met Phil Belsito, a vice president with CMI, at the airport in New York and on board we met, John Hodge, Executive Vice President at CMI and Lance Parker, a client with CMI. Needless to say, everyone was pumped. We chattered excitedly all the way across the big pond.

What had started out as a hunting expedition in the U.S. quickly turned into an outright adventure the minute the wheels of Pan Am Flight 30 hit the runway in Moscow. It took a minute for reality to sink in as we taxied down the pockmarked runway to the terminal. We were surprised by how dark and dreary the terminal looked compared to the airport terminals in the United States. Not much lighting, no little shops and eateries, and the interior of the terminal reminded me of the inside of a storage shed.

We arrived in Moscow at 9:30 A.M. on Saturday, the 28th. We were met at the airport by Dmitri Sikorski, a CMI contact in Russia, a tall young man in his late twenties. I was surprised by how well he spoke English. A lot of people who learn English as a second language have quite an accent but he had very little. And he spoke American English, not British-sounding English, as most of our interpreters later on did. And even more amazing was the fact he had pretty much learned the language on his own and not in some formal program at a school or university. Dmitri said he would be our interpreter and tour guide for the next two weeks. He had made all the arrangements for our in-country travel, hotels, and stays at the hunting camps.

One thing I found out right away is that Dmitri is from the Ukraine. "I'm not a Russian," Dmitri corrected me when I introduced him to the rest of the gang. "I'm Ukrainian."

It's a distinction that people from the Ukraine and other Soviet Bloc countries repeatedly pointed out to me on this trip. If they were from a Soviet Bloc country like Romania, Czechoslovakia, or the Ukraine, and not from Russia, they didn't want to be called Russians. In fact, they even seemed a little offended by it. I asked Dmitri why the big fuss: "After all, in the U.S. we are all from different states but we still refer to ourselves as Americans. Why do people from the different countries who joined the Soviet Union not want to be called Russians?"

"Denny, there's a big difference in the way the states in America joined the union and the way the states of the Soviet Union joined," Dmitri pointed out. "In the U.S., the states all petitioned to become part of the union. We didn't petition to become part of the Soviet Union, we were annexed!"

Yes, I guess you could say that is a big difference! Just one of the many things I learned about the former Soviet Union and Russia on this trip.

After retrieving our baggage, we headed for the customs booth. Let me back up just a bit . . . Before leaving for Russia, I had asked Belsito if there was anything special I should take along on the trip to make things easier and more comfortable. I was told to take some toilet paper and a carton of Marlboro cigarettes.

"Toilet paper and cigarettes?" I asked in disbelief. "Why?"

"The toilet paper over there is like recycled sandpaper," Belsito told me. "You might want to take your own. And, as far as the cigarettes go, all the Russians smoke. They love our Marlboros but they can't buy Marlboros over the counter in Russia; only on the black market, where they are very expensive. Their cigarettes are really bad. A pack of Marlboros will grease a lot of wheels in Russia."

He was spot on. After retrieving our baggage and hooking up with Dmitri, we got in line to go through customs. While in line I overheard the customs agent ask the guy in front of me—somebody from England or Germany or something— if he had any cigarettes. He said he didn't. The customs agent took his passport, visa, and customs declaration and scrutinized them very thoroughly. He asked a lot of questions in broken English and scribbled and checked and putzed for five minutes before finally clearing the guy. By the time I shuffled up to the window, I had already fished a pack of Marlboros from my carry-on bag. I could see what was going on here.

"Do you have any cigarettes?" he asked me in broken English as I stepped up to the booth.

"Yes I do," I said with a big smile on my face, handing him a fresh, crisp pack of Marlboros. He took the cigarettes, stashed them in a corner of the booth, and promptly stamped all my papers and handed them back to me. Then he said with a big, wide grin: "Welcome to Russia!"

Belsito was right! A pack of Marlboros will grease a lot of wheels in Russia! Cigarettes in hand, we hustled through customs and headed for a big van Dmitri had waiting for us outside the terminal. The ride through downtown Moscow to the hotel was a real shocker. It was like traveling through a time warp! The buildings were all at least 100 years old, run-down, and dirty. This city was in bad shape and in dire need of a face lift.

The hotel was old and run-down as well. Everything was so dull, dreary, and colorless and the check-in process was long and tedious. The clerks in the hotel spoke no English so everything had to be translated through Dmitri. It was obvious an American on his own here would quickly get lost in the shuffle.

After finally checking into a hotel room and grabbing a bite to eat (grabbing a bite to eat was an adventure in itself and will be detailed in a later chapter), we flagged down a cab and headed to Red Square.

A visit to this iconic Russian landmark was high on everyone's priority list. Unlike the rest of the city, Red Square is very ornate and steeped in tradition. It was by far the most colorful place we visited in Moscow. Never thought I'd be walking around in Red Square! I remember seeing it on TV as a kid, with all its pomp and pageantry during the country's May Day celebrations. Long lines of soldiers, tanks, anti-aircraft missiles, and other military hardware passing in front of Khrushchev as he briskly saluted them. Wow! I was standing right where the missiles went through!

There was a large crowd of people in the square. There were also a lot of policemen and army personnel, a definite holdover from the recent coup. There were even a couple of tanks and several wreaths of flowers on the corners where people had been killed during the demonstrations against the communist-led coup. We were standing right in the middle of a titanic chapter in history! It sent a cold chill up my spine.

We also ran across quite a few panhandlers, who were trying to sell us everything from Soviet military watches and uniforms to "Gorby" dolls. We soon discovered that the American dollar is highly coveted. We were offered 35 rubles for one dollar – black market price. One of the highlights of the visit to Red Square was watching the changing of the guard in front of Lenin's tomb.

Tour over, we caught a flight out of Moscow to a place called Sverdlovsk in western Siberia the next morning. This flight turned out to be an adventure in itself. First of all, the airplane we flew on wasn't exactly the latest model, hot off the Aeroflot assembly line. The tires on the plane were showing a lot of wear and tear. I don't know how many plies an airplane tire is supposed to have, but at least two were showing! This made us all a little nervous.

Our travels through the Soviet Union were done on very old small prop planes with bald tires. (Denny Geurink photo)

We noticed that the flight attendants were very curt and cold. Not a lot of smiling and "how can we make your flight more comfortable" attitude. And when the plane touched down at the Koltsovo airport, and all the Russians began clapping their hands, we wondered if this meant we were lucky to have made it! Looking out the windows of the plane and seeing close to a dozen wrecked airplanes bulldozed off the runway didn't do anything to allay this suspicion.

Later we learned that the Russians and, as it turns out, the people in a lot of other European countries, like to give the flight crew a round of applause upon landing to thank them for a good trip. It's a custom we are not familiar with in America.

When we asked about all the wrecked airplanes lining the runway, we were told that when a flight comes into this part of Siberia, they sometimes run into bad weather, with big snow drifts and ice on the runway. Because the airport is in such an isolated part of the world, there is nowhere else to divert the flight to so they just land and hit the snowdrifts or skid off the runway. If the repairs are more than the plane is worth, they simply bulldoze them to the side and use them for spare parts. When we tried to take pictures of the wrecked planes, we were told to put our cameras away.

I'm beginning to think that all the clapping wasn't just a thank you to the flight crew!

Dmitri told us that Sverdlovsk is the unofficial capital of Siberia, which starts east of the Ural Mountains. This is where Boris Yeltsin got his start as a big shot in the Communist Party. Yeltsin was the communist boss of the Sverdlovsk region until 1985. This place was hard-core pro-Soviet so it is very ironical that Yeltsin would be the guy to lead the resistance movement against the communist coup just a few weeks earlier in Moscow.

Dmitri also told us that President Franklin D. Roosevelt had reportedly stopped here on his way back from the Tehran Conference in 1943, where he met with Churchill and Stalin to discuss the reconstruction of post-war Europe. We were once again smack dab in the middle of an area of historical significance! It was a fact that wasn't lost on any of us.

After deplaning and gathering our gear, we jumped into a couple of waiting army "jeeps" and took a long, bumpy ride through the forest to camp. We were amazed to see that most of the people out here were still living in log cabins! It's like we had stumbled onto a set of the *Little House on the Prairie* TV show. I was expecting to see Laura Ingles Wilder walking around in front of one of these log homes at any time. It was like a step back in time.

We arrived at our hunting lodge late that night and fell exhausted into bed. The following morning, after a hearty breakfast of bear meat and noodles, the guides told us to load up and get ready to go out hunting.

They didn't have to tell us twice. We were pumped and ready for the hunt to begin. We grabbed our gear and headed outside to where the jeeps we had traveled to camp in the previous evening were parked. As I opened the door to one of the jeeps to climb in, Dmitri said: "No. No. Over there. Over there. Load up over there." He was pointing to an old, stripped down, army personnel carrier parked out in front of the lodge.

"That?" I asked with a puzzled look. "We're going out hunting in that thing? You've got to be kidding me!"

"Yes, that thing," Dmitri said, chuckling.

"Must be they are going to take us out in the tank and drop us off somewhere," I thought to myself as we climbed aboard. But I soon found out that wasn't the plan at all.

"They taking us out to the hunting area in this thing?" I asked Dmitri as the tank rumbled out of the yard.

"No, you are going to hunt from the tank." Dmitri grinned. "What do you think of that?"

Hunt from a tank! No way! That's when it struck home! We were going to head out into the woods to do some "road hunting" Russian style! Holy crap! "Hunt what?" I queried, still a bit in shock.

"If something runs across the trail, shoot it!" Dmitri explained.

"Whoa! You're kidding me?" I shot back in total disbelief. "So you're saying the deal is . . . if it's brown, it's down and if it flies, it dies!"

"Yes! Real Russian hunting!" Dmitri chuckled.

"I sure hope they don't have skunks and possums around here," I mumbled to myself as we rumbled out of the yard and into the woods. "Cause I know whatever we shoot, we're going to eat! And what about road kill? Ahhhgg!"

"I can't believe I am actually riding a Russian tank!" I shouted to Terry over the roar of the engine as we clunked through the forest. "I figured the only time I'd ever see one of these things was in some rice paddy in Vietnam – looking up the barrel!"

Road Hunting Russian style! Photo of the "tank" the Russians wanted Denny and crew to hunt with. (Denny Geurink photo)

We soon found out why the tank was used . . . the roads were not negotiable by truck or jeep. They were full of ruts and extremely muddy. Heck, we even got the tank stuck a couple of times! The tank ride actually proved to be quite a thrill. Everybody should try it – once! It makes the Demon Drop at Cedar Point look like a kiddy car ride! Going 25-30 miles an hour down muddy trails and through the woods knocking down trees and careening off old stumps was quite an experience. We hung on for dear life!

Needless to say, we didn't shoot anything from the tank. It made so much noise roaring through the woods like an angry dragon that it scared everything away for miles around, long before we got to it. I think the Russians were just taking us on a joy ride, to see the countryside on our first day in camp. And, just maybe, to see if they could scare us a little! I do have to admit, it was exciting and I will never forget it. Heck, I'm writing about it now!

That evening, Boris Shiryaiev, one of our guides, asked me if I wanted to hunt moose. I explained to him, through Dmitri, that while I enjoyed the tank ride a bit earlier, being an editor for a large outdoor magazine, I'd have a hard time selling a hunting story which involved shooting game from the front of a tank! Could we hunt them on foot? No problem, says Boris.

An hour later, we left the lodge on foot. Dmitri, however, stayed behind. "This ought to be interesting!" I thought as we headed for the woods. "No interpreter! I don't speak any Russian and Boris doesn't know any English. Now we're talking adventure!" It turned out to be one of the most exciting hunts I've ever been on.

As soon as we hit the woods, we came across a fresh set of tracks. Boris studied the tracks for a few seconds then stood up and started into what looked like a game of charades. He spread his arms out wide over his head and shook his head, "No". He then cupped his hands over his chest and nodded his head, "Yes". After doing this a second time, a big smile crept across my face. He was telling me this moose was not a bull. It had no rack. It was a cow. It had, well . . . it was a cow. I nodded my head, "Yes". I understood.

About 10 minutes later, we came across another set of fresh tracks. This time Boris put his arms up and spread them wide, nodding his head, "Yes". This was a bull. I figured these might be a bull's tracks, as they were quite a bit larger than the first set. Boris jumped on the tracks like a beagle on a bunny trail.

After following the trail for several hundred yards, Boris got down on one knee and pointed to the tracks. He showed me how they were spaced farther apart now and there was mud kicked up in front of the toes. He then pointed to his nose to let me know the bull had winded us. He pumped his hands up and down quickly to show me that the bull was running. This was cool! It was amazing how well we were able to communicate just using hand signals.

After following the tracks for several hundred more yards, Boris stopped to show me how the tracks were now closer together again. He pumped his hands up and down slowly. The bull was walking again. He then pointed to some willow leaves, which had just been nibbled on. The bull wasn't spooked anymore and was feeding. I understood everything he was showing me. We were in sync.

Then, suddenly, Boris grabbed my arm, brought one finger up to his lips, and signaled for me to walk very quietly. The moose was close. We moved along the trail very slowly. Boris froze and motioned for me to get my rifle ready. He then motioned that the bull was right around the next bend in the trail. I had no idea how he knew this but, by now, I believed everything he was telling me via his hand signals. I brought my rifle up as we eased around the bend.

Sure enough, there in the woods about 75 yards away, stood a large bull moose. I eased my rifle to my shoulder and squeezed the trigger. A solid "whump" told me that the bullet had found its mark. The moose ran off into the brush.

Boris turned and looked at me with a questioning look on his face and shrugged his shoulders. He was asking me if I thought I had made a good shot. I took my right fist and smacked it into my left hand and nodded my head, "Yes", I had made a good shot. Boris grinned from ear to ear and we went to look for the bull. We found him piled up in the brush less than 100 years away. After a round of back slapping and hugging, we went to work field-dressing the bull. Day one and I had my moose. What a great hunt!

It wasn't a record book bull by any stretch of the imagination but it was a trophy to me. A Russian moose! Besides, I sensed that if I hadn't shot this bull, Boris would have shot me. The Siberian winters are long and cold and a moose in the freezer gives these people a warm, fuzzy feeling. They live on what they harvest, as was evidenced by our every meal. We ate bear, moose, rabbits, fish, game birds, and some "mystery" meat during our entire stay.

The next morning we found out that there was only one moose tag in camp. This was a major oversight, buying just one license at a time. The guys from CMI explained to the Russians that there must be one tag in camp for each hunter. We were promised more tags the following morning. Unfortunately, the tags didn't make it to camp until Thursday, our last day in Siberia. Too late for us to shoot another moose.

While waiting for the moose tags to arrive, we spent our time hunting birds and bear. There were a few fresh bear tracks around but we soon realized that most of the bruins were denned up for the winter. As we had feared, because of the coup we had missed the best time for bear.

"You come back next year in August and you will get a bear," Boris told us. "I guarantee it 100 percent! And moose, too!"

Sure hope I get a chance to check out that guarantee someday.

The birds we hunted were called wood grouse or capercaillie. They were odd-looking critters. The males were about the size of a big chicken. They have heads like a duck, a feathery beard under their chin, sharp beaks and claws like a hawk, bluish-green metallic-like feathers, and they fan their tails like a turkey gobbler. They looked like something a taxidermist might concoct after an all-nighter at the Dead Reindeer Saloon! The females resembled a North American sharp-tail grouse. They sure make an odd couple.

We later learned that the capercaillie is a much sought-after species of grouse by European hunters. They are the largest species of grouse in the world and are very rare, even close to extinction in some countries. They were, however, everywhere in this part of Siberia. We shot and ate them for lunch!

Late one afternoon, as we were lounging around in the cabin, I looked out the window and saw a big black Mercedes pull into the driveway. Three men in suits and ties stepped out and walked towards the house. It was obvious one of the guys was pretty important and the other two were probably body guards

"Who are these guys?" I asked Dmitri.

"It's the head of the Department of Hunting for this part of Siberia, and a couple of his associates," Dmitri replied. "They are here to greet you and welcome you to this region.

You are the first Americans to ever hunt in this area and they want to meet you."

"Wow! I wish we had known they were coming, we could have dressed up a little," I said. "They're all dressed up in suits and ties and we are sitting here in T-shirts and three days' worth of whiskers. I'm a little embarrassed!"

"Oh, don't worry about it, Denny. They know you guys are out here hunting and not at a birthday party," Dmitri replied.

As we gathered around the dinner table a few minutes later, the head of the hunting department, whose name was Anatoli Kiselev, welcomed us and made several vodka toasts to celebrate the occasion. This was our first introduction to Russia's national drink. (More on this ceremonial Russian custom a bit later.)

After a toast welcoming us to this part of Siberia, and another to our health, and a third toast wishing us a good hunt, an awkward silence filled the room as Kiselov looked at all of us whimsically. Dmitri then leaned over to me and whispered: "Denny, they are waiting for one of you guys to make a toast. It's Russian tradition. The host makes a toast or two then the guest must make a toast."

"What kind of toast should I make?" I whispered.

"It doesn't really matter," Dmitri whispered back. "Just make something up."

Talk about being put on a spot. I wished I had known they were coming . . . and that I had to make a toast to the chief of the Hunting Department of Sverdlovsk! Not some intern or political science student, but the freaking head of the hunting department for the entire region. Holy cow! Wish I had more time to think about it. This was a pretty important part in the history of Russian/American detente as I saw it. We were the first Americans they had ever seen. I'm sure they had heard a lot about us and probably most of it bad. I didn't want to confirm this with an improper or stupid toast.

After thinking about it for a minute . . . that's all the time I had as the silence that was starting to creep over the room was deafening . . . I stood up and gave it my best shot.

"I'd like to propose a toast!" I announced, mustering all the courage I could. "I want to thank Mr. Kiselev for coming here to greet us tonight. This is a proud and momentous occasion. We are proud to be the first Americans in this area. We have really enjoyed our stay. You have made us feel very welcome. Your hospitality is much appreciated. All the Russian people we have met have been very kind and helpful. On this trip we have found out that Russians and Americans are really not all that different. We are a lot alike. Especially those of us who love the outdoors and like to hunt. We share a kindred spirit."

Everyone stood, touched shot glasses together, and chugged the poison, er, ah, vodka. Kiselev looked very pleased, as did my comrades. "Good toast, Denny," they complimented me. "Good toast."

Anatoli Kiselev, Head of the Sverdlovsk Regional Hunting Department, presents Denny with Capracallie Medal making him an honary member of the Sverdlovsk Urals Hunting Society.

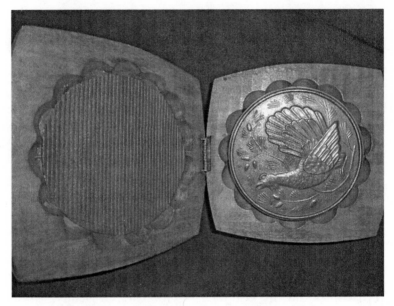

Close-up of medal in case on right. (Denny Geurink photos)

After a few more toasts, Kiselev came up to each one of us, shook our hand, and presented us with a beautiful, round, silver medallion with a capercaillie etched on its face and a very important-looking inscription etched on the back. Then he handed us a small, red, hard-covered, passport type of document. Inside, next to a picture of Lenin, was a photo of us and some more official-looking documentation written in Russian. Ah, so that's what Dmitri wanted the extra passport-size photos for!

"You guys have been made honorary members of the Communist Party," Dmitri quipped. "How do you feel?"

"You're kidding me, right?" I said in disbelief.

"Actually, I am kidding." Dmitri chuckled. "He's made all of you guys honorary members of the region's Society of Hunters. It's a very prestigious honor."

Wow! We were all pretty taken aback by what was going on out here in the middle of Siberia. This was beyond our wildest dreams. An honor indeed!

On our last day in camp, we decided to leave Boris a nice tip for all the hard work and hospitality he had shown us at his hunting lodge. Tipping is an American tradition. That evening we didn't even recognize Boris when he showed up at the dinner table. He had scraped the scruffy whiskers from his face and was wearing a suit and tie. He was grinning from ear to ear and smelled of vodka.

"What's up with Boris?" I asked Dmitri. "He seems pretty pleased tonight. Is he glad we are all finally leaving?"

"No!" Dmitri said, with a hint of disgust in his voice. "Do you guys know you gave him almost a year's wages in tips today! This guy makes about $200 a month and you guys gave him over $2,000 in tips. You shouldn't have tipped him so much. You're going to spoil him. Now he's going to expect that much again if we ever come back. Look at him! He's so drunk he can hardly walk!"

Yeah, I'd have to say Boris was getting a little wobbly! And he was trying to get us wobbly right along with him! He kept proposing all kinds of toasts, each of which was consummated with a shot of vodka.

We learned a lot more about old, Russian traditions that night. The reason vodka bottles don't come with screw-on caps is because once you take the cap off, you're supposed to keep on having shots until the bottle is empty! Also, you must keep the shot glass on the table when you fill it; you can't hold it in your hand. And you can't leave an empty vodka bottle on the table; it must be placed on the floor next to the table. The first toast always has to be to your health! And, oh yea, you can't just sip the vodka from the shot glass. Bad manners! You are supposed to slam it! Needless to say, we all slept in late the next morning!

Our hunt in Siberia was over. Next stop . . . Crimea.

CHAPTER 2

HANGING OUT
WITH THE KGB

FTER SURVIVING A LONG evening of vodka toasts and a first-hand introduction to Russian culture, our entourage of intrepid American hunters flew out of Sverdlovsk late in the afternoon on October 3, 1991. The next morning, Friday, October 4, we landed in the resort city of Simferopol, located on the southern tip of the Crimean Peninsula. Simferopol is an old, Russian navy town nestled along the scenic shoreline of the Black Sea.

What was ironic about us landing in Simferopol is that it is located near the city of Foros, where Gorbachev had been placed under house arrest during the coup attempt several weeks earlier. Again, we were right in the middle of a time and place of historical significance.

We were met at the airport by Sergey Kolpack, an interpreter who had been hired to accompany us on the next leg of our journey. Kolpack is an English professor at a nearby university. Along with Dmitri, this would give us two people who could translate for us at the next camp.

I was the first guy through customs and, as soon as I cleared, I was approached by Kolpack, a short, slender man in his early 30s. He introduced himself and then looked up at me and queried, "Are all Americans as big as you?"

I'm 6'2" and weigh 210 pounds so I'm not exactly a small man, but I don't consider myself exceptionally big compared to many other Americans. After Kolpack asked me this question, I did a quick look around the airport and noticed that most of the people were rather short in stature. I guess I did look big in this crowd. "I'm not really all that big compared to a lot of other Americans," I told Kolpack. "You should see my cousin."

About that time my cousin, Terry, walked towards us. Terry is 6'5" and weighs in at 250. Sergey's jaw dropped to his chest. "Wow! You Americans are really big people! I'm glad we didn't fight you!" Kolpack chuckled, referring to the tensions that have existed between Russians and Americans during the Cold War era. We all had a big laugh over that one. It wouldn't, however, be the last time we would hear this comment.

After everyone cleared customs, we made our way out of the airport towards a waiting van. On the way to our hotel, Kolpack, still obviously intrigued by meeting a group of Americans for the first time, came up with another astute observation. "You are the first Americans I have ever seen," he said, eyeing us up and down. "I'm quite surprised how much Russians and Americans look alike. I thought you would look different."

"What did you think we would look like?" I laughed. "Did you think we had one eye in the middle of our forehead?"

"No, no!" Kolpack quickly replied. "It's just that in many other countries, the people look a lot different than Russians. For example, Koreans don't look like Russians. Neither do the Japanese or Chinese. But there isn't a whole lot of difference between the way Russians and Americans look."

Except in the way we dress . . . as I had found out about a week earlier on a bus ride through Moscow with Dmitri. "How do these people know I'm not just another Russian?" I asked Dmitri after I noticed how a lot of people on the bus were staring at me and whispering to each other. I heard the word "American" whispered several times. "I haven't said a word to this point but these people know I'm an American and not a Russian. Same thing when we are walking down the street. How can they tell?"

"For one thing, look how you are dressed," Dmitri responded. "You have colorful clothes on and are wearing blue jeans and tennis shoes. Do you see anyone around you dressed like that? Notice they are all wearing dark, drab clothes. No tennis shoes and no blue jeans. Plus, Americans are always smiling. Do you see anyone smiling on this bus? Life in Russia is very difficult. Russian people are very stoic; very serious. They don't walk down the street and ride the bus with a big smile on their face. They are good, kind people but just don't wear their emotions on their shirt sleeve."

I looked around. Dmitri was right. That's when I noticed two grandmotherly ladies right across the aisle from us looking directly at me with their fingers in their ears. That was weird! "Why do they have their fingers in their ears?" I queried, a bit perplexed.

"They know that you are an American and they have always been told that all Americans do is cuss and swear." Dmitri smiled. "They don't want to hear it."

Good grief! How could so many misconceptions between Russians and Americans have developed over the years! That little bus ride was quite an eye-opener.

As it turned out, we were the first Americans in pretty much every place we went on this trip. We felt a lot of pressure to leave a good impression. We didn't want to look like the "ugly Americans" so many cultures seem to picture us as being. We did hear the comment "spoiled Americans" a few times. Unfortunately, these kind of rude, obnoxious Americans do travel to countries like Russia. We ran into a few of them on the airplane ride over and back.

Meanwhile, back in Simferopol, we had reached the hotel. Again, no one in the hotel spoke English. I guess that's understandable as we were in a country which has been pretty much closed to citizens from the United States for decades. This was not a tourist destination for Americans; it was a Soviet Navy town, so there was no need for anyone to speak English. After another lengthy check-in process, we stashed our gear in our rooms and grabbed a bite to eat.

The next morning we were taken to a small helicopter pad and flown up to the top of a large, rugged mountain overlooking the resort town of Yalta. This, Dmitri informed us, is where we would be staying on the next leg of our journey. As we landed on the helicopter pad next to the lodge, we found out that our "camp" was located on a giant naval base in the southern part of the Crimea. Things just kept getting more interesting by the minute!

While we were unloading our gear from the helicopter and stashing it in the lodge, we noticed a big, black Mercedes pull up out front. Out popped two men dressed in suits and ties, wearing dark glasses, and carrying brief cases. When I asked Dmitri who these guys were, he told me they were with the KGB! I didn't know whether to believe him or not as Dmitri was turning out to have quite a dry sense of humor but they sure looked like they could be KGB. And we were, after all, on a giant Soviet naval base. I figured if they look like KGB, act like KGB, and Dmitri says they are KGB, they must be KGB!

So, the way I see it, we were going to be hunting on a Soviet naval base with two guys from the KGB. Incredible! I had to pinch myself to see if I was dreaming! Ouch! Nope!

The KGB is watching! Guy on far left in suit and tie with briefcase is a KGB agent keeping a careful eye on Denny and crew. (Denny Geurink photo)

As we settled into our new surroundings, we found out from Dmitri that pretty much the only people who are allowed to own guns and hunt in the Soviet Union are military people and Communist Party officials. A whole lot different than the way we grew up here in the US, where hunting is a rite of passage for millions of Americans. When I told him that on opening day of the firearms' deer season in Michigan there are around 700,000 hunters in the woods, he was dumbfounded.

"There aren't that many hunters in all of Russia," Dmitri said in disbelief. "And Russia covers 11 time zones!"

Our headquarters for this leg of the journey was a very comfortable lodge overlooking a steep, wooded valley, which is home to the Crimean red deer that we will be hunting. The Russians refer to these animals as a "stag". There are a number of different species of red deer spread around the world, including this one and the American wapiti, or elk. While our elk and this species of red deer look a lot alike, there are some subtle differences. These stag are about three-fourths the size of our elk and the bulls have antlers that go straight up and crown, rather than antlers that slant back with points coming off the main beams, like our elk. The cows and calves look just like our elk cows and calves, only a bit smaller.

Also found in this area are roe deer, a small deer about the size of a large German shepherd, with little antlers. And there are a few mouflon sheep and wild boar around as well.

After a quick lunch of hot soup and sandwiches, we were introduced to our guides and prepared for the evening hunt. All of the guides were obviously military personnel. They wore Soviet military camouflage and carried Russian SKSs. My guide's name was Sergey (not the interpreter, another Sergey). He was the head guide in this camp, according to Dmitri.

That evening as Sergey and I sat beside a well-used game trail on the edge of a small clearing, I had my first introduction to stag hunting. I had never hunted them before so I really didn't know what to expect, and certainly had no clue as to what they sounded like. I just figured that because they looked a lot like our elk, they probably sounded a lot like our elk. Wrong!

Just before dark, a deep guttural roar echoed through the woods. It sounded like a grizzly bear with a toothache. It sent a shiver up my spine. I wasn't figuring on running into any bears in this camp. "Bear!" I whispered to Sergey. Actually, I guess it was more of a question. "Bear?"

Sergey looked at me and smiled. "No, stag. Not bear. Stag!"

Stag? That's what a stag sounds like! You're kidding me! Boy, did I feel stupid. Here I was, supposedly a big-shot writer with the world's largest outdoor magazine and I didn't know that a stag doesn't bugle . . . it roars. Well, I do know one thing for sure, I'd hate to be out in the woods alone after dark and hear a stag roar for the first time!

"Stag?" I replied, a bit puzzled.

"Yes, Denny, stag!" Sergey grinned.

Our outfitter, Dmitri Sikorski, poses in front of a big stag we found on a later trip that was starving to death and couldn't even stand up when we approached. (Denny Geurink photo)

About that time, the big bull shook the trees again with a loud roar then it started grunting like a pig! Holy cow! These things sound pretty gnarly. Another guttural roar echoed through the woods. He was getting closer! Problem was, it was also getting darker by the second.

Right at dark, the big bull roared along the edge of the woods but refused to step out into the clearing. Either it smelled us or he just wasn't going to expose himself. It exhibited the same sort of sixth sense our big whitetail bucks have back home in Michigan. Whatever it was, we never got a chance to see it. While I was disappointed that I didn't get to see the animal, I considered this to be a great hunt. Hey, it was my first stag hunt. I had a chance to hear what a big bull in full rut sounds like . . . plus, I was hunting in the Soviet Union with a big shot in the Russian Navy. What's not great about that!

Back at camp we found out that Terry had drilled a large red stag just before dark. He was grinning like a Cheshire cat as he told us the story. As it turns out, everybody had either seen or heard a stag on our first night in the woods. Needless to say, expectations were running high for this phase of the trip. The place was infested with stag. We were told that there were five red deer per hectare in the habitat surrounding the lodge. Five per hectare! I liked those numbers.

That evening as we gathered around the table for a wonderful meal, I noticed that the two guys with suits and ties were gone. They had driven back to Yalta, according to Dmitri. So, no more KGB to worry about! I was feeling a little more at ease about our stay here in Crimea until a short time later when Dmitri leaned over and whispered . . . "Denny, your guide, Sergey..." he said with a short pause, "KGB!"

"Ya, right!" I chuckled, figuring Dmitri was pulling my leg. Seeing I was relieved that the suits and ties were gone he wanted to stir up the pot.

"I'm not kidding!" Dmitri replied in a very serious tone of voice. "Big shot, KGB. Five years ago you go in woods with Sergey, you don't come back out!"

Whoa! Now that will bring the hairs on the back of your neck to attention! I had just spent the afternoon in the woods with a big shot from the KGB! I was carrying a rifle and he was carrying a rifle but we weren't pointing them at each other. We were hunting buddies! Think about that for a minute!

So that's why the suits and ties left camp. They had one of their own on the ground and in the field with us. What better way to keep track of us?

Things got even more interesting a few minutes later, after we had finished eating. That's when Sergey started asking me some questions through Dmitri. His first question was kind of an ice breaker. "Ask Denny if all marines are like Rambo!" Sergey deadpanned. We had found out a bit earlier that in this era of Glasnost and Perestroika, the Russians were now getting a chance to watch some of our movies and TV shows. Obviously, Sergey had watched *Rambo, First Blood*.

"Yes, of course!" I grinned, figuring Sergey was joking around. He was.

"Man, glad we didn't fight you!" Sergey chuckled.

We all had a good laugh. That's the second time a guy named Sergey said that and it was just as funny this time around. A bit later Sergey started to get a little more serious.

"Tell Denny we never hated the Americans," Sergey said. "We really didn't want to go to war with America. All we want to do is have a place to live, enough to eat, a good job, and be able to take care of our families. We just want to live a normal life and be happy."

"So do we!" I replied. "We didn't want to fight you either. It's all politics. We are just like you, we just want to live a normal life and be happy."

"Let the politicians fight each other." Sergey chuckled.

"Yeah, let them fight!" I laughed.

"Besides, if we had gone to war with America, you would have defeated us in two weeks," Sergey continued.

"Yeah, right!" I laughed. "Russia has the largest standing army in the world, more tanks than any other country, more missiles, more guns . . . "

"Yes, but no gas for tanks, no bullets for guns, and no food for the soldiers." Sergey laughed. "You defeat us in two weeks! Time to be friends!"

I hadn't thought about that. This country is really run-down. I can see how this might be true. No gas for the tanks, no bullets for the guns . . . Wow!

"And now you have the Star Wars missile defense system," Sergey added. "You fire missiles at us and blow us all up. We fire missiles at you and you stop them with protective shield. We don't have Star Wars. Time to be friends."

"Ha! Problem is, we don't have a Star Wars protective shield either." I laughed. "It's just a theory. We are working on it, but it hasn't been perfected yet. But, it is time to be friends."

"Now if we have a nuclear war, we all die," Sergey said somberly. "We have a lot of nuclear weapons and the U.S. has a lot of nuclear weapons. Politicians start pushing buttons, we all die. Time to be friends."

All the Russian guides and all the Americans sitting around the table raised their glasses to this astute observation and toasted: "Time to be friends!"

A little later that evening, Dmitri told me some more interesting news. Apparently the waiters in white shirts and bow ties who were serving us our meals were not really waiters at all! "There has been a lot of poaching and organized crime in this area recently," Dmitri explained. "So one of our friends from Sevastopol has provided us with armed body guards, who are posing as our waiters. They are here to make sure we are safe and nobody bothers us."

Wow!

I know I keep saying "Wow" and "Holy Cow" and stuff like that on this trip but I don't know how else to describe my reaction to a lot of these things. It's all been kind of mind blowing. I do know one thing, I'm glad my mother said she was going to have the whole church congregation pray for us while we were gone! It was starting to look like we might need a little divine intervention to pull this thing off!

Needless to say, Mom was not all that pleased I was going to the Soviet Union for two weeks! She kept trying to talk me out of it. She had grown up during the heart of the Cold War and the thought of her, or anyone in her family, going on a road trip to the Evil Empire was something that never crossed her mind.

Dmitri hired a body guard and had him dress up like a waiter to protect us that first trip because everything was so unstable after the coup. It was a very volatile time in the history of Russia. (Denny Geurink photo)

Later that evening, a few of us decided to get a poker game going to pass the time. One of the waiters/bodyguards began watching us with great curiosity. We were using rubles we had exchanged for some of our dollars in Moscow to make our bets. None of us would have played poker for U.S. dollars because we aren't the betting kind but we didn't have poker chips and the rubles looked more like play money than real money so we used them. We asked the waiter/bodyguard if he wanted to join us. He declined, saying he didn't have enough rubles to spare on a poker game. We told him "no problem," we would each give him some of ours.

The look on his face was priceless as we each pushed a pile of rubles in front of him. We had no idea how much they were worth but, apparently, it was quite a bit as he looked shocked when we did it. We noticed that he bet very sparingly as the game went on. He just couldn't get himself to part with his newfound wealth. The real clincher came when at one point, the pot got rather large . . . and I had a hand full of aces . . . so I pushed my entire pile of rubles into the center of the table and quipped: "I'm all in! Heck, it's only rubles!"

Mr. Waiter/Bodyguard gasped and stammered: "Only rubles! Only rubles!! My God! That's two months' wages!"

Whoops! We had done it again! First with our guide, Boris, in Sverdlovsk, and now with this guy in Crimea. We keep forgetting what little money these guys make in comparison to what we make in America. Well, the game ended when I won the pot. The waiter/bodyguard tried to give the rubles we had laid on him back to us but we told him to keep them as a tip. Big mistake! Out came a fresh bottle of vodka! Let the toasting begin!

The following morning Ed and Bob each dropped a huge bull. Bob's was exceptionally large, one of the biggest bulls ever taken in this area according to the guides. My turn came that evening when I downed a nice stag just before dark. The guides were almost as excited as we were, telling us we had all taken "gold" and "silver medal" stags. (Europeans have a scoring program that ranks animals as gold, silver, or bronze medal animals.)

During the next few days, we tagged two roe deer and a number of very small quail, called a steppen quail by the guides. Don't really know what species of quail they are scientifically, all I can tell you is that they are a bit smaller than our bobwhite quail. While they don't look like our bobwhites, they do taste very good . . . just like our bobwhite quail!

We also tried for wild boar, but soon found out that these animals had already left the area – another casualty of the coup! We jumped several mouflon sheep but were asked not to shoot them because they had just been released into the area.

At the end of the hunt, we were paid another visit by someone in a black Mercedes and dressed up in a suit and tie but this time it wasn't the KGB. It was Igor Markevich, President of the Soviet Black Sea Navy Hunting and Fishing Society. When Dmitri told me this guy was coming, I was again flabbergasted that such a high-ranking government official was coming to greet us.

Photo of The Tea House Lodge. (Denny Geurink photo)

"Dmitri, I can't believe all these dignitaries are coming to these camps to meet us," I said in utter disbelief. "They act like we are some kind of ambassadors or something. We're just a bunch of peons compared to these guys. We are just plain, ordinary Americans."

"No, you guys are ambassadors," Dmitri replied. "You are the first Americans these people have met. You are the first Americans to visit these places. So you are ambassadors of America. They want to make sure you feel welcome."

View from the porch of the Tea House Lodge overlooking the scenic Crimean mountain range. (Denny Geurink photo)

That will humble you and make you mind your manners. And, yes, we were feeling more than welcome!

That evening around the dinner table, Markevich led us in a round of toasts. He then gave each of us a laminated card with a lanyard to hang around our necks. The cards gave us honorary membership of the Crimean Society of Hunters.

The hunt ended all too soon on Wednesday, October 9. Before heading back to Russia, we spent a couple of days in Yalta, a beautiful resort city on the Black Sea that the Soviets like to compare to the French Rivera. This is where the elite come to play and relax in the sun along the sandy beaches of the Black Sea.

While in Yalta we also had a chance to visit the spot where the famous Yalta Conference of 1945 took place. This is where President Franklin D. Roosevelt, Prime Minister Winston Churchill, and General Secretary Joseph Stalin met from February 4–11, 1945, to discuss Europe's post-war reorganization. It was the second meeting between the

Big Three to discuss the fate of post-war Europe; the first meeting was in Tehran in 1943. The Yalta Conference is what many believe led to the start of what we call the Cold War.

After leaving Yalta, we flew into St. Petersburg to spend a couple of days there touring. St. Petersburg is a beautiful city steeped in Russian culture and tradition. Here we had a chance to visit one of the largest and most prestigious museums in the world—the Hermitage. You really need more than one day to take in everything there is to see in this museum. It was incredible.

We also visited St. Catherine's summer palace, which was the lavish summer residence of the Russian tsars. And then we visited the Winter Palace, which was originally built by Peter the Great in the late 1700s. It served as the official residence of the Russian Monarchy until the Bolshevik Revolution in 1917.

We left Russia and headed for home on Friday, October 11. What started out as a hunting trip had turned into a whole lot more! I learned a lot about Russia, its people, its culture, its history, and its wildlife during my two weeks there. There was so much more about this trip than I could ever hope to write in a few short stories. I shot over 12 hours of video and put together what is, as far as we know, the first ever hunting video filmed in Russia. I also took over 1,000 slides on this trip. These will help preserve the many fond memories and many exciting moments I experienced in the Land of the Bear!

CHAPTER 3

LAND OF THE BEAR

RUSSIA IS CALLED THE Land of the Bear for a reason. Out of the 200,000 brown bears roaming the northern hemisphere in a dozen or more countries, approximately two-thirds of them, or 120,000 bears, reside in Russia. Compare that to the 32,000 found in the United States—of which 95 percent live in Alaska – and the 21,000 found in Canada, and you get a pretty good picture of why the brown bear is so closely identified with Russia culture. The brown bear is one of the most widespread and popular animals in Russia, where it has been long considered to be the country's national symbol. It appears on coins, flags, street signs, maps, billboards, and even beer bottles. In 1980 the brown bear was chosen as the official mascot of the Moscow Olympics.

On a number of occasions while visiting Moscow and St. Petersburg, we have run into people with trained bears, standing on street corners where tourists can take pictures of them. Most of the bears are cubs, but once in a while someone has a very large bear. While the bears are muzzled, they can still be very dangerous. On one occasion we saw a large bear try to steal an ice cream cone from a passing tourist. The handler had all he could do to keep the bear in check as it slapped the cone from the frightened tourist's hand. Had the bear been agitated or angry, the person could easily have lost her hand . . . and her arm! We gave this guy and his bear a wide berth!

Brown bears are one of the most majestic and awe-inspiring creatures in the world . . . and also one of the most dangerous. Scientists tell us that the brown bears found in

North America are direct descendants of brown bears from Russia. They both belong to the same species, *Ursus arctos.* Somewhere way back in time, they crossed a land bridge over the Bering Sea and made their way into Alaska and then down into Canada and the lower 48 states.

The brown bear we call a grizzly is a subspecies, scientifically known as *Ursus arctos horriblis.* Some scientists believe the grizzly evolved from the bigger coastal brown when it moved inland and started feeding on other things besides salmon. Others believe there may have been two separate brown bear migrations into North American from Russia.

They believe that grizzlies stem from the narrow-skulled bears found in northern Siberia. These bears, they contend, migrated into central Alaska and into the interior of Canada and the lower 48 states. Meanwhile, the big coastal Alaskan brown bears, or Kodiak bears, are direct descendants of the broader-skulled bears found in Kamchatka. Brown bears were at one time quite widespread in Canada and the lower 48, with fossil remains found as far east as Ontario and Labrador in Canada and as far east as Kentucky and Ohio in the United States.

What a bear eats has a lot to do with its size. Brown bears living along the coast in Russia's Far East, for example, can grow very large, living on a steady diet of spawning salmon. Weights of up to 3,300 pounds have been recorded. That's almost a ton and a half! Meanwhile, the interior version of a brown bear, which we call a grizzly, may only top out at 700 pounds in the Yukon. These bears live off pine nuts and berries, and whatever else they can find. Without the protein-rich salmon the coastal bears feed on, a grizzly just can't grow as large. So, despite the common misconception that the grizzly bear is larger than a brown bear, the fact is that the grizzly is a brown bear, just a smaller version. I think it's the grizzly's nasty reputation that makes it seem larger than life.

There are several reasons why there are so many brown bears in Russia. First, the habitat is perfect for them. The country is covered with dense forests and wilderness areas flush with the perfect bear foods, from the salmon-rich Kamchatka Peninsula to the pine nut rich forests of Siberia. Secondly, the human population in Russia is very widespread. Once you get outside the major cities, the population is very rural. Thirdly, after the Bolshevik Revolution in 1917, guns and hunting disappeared from Russia. This allowed bear populations to explode. While this was good for the bears, it wasn't always so good for the rural Russian population.

According to Dmitri, many rural villagers live in fear of the bears. Many are killed or injured when they go into the woods to forage for mushrooms or to the rivers to catch fish. With no way to defend themselves, they are afraid to roam too far from their homes. This fact was driven home on our very first grizzly hunt back in the early 1990s.

We were staying with an older couple in their home in a small village several hundred miles east of Moscow. One day as we were sitting at the dinner table, there was a frantic knock at the door. The entire village knew that there were several American hunters staying in this house and one of the villagers had come to plead with us to go with him to his home to shoot the bear that had killed his milk cow.

Seems the bear had killed the cow and had been dragging the partially-eaten carcass into the woods when the man and his neighbors ran the bear off with pitchforks and sticks. They had made such a commotion that the bear had been scared off. The farmer retrieved what was left of his cow, loaded it onto a wagon and brought it back to his barn, where he planned to butcher it and eat what was left of it. There was no sense in letting the bear have it when his family was in dire need of the meat.

Unfortunately, during the night, the bear had returned to drag the cow back into the woods. The farmer was afraid to go and get it. He didn't have a rifle, but we did. He wanted us to shoot the bear and retrieve what was left of his cow. That evening, just before dark, one of my clients killed the bear. There was joy in the village that night because many other villagers had had their livestock attacked by this same bear recently.

Bear searching for food along Sea of Okhotsk near Magadan.
(Tom Thompson photo)

On another hunt, one of the villagers told us about how his grandmother had been attacked and killed by a bear when she had gone out to the barn to milk the family cow. Dmitri told us this happened all too often in these remote villages. The bears find the domestic animals on a farm to be easy pickings compared to trying to find something in the wild to eat. Many oat crops are also destroyed each year by bears chowing down on the grain in preparation for hibernation.

With so many bears in Russia, and so many remote villages located in bear habitat, it's no wonder that there are five times as many people killed by bears in Russia as there are in the United States. Studies show that, on average, there are two recorded fatal bear attacks a year in the United States; there are at least 10 fatal attacks a year in Russia. A lot more people are attacked and not killed. In years there is a poor salmon run or pine nut crop, these numbers can double.

There are documented cases in Eastern Siberia where some bears have become man-eaters during times when natural foods are scarce. At least two bears in this region have been identified as killing and eating 12 people each.

In the next few chapters, we will take a look at some of the bear stories we've run across while traversing Russia the past few years. Be forewarned: some of these stories are pretty gruesome.

Bear emerging from den site near Magadan. (Tom Thompson photo)

CHAPTER 4

GIRL CALLS TO SAY GOODBYE AS BEAR EATS HER

A LOT OF THE BEAR encounters which occur in Russia happen along salmon streams where people and bears both come seeking food. I have heard about a number of these attacks over the years from guides, interpreters, and local residents of the many small villages which dot the Siberian landscape. Most of the attacks occur in July and August, during the big salmon runs. People from the villages often camp along these salmon-rich streams for several days while they seek to supplement their winter food supply. The bears are doing the same thing. They congregate in large numbers, seeking to build up their fat reserves for a long winter's nap. It's a recipe for disaster!

Over the years I've had the chance to fish a number of salmon streams in Russia's Far East with great success. On most of these trips, we would either see bears or a lot of bear tracks along the streams. We always knew there were plenty of bears in the area but, unlike most of the Russian villagers, who don't have guns, we always carried a high-powered rifle for protection. Fortunately, we have never had to use them, and I hope we never to have to. That's because, generally speaking, bears will avoid human contact . . . and we certainly try to avoid contact with the bears! But it doesn't always work out that way.

One of the most heart-wrenching bear attack stories I have ever heard happened in August of 2011. The story was reported by a number of news agencies, including the *Moscow Times*, the *Daily Mail* and featured in a story written by Spencer Hawken in *Newsflavor*.

According to these news sources, a 19-year-old Russian girl, Olga Moskalvova, and her stepfather, Igor Tsyganenkov, were camping and fishing beside a river near their home in the village of Termalniy on the Kamchatka Peninsula. Termalniy is a small village located near Petropavlovsk on the southern end of the peninsula. They were in the process of retrieving a fishing pole Igor had left in the tall reeds along the river when a large female brown bear burst out from the reeds and attacked him.

Olga watched in horror as the big bear knocked her stepfather to the ground, grabbed him in its powerful jaws, and crushed his skull and broke his neck. As Olga turned to run, the bear saw her and ran her down, grabbing her by the leg. At first the bear just toyed with her, biting and chewing on her leg. That's when Olga managed to get her cell phone out and call her mother, Tatiana Tsyganenkov. "Mom, the bear is eating me!" she screamed into the phone. "Mom, it's such agony! Mom, help!"

At first Tatiana though her daughter was just joking, because she liked to kid around. But, she quickly realized this was no joke. She knew her daughter was in big trouble as she listened in panic to her daughter's screams for help. "I heard the real horror and pain in Olga's voice and the sounds of a bear growling and chewing," says Tatiana. "I could have died then and there from shock!"

Suddenly, the phone went dead. She had lost the call. At this point Tatiana desperately tried to call her husband to ask him to help Olga, not knowing he was already dead. The phone just rang and there was no answer. Then Olga called back. "Mom, the bears are back!" Olga cried. "She came back and brought her three babies. They're eating me!"

When this call was also cut off, a distraught Tatiana phoned the police station and relatives in Termalniy, and pleaded with them to rush down to the river and save her daughter.

A bit later the phone rang again. It had been almost an hour since the first call. This time Tatiana listened helplessly as Olga spoke to her for the last time. The long ordeal was nearing an end. After viciously attacking and mauling her for nearly 60 minutes, the bears had apparently walked off and left her for dead. "Mom, it's not hurting anymore." Olga spoke in a weak voice. "I don't feel the pain. Forgive me for everything. I love you so much."

These were the last words Tatiana would ever hear her daughter speak. All she could do was cry.

A half hour after that last call, Igor's brother, Andrei, and several policemen arrived at the river. When they got to the scene of the attack, they found the mother bear and cubs still feeding on Igor's partially-eaten body. They found Olga's body a short distance away. She had been badly mauled and was already dead.

"My daughter was such fun," said a grief-stricken Tatiana. "She was so cheerful, friendly, and warm. She had just graduated from music school, and had just gotten her driving license."

Local authorities sent six experienced hunters to the scene to track down the mother and her three cubs and kill them so this kind of tragedy would not happen again. Once a bear loses its fear of humans, it's more prone to attack and kill again.

BEAR DRAGS OFF SLEEPING BAG WITH MAN INSIDE

Elaina Bulatoba, one of my interpreters from Petropavlovsk, told me a similar story a number of years ago. It was a horrible experience her father, Sergey Bulatoba, had while camping and fishing along the Zhuponova River late one summer.

When Sergey and his friends arrived at the Zhuponova in July of 2004 to do some fishing, they fully expected to see bears along the stream during their visit. They had fished the river several times before and had always encountered bears on these trips but they found that if they left the bears alone, the bears would leave them alone. At least that's the way it had always worked in the past. As they were soon to discover on this trip, however, this uneasy truce between man and beast can turn deadly in a big hurry.

Sergey, who is a police officer in the small town of Yelizova, had brought his police-issue revolver to camp with him. Not much of a bear gun to be sure but better than no gun at all. As they planned to avoid any confrontations with the local bear population, they figured they wouldn't need the pistol anyway. In the past the bears had always given the anglers a wide berth so they were not expecting any problems on this outing.

While the anglers were storing their gear in one of the small wooden fishing shacks located in the camp, they noticed a sow and her two young cubs nearby, scrounging around for food. The mother bear did not seem to be scared of the men, who were busily preparing to fish, nor did she appear to be aggressive, so the fishermen went about their chores, not overly concerned with the bear's presence yet keeping one eye on her to make sure she didn't get too close to camp.

Bulatoba and his friends were planning to stay on the river for several weeks, hoping to gather a larder of fish and caviar for the long winter months that lay ahead. As usual, the fishing was good and it wasn't long before they had dozens of fish drying on big wooden racks in the hot July sun. And it wasn't long before the mother bear and her two cubs began sneaking in and pilfering fish and caviar from the camp. The bears had a den nearby and they found the camp fish to be easy pickings.

The men ran off the bears every time they caught them near camp. After a couple of days of camp raids, the bears finally seemed to move off and the fishermen began to forget about them.

One particularly hot summer night, Bulatoba had a hard time sleeping in the stuffy wooden shack so he took his sleeping bag outside and lay it down on the ground next to the shack. He had done this many times before in the past as he enjoyed sleeping under the stars. He always took his pistol with him and kept it right inside his sleeping bag . . . just in case.

Sometime during the middle of the night, Bulatoba was awakened from a deep sleep by a strange sensation of movement. At first he thought he was just dreaming but, as he slowly began to wake up, he realized that something was dragging him and his sleeping bag across the ground. He still didn't know what was going on until he heard a low growl. Immediately, a cold chill began to spread across his entire body. His pulse raced wildly.

"All of a sudden, I became aware of the sound of heavy breathing," Bulatoba recalls, "then the stench of dead, rotten fish filled my nostrils. That's when it hit me. My God! I was smelling the breath of a bear! I was about to be eaten alive!"

Bulatoba's heart hammered against his rib cage as the bear began dragging him farther and farther away from camp. He was paralyzed with fear. He couldn't even scream or yell for help. His mind raced as he thought about the horrible death he was about to experience. Somewhere in the pandemonium he realized that it was the mother bear dragging him off to her den to feed her young cubs.

"Just then I remembered that I had my pistol in my sleeping bag with me," Bulatoba continues. "I tried to get my hands on the pistol but my body was moving in slow motion. I couldn't make my arms and hands work. It was like I was trapped in the middle of a bad dream. Only this wasn't a dream! My palms were sweating but the rest of my body was as cold as ice. I was shivering and sweating with fear."

Finally, as he desperately groped for the pistol, he felt the distinct sensation of cold steel against his outstretched fingers. His instincts began to take over. He slid the handle of the pistol into his hand and arched his finger around the trigger. He slowly pulled the pistol out of the bag and aimed it at the body of the mother bear. He then pulled the trigger again and again and again. Strange feelings of fear and pity rushed through his head as the report of his pistol shattered the quiet moonlit night.

The bear roared in pain and fury as it dropped the sleeping bag and charged off into the forest. The mortally-wounded beast sounded like a bulldozer clearing brush as it plowed through the trees, snapping twigs and cracking branches.

As the sound of roaring and crashing faded off into the distance, Bulatoba pulled his shaken, bruised body from his torn sleeping bag. While his nerves were shattered, his body was intact. No broken bones and no bite marks. He was alive!

Bulatoba slowly groped his way through the inky blackness back to the shack, hoping that his bear encounters were over for the evening. Problem is, this was the time of night the river bank was crawling with hungry bears looking for something to eat!

At last he was back at the shack where he found his frightened friends waiting for him. They were worried sick and extremely happy to see him alive. When they heard the shots and the roaring bear, they expected the worst.

After a long, sleepless night, the men cautiously headed out the next morning in search of the bear. They found it dead, near the entrance to its den. As they cautiously approached the dead sow, they could hear the young cubs whining and whimpering inside. At this point the overwhelming sense of fear gave way to a feeling of sadness for the orphaned cubs.

Knowing that the young cubs would not survive without their mother, they caught them and carried them to a nearby Forest Service office. Later, they found out that one of the rangers was able to get an older sow with one cub to adopt the two young bears. Soon, the cubs were back along the river, feeding on fish once again.

"I was just happy that the cubs were able to survive," says Bulatoba, "and that they had something else to eat beside me!"

KILLER BEARS

I heard another bear attack story from Sergey Mashkantsewe while in a hunting camp near the town of Magadan along the Sea Of Okhotsk in Russia's Far East, back in 2005. Mashkantsewe was the head guide in the camp and, with all the time he spent in the woods hunting and trapping, he certainly had plenty of big bear stories to tell. Again, it was the volatile combination of salmon stream, bears, and fishermen that created the tragic story he told me that day.

Like most young Russian military inductees, Mashkantsewe grew up lean and tough. You don't have a choice when you are sent to a military outpost in the middle of Siberia to man a remote weather station. You either survive or you are sent back to the city in a pine box. That is, if the bears don't find you and eat you first.

"My job was to provide food for the outpost," Mashkantsewe, then in his early 40s, told me through an interpreter. "I was a professional hunter. I went out and shot moose, bear, wolves, fox, waterfowl, and anything else I could find for food and hides. The meat we would eat and the furs we would sell to the natives in the remote villages for a few dollars to buy more supplies. If there were streams around, we caught fish. When the blueberries and red berries were ripe, we went out and picked them. We had to live off the land because we didn't receive supplies but once every three or four months from the city."

He told me that even when supplies arrived from the city many hundreds of miles away, they were usually sparse and consisted mostly of bread—which went stale fast—sugar, salt, and hard tack. So it was pretty much shoot something for the table or starve. Sergey became very good at what he did best . . . hunting moose and bear. And there were a lot of bears around back then. A lot.

But, even the many close encounters he had with ill-tempered bears did not prepare Sergey for the ghastly scene he came upon one gloomy afternoon in October of 1996.

He was still having trouble talking about it as he told me the story.

"We were working our way down a wide, shallow spot on the Renzhina River when we noticed a big bear feeding on something along the bank," Mashkantsewe said in a low, sad voice. "We decided to cut our engine and try to float in close to see what the bear was eating. The bear spotted us and slowly walked off, not really all that afraid of us. It was more annoyed than afraid. That's the sign of a big, dangerous bear. That's when we saw the body of a partially-eaten man in the bushes. His face had been eaten away."

Mashkantsewe paused for a second and swallowed hard. He was visibly shaken. After a few minutes, he composed himself and continued.

"The scene sent a cold chill down my spine." Mashkantsewe spoke in a barely audible voice. "We knew we were dealing with the worst kind of bear possible, a man-eater. We knew we had to destroy him or he would kill again."

Mashkantsewe and his two partners quickly formulated a plan. They knew the bear would be back to reclaim his kill so they set up a blind about 50 yards away and waited. As they waited in silence, every nerve in their bodies was on edge. All the hunters had for firepower were military issue 7.62 carbines. They were using standard issue, full metal jacket cartridges with minimal powder. This is what they had always used to hunt bear but, somehow, it seemed inadequate right now. They were thinking about how nice one of the carbines of their American hunters would be. A .338 or .375, with a 220-grain bullet, would have made them feel a lot better.

Just before dark the hackles on the back of their necks stood up when they heard a twig snap. The bear was coming in from behind them! The bear had caught their scent and was now hunting them, intending to make Mashkantsewe and his friends his next meal. They were in a bad situation. The brush was so thick behind them that they would not see the bear until it was less than 20 yards away. Their skin began to crawl as the big bear stalked closer and closer. They could hear it sniffing the air for their scent as it worked towards them. Their hearts began to race as they thought about what had happened to the man whose partially-eaten body lay beside the river in front of them. Would they soon join him on the stream bank?

Suddenly, in the waning daylight, they saw a dark form slipping through the shadows. They didn't wait for the bear to clear the brush. With nerves sparking like an electrical short, they opened fire with their banana clips. The big bruin roared and bellowed like a freight train as it charged towards the men.

"I don't know how many times we shot," Mashkantsewe blurted excitedly. "Maybe 20 times! Maybe 30 times! We didn't stop until the bear quit moving right at our feet. It was a big, old bear with very bad teeth and a very bad hide. That's why it had become a man-eater. We found the arms and hands of the man inside its stomach. It made us sick."

Mashkantsewe found out who the man was a few weeks later when he was back in town. It was one of his friends, with whom he had spent a lot of time fishing. "I still have a hard time talking about this today," Mashkantsewe whispered as he slowly walked from the tent.

CHAPTER 5

THE PEOPLE

"WE ARE JUST LIKE Americans," one of my guides, a KGB operative named Sergey, told me back in 1991. "We just want to be happy. We want to have enough food to eat, clothes to wear and a place to live. We never hated the Americans. We never wanted to fight you. Let the politicians fight each other. We want to be friends. We just want to live a normal life."

Amen. That is one statement that has stuck with me through my many years in Russia. The Russians are just like us; they just grew up under a different system of government. They have the same hopes, dreams, and needs we do. It's just that they were always told what to do and when to do it, who they should love and who they should hate. You talk about "Big Brother Is Watching You!" That was the communist system.

"We never hated you either," I told Sergey. "We were told bad stories about you too. But we never hated you or wanted to fight you either. You're right! Let the politicians fight."

Over the past two decades, I've made many friends from all walks of life in Russia. One of the most unique friendships was with a colonel in the Russian army back in the late 1990s. Because of the sensitivity of an American businessman hanging around with a Russian colonel at that time, the colonel has asked me not to use his surname in this story. While we doubted there would be any repercussions, we decided not to take a chance.

It all started a number of years back when one of my interpreters, Vladislav Shurin, told me about this high-ranking military colonel he knew from Moscow. "His name is Igor," Vlad told me one day. "He's a colonel in the Russian army. I went to school with his wife, Larisa. She was a good friend of mine and we are still friends today. Would you like to meet with him and his wife? They would like to meet you and talk to you. Let's go out to dinner with them while we are in Moscow."

"That sounds really cool," I told Vlad. "A Russian colonel. Wow! That'd be great! Let's do it."

That evening Vlad and I took a taxi to a nice restaurant in town where we met Igor and Larisa. Igor was a handsome man in his early 50s, all dressed up in a dark suit. His wife, Larisa, was a pretty lady, wearing a nice dress and fine jewelry. I felt sorely underdressed in my jeans and Outdoor Adventures shirt, but they were very friendly and actually spoke a little bit of English. Between Vlad's excellent command of the English language, their spotty English, and my spotty Russian, we communicated very well.

As an American in Russia, I felt no animosity at all from the colonel and his wife. I felt that if anyone had been subjugated to a steady stream of anti-American sentiment throughout his career, it would have been Igor; but it didn't show.

We had a great dinner and interesting conversation. Igor and his wife were extremely curious about life in America. What was the food like? Were the restaurants in Moscow as nice as the ones in America? Were Russians as well off as Americans? What kind of sports did I like? What was the incredible passion for football in the U.S. all about? And so on. They were extremely curious about my opinion of Russian life, food, housing, clothes, technology, etc.

It was the dawning of the computer age and they wanted to know if all Americans had a computer. The Russians were just getting them but he felt they were inferior to the ones the Americans were buying because the Russians couldn't afford to buy the expensive ones that Americans could afford. Like so many other Russians I have come in contact with, he seemed to have this perception that all Americans were millionaires . . . or cowboys . . . or both.

The next night it was just Igor, Vlad, and me on a guys' night out. First we went bowling and then we played some pool. There was, of course, some vodka involved, not much but just enough to lead to some more interesting conversations. But, at no point did I feel intimidated, as I should have been being with a Russian army colonel. Igor was a warm, compassionate human being, totally unlike the perception of a Russian career army officer I had grown up with.

Of course, back then, when I told some of my friends about hanging out with a Russian colonel, they said, "Denny, maybe he's with the KGB and he's just trying to get information out of you." There was plenty of suspicion on our side of the pond as well.

My friendship with Igor and Larisa lasted for several years. On later trips to Moscow, Vlad and I would meet with the colonel and his wife several times. Once, the colonel took us to the horse races. I couldn't believe they actually had a horse track in Russia! My, how quickly capitalism was catching on! We sat in a special box reserved for VIPs.

Another time we went to Moscow to attend a tennis match, where tennis stars from around the world were competing in an international tournament at the old Olympic Stadium. It was called the Kremlin Cup. The tourney was established by the first President of Russia, Boris Yeltsin, who was an avid tennis fan. He is generally credited with the big surge in the popularity of tennis that took place in Russia in the early 2000s. This eventually led to the domination by Russians of the international tennis scene for many years. I was thrilled when they announced his name and he stood to receive an ovation from the crowd. "Wow! I'm at a tennis match with a Russian army colonel and Boris Yelstin!"

I was privileged to watch some of the best Russian tennis players in the world compete. Among the women playing that day were Elena Dementieva, Nadia Petrovo, Anastasia Myskina, and yes, even Anna Kournikova. Many say she was just a flash-in-the-pan tennis player, who really never played tennis that well. To set the record straight, she won the Kremlin Cup doubles tournament in 2001 and two Grand Slam doubles titles, one in 1999 and another in 2002.

I was thrilled one year when I found out that she was on the plane with us on one of our trips from the U.S. to Moscow. While I wasn't lucky enough to talk to her, I did catch a glimpse of her up there in first class . . . as did everyone else on the plane! If I had known she was going to be on our flight, you can bet I would have purchased a first class ticket!

One of the most exciting evenings I spent with the colonel was when he invited Vlad and I to his flat for dinner one evening. He met us in town, all dressed up in full military colors. I was impressed by how rugged he looked and his air of command. This was the first time I had seen him in military uniform.

"Now, Denny, when we get to the military base where I live, do not speak English," Igor instructed as we hopped in a taxi and headed for his flat on the base. "Do not speak English until we get to my room."

"No problem," I said. "I'll try to keep my mouth shut. You know that won't be easy!"

"They might think you are CIA!" Igor chuckled.

Didn't think of that! Well, not immediately. Not until we got there. We were dropped off at the entrance of a very intimidating military compound. We were met at the closed gate by two sentries. They briskly saluted Igor, and he saluted back. They opened the gate and gave me and Vlad the evil eye as we walked past. Now I felt intimidated!

A couple more times, as we progressed up the sidewalk to the building, we were met and saluted by other Russian soldiers. Then again at the door to the building . . . and even in the elevator! I was definitely getting the once-over. Igor didn't have to worry about me speaking English. I don't think I could have said anything if I wanted to! I was beginning to think we should have found another restaurant in town.

Finally! We arrived at his flat. We were greeted at the door by Larisa, who motioned for us to come into the room.

"OK Denny, you may speak English again." Igor chuckled. "This is my flat. Sorry it doesn't look like much for a Russian colonel, but this is what we have. We don't make nearly as much money as an American colonel would. But it's comfortable."

Photo of me (far right) and friend, Dale Fulkerson, on visit to The Colonel's apartment. We edited his face out at his request. While I don't expect any repercussions, we didn't want to take any chances.

It was comfortable and Igor and his wife were gracious hosts. First we were treated with the typical Russian appetizers of meat, cheese, caviar, bread, and . . . of course . . . vodka. There were also bottles of cognac and wine on the table. Later we had a tasty meal of meat, fish, and potatoes, cooked by Larisa. It was an excellent night out. And, before it was over . . . and I had participated in several vodka toasts . . . . I conjured up the nerve to ask Igor if I could have my picture taken wearing his Russian military officer's jacket and hat.

"No problem," he said, chuckling. "But you can't take it with you. You might look suspicious wearing that when you leave."

Photo of me in Igor's uniform. Do I look like a Colonel in the Russia army? (Denny Geurink photo)

I can only imagine.

After that we had a few more meetings but, eventually, I lost contact with Igor and Larisa; the main reason being my company wasn't working with Vlad's outfitter as much, so I just didn't see him very often.

Oh, one more thing. After one of our dinner meetings, Igor handed me a business card with his name on it. "Denny, if you ever have a problem with anybody in Russia, like the police, or some business guy, or whatever," he said, chuckling, "just show them this card. No problem!"

A "Get Out of Jail Free" card! Never know when you can use that!

Another interesting person I met on one of my expeditions to Russia was Kirsan Ilyumzhinov, the President of the Republic of Kalmykia. I met Ilyumzhinov in January of 2002. Kalmykia is part of the new Russian Federation which was created after the fall of the Soviet Union and it is the only Buddhist region in Europe. In addition to being President of Kalmykia, Ilyumzhinov was also the President of the International Chess Federation. He is credited with creating a huge interest in chess in Russia during his association with the International Chess Federation.

I had the opportunity to meet Ilyumzhinov while on a trip Dmitri Sikorski had arranged with the head of the

Kalmykian Hunting Department. Dmitri wanted to know if I would be interested in meeting the president, who he said wanted to greet us and welcome us to his country. Of course I was interested, especially as I had just started a new TV show back in the U.S. and was hoping to film this hunt for an episode on my show.

"You think it would be OK if I took my TV camera along to get some film of the president?" I asked Dmitri. "Can you imagine how impressive that would be? Tell him it will help bring more tourists to Kalmaykia! Give him your best sales pitch!"

"I'll see what I can do," Dmitri answered. He did very well! I was given permission to film our meeting!

Photo of Denny and the president of Kalmykia, Kirsan Ilyumzhinov, taken during meeting in 2002. (Dmitri Sikorski photo)

I'll never forget walking into the president's office and seeing the colorful country flag, a large collection of

Buddhist photos, paintings, statuettes, and a long, impressive conference table. And there, sitting behind a huge wooden desk, was Ilyumzhinov, looking very presidential! I was a little intimidated. After a short, formal meeting at the conference table with the head of the hunting department, and some other department head, I mustered up the nerve to ask Ilyumzhinov if he would say a little something I could use as an introduction to the show I was filming. He agreed.

I figured I would have Dmitri translate what he said and dub in the translation when I edited the show. To my surprise, Ilyumzhinov followed up his Russian greeting with one in English! Excellent English, by the way. "I would like to welcome our friends, especially those from America, to come and visit our beautiful country," he began. He went on to say how beautiful Kalmykia was and how many natural resources from flora to fauna can be found in this region. I was impressed!

But the surprises and presidential hospitality were not over yet! Later that evening, much to our delight, Ilyumzhinov had a native dance troupe come to our hotel to perform some of the country's traditional dances in the hotel ballroom. Several of the dances dated as far back as the 16th century when the ancestors of the present day Kalmykians migrated to this part of Russia from China. You can bet I had the camera rolling!

The next day we were taken to a Buddhist temple in downtown Elista, the capital of Kalmykia, to ask for a blessing for our trip. Before entering the temple, we went through a ceremonial ritual where we had to touch a dozen or so large, colorful photos and paintings, which were lined up about 40 yards from the entrance. Then we were told to walk into the temple, ask for a blessing, and then walk backwards out of the temple. To this day that trip remains one of the most memorable I have ever taken.

Another close encounter I had with the head of a country came in January of 2000. While I didn't get to meet him personally, I had the chance to hunt stag on the estate of Leonid Kuchma, the President of the Ukraine. Accompanying me on that trip was Jay Link from the Jack Link's Beef Jerky Company in Minong, Wisconsin. He was joined by several of his long- time hunting buddies.

As I mentioned, we never did get to meet the president but we had a close encounter. One day he stopped by the main residence on the estate while we were in the hunting lodge about a mile away. Someone came to the lodge and told us we needed to stay inside and keep the hunting rifles locked up in a storage room. He would watch them until the president left. We were fine with that! There was no way any of us wanted to be out roaming around in the woods with a rifle while Kuchma and his entourage of heavily-armed body guards patrolled the area!

Several hours later, Kuchma left the estate and we went about our business.

Besides Dmitri, I have had two other main outfitters that I worked with in Russia over the years. One of them was Michael Silin a short, thin man from Moscow, who had organized hunting and fishing trips for the Communist Party elite and the military while the country was still the Soviet Union. Michael had close friends in the hunting department and was able to get us in and out of sensitive areas to hunt moose, sheep, and bears.

I always enjoyed Michael's company because he was an easy-going guy with a good sense of humor. But Michael sure could get nervous helping us clear customs at the airports! That had a lot to do with us being heavily armed and entering sensitive military areas. As I mentioned earlier, about the only people who were allowed to hunt in the Soviet Union were Communist Party elite and the military so a convoy of Americans roaming around the countryside with high-powered rifles and several boxes of shells was not something the local police departments and military personnel were used to seeing.

Fortunately, Michael had good contacts in the government . . . and also knew how the system worked. There were a number of times when he asked me for a "little money to grease the wheels." I would hand him a 50 or a 100 dollar bill and he would take care of the problem. When we ran into these situations, Michael would look at me and say, "Denny, what can I do. It's Russia!"

The other outfitter I have worked with extensively over the years is Andrey Konvolov. Andrey lives in the small town of Yelizovo, which is located just outside the city of Petropavlovsk on the Kamchatka Peninsula. I always enjoyed working with Andrey because I knew that he was covering all the bases. He is a very detail-orientated man who takes his job seriously. Andrey also knew how to get things done under the table when need be.

In addition to working with me on bear and moose hunts on the Kamchatka Peninsula, Andrey is one of the top agents in Kamchatka for angling trips. The Kamchatka Peninsula has become the premier destination for fly fishermen over the past two decades. The salmon and rainbow trout fishing here is second to none. These wild pristine streams produce thousands of fish a year to anglers from all over Europe and the United States.

Andrey arranges many of these fishing trips through an organization called Wild Salmon Rivers (WSR), which works closely with the Fly Shop. There have been years when WSR has booked over 200 anglers to various streams located on the Peninsula. One of the most famous streams here is the Zhuponova River, just north of Petropavlovsk. It's a stream where I have also taken clients, with Andrey's help. I can honestly say that I have never caught more trout and salmon on a fly rod in one week than on the Zhuponova.

I had a chance to meet one of Kamchatka's most prominent fly-fishing aficionados a number of years ago. I'll never forget Andrey coming up to me with a big grin on his face as we made our way out of the small airport in Petropavlovsk. "You know who that is, Denny?" he said, pointing to a tall gentleman standing just outside the door.

"Well, I'll be . . . it looks like Bobby Knight!" I said excitedly. "He used to be the coach at Indiana and is now with Texas Tech. How do you know who Bobby Knight is?"

"That's him," Andrey replied. "That's Bobby Knight! He's been here before, back in the late 90s. He was at the Cedar Lodge, where you fished with me. I worked as an interpreter then and was at the Cedar Lodge when Bobby Knight was there. He likes to fly fish here in Kamchatka. Have you ever met him?"

"No, I haven't," I said. "But I'm going to take care of that right now. Hi, my name is Denny Geurink," I said as I walked up to Knight and extended my hand. "I used to go to school at one of your Big Ten rivals. We played some exciting games against you when you were at Indiana." I smiled.

"Which school was that?" Knight came back, grinning.

"The University Of Michigan," I replied. "While I did play basketball in college, it wasn't at Michigan. I took graduate courses there, though, so I always rooted for them when they played Indiana. Indiana was really good back then!"

"Yeah, those were some good games," Knight replied. The conversation then turned to fishing. After talking for a few minutes, we shook hands, wished each other luck, and parted ways. I never ran into him again.

Another famous visitor to the Zhuponova River back in 2004 was President Jimmy Carter and his wife Rosalynn. They fished the Zhuponova from July 9–16, 2004.

Among some of the nicest people I have met in Russia are the various interpreters, guides, and cooks who have accompanied me and my clients on our journeys. Because we've used the same camps for many years, I've gotten to know a number of them very well. I'll never forget the first year we were in a spring bear camp during the Russian "Victory Day" celebrations.

Victory Day is the equivalent to our Fourth of July. It is celebrated on May 9 to commemorate the day the German military surrendered to the Soviet Union in World War II. It is a day to honor those who fought and died in the war. The holiday is celebrated with huge military parades in Red

Square, and the laying of flowers and wreaths at grave sites. It's a poignant reminder of the casualties of war.

Some of the nicest people I've met in Russia were some of our guides. I especially enjoyed swapping stories with our Yakutian guides seen here standing next to our tents with Gerald and John Crever. (Gerald Crever photo)

When May 9 rolled around as we sat in bear camp one year, the guides became very somber at the evening dinner table. They wanted to have a vodka toast to honor those who had fought and died in combat. Some of the guides had fathers, friends, and relatives among the casualties. After the first toast, one of the guides stood up to toast the American soldiers who fought and died as well because, as he pointed out, the Russians and Americans were allies in World War II. The guides made a very big deal out of this alliance. It was the one time in history where Russians and Americans stood side by side to defeat a common enemy.

After that toast, I stood up to make a toast to Russian and American friendship. I told the guides that my father was a veteran of World War II; that he had landed on Omaha Beach in France and survived that day . . . which was known in America as "D-Day" . . . only to be mowed down later by a German machine gun. He took four bullets. Two of them took out a lung, one went through his hip, and another through his elbow as he fell to the ground. Somehow he survived and lived to tell about it.

You should have seen the look on the guides' faces. This really struck a nerve. It revealed how much Russians and Americans had in common. From that day on, every year we were in camp, the guides always made sure they made a toast to my father. One year, two of the guides who were in a camp about 30 miles away with some of my other clients, drove their snowmobiles over a mountain to come to the camp where I was staying so they could toast me and my father on Victory Day!

As alluded to several times already, the Russians like their vodka. A lot has been written about the Russian's love affair with this potent alcoholic beverage over the years and I can tell you from personal experience, most of it is true! It seems to have become an integral part of their society. They celebrate with it, mourn with it, party with it, and toast everything you can imagine with it. It's on the table for every occasion. And, of course, it's always in camp. The guides are always toasting something.

Those first few years, the guides would haul out the vodka bottle and the shot glasses and say: "Denny, wadka! Wadka!" I didn't want to offend them by not joining with them in a toast, so I would say, "OK, but choot choot!" This means "just a little bit" in Russian. "Denny wants choot choot wadka!"

The guides would look at me, chuckle at my lame attempt at speaking Russian, and then pour me a full glass anyway. But, undeterred, I kept asking for a "choot choot" shot every time they hauled out the bottle. That's because I had such a hard time getting the nasty stuff past my lips! It burned all the way down to the pit of my stomach. Some of the really cheap vodka the guides brought to camp would bring tears to a glass eye!

After a few years of asking the guides for a "choot choot" shot every time they hauled out the "helicopter fuel," as

Dmitri called it, the guides began smiling at me and, instead of saying, "Denny wadka! Denny wadka!"; they began saying, "Denny, choot choot! Denny, choot choot!"

It didn't take long before the nickname stuck. And that's how Russian vodka became known as "choot choot" in our camps.

One of the first things we usually do after arriving at a camp is meet up with the guides and sight in our rifles. We want to make sure everything is working properly after our long, arduous trip from the States to the Middle of Nowhere, Siberia. The guides are just as interested in making sure our rifles are still firing accurately as we are. After all, a bad shot could spell a lot of trouble for the guide as well as the hunter.

Our Russian guides were as tough as nails. Notice this one even has the tip of a finger missing! Not an unusual occurrence. Many were missing body parts. (Merle Barnaby photo)

Those first few years the guides were especially interested in seeing what our rifles could do. They were used to old SKS military issue rifles. None of them had scopes, and some were so old they were actually held together with duct tape and baling wire! I'm not kidding! The guides were fascinated by how big and shiny our rifles were. They especially marveled at the scopes and the size of our shells.

"That's not a bullet, it's a bomb!" one of the guides gasped in amazement our first year in Russia as he looked at one of my cousin Terry Geurink's shells. "May I shoot your rifle?"

"Sure," Terry said, handing the guide his 300 mag.

The guide pulled the rifle up, aimed at the target, and pulled the trigger just as Terry tried to warn him about the recoil. Too late! The guide got whacked on the eyebrow with the scope! He handed the rifle back to Terry, wiped the blood off his brow, and shook his head.

"Russian hunters don't need such big rifles," he said sarcastically. "We are so tough we can kill bears with a little gun!"

To be sure, our Russian guides are some of the toughest, hardest-working, grittiest individuals you'll ever meet. On one occasion, two of my Kamchatka guides traveled from their village over snow-covered mountains and through dense wilderness for two weeks, just so they could get two extra snowmobiles in camp for my hunters. They ate fish they caught in the streams and squirrels and hares they shot (and who knows what else!) to survive so that they wouldn't have to eat the food that was designated for camp. At night they slept on the sleds they were towing behind their snowmobiles, waking up frequently to chase off bears and wolverines from their campsite. These guys are tough SOBS!

Several times we had guides do the same type of thing for our sheep hunts in Yakutia only this time they were taking in strings of pack horses instead of snowmobiles. Again, it was a two-week ordeal; basically living off the land. We have no comprehension of how tough life was – and still is – in many remote areas of Siberia. These guys do this all the time without giving it a second thought; it's part of their normal way of life. And we complain if our TV remotes don't work!

Life is harsh in the remote villages of Siberia. You can especially see it in the faces of the elderly. (Ken Horm photo)

Besides having a good command of the English language, making them easy to communicate with, my interpreters have always had an insatiable appetite to learn more about America. Combine that with my insatiable appetite to learn more about Russia, and you have the basis for a good relationship. I've learned to speak and understand quite a bit of the Russian language over the years, thanks to my interpreters.

One of the most interesting interpreters I've had the pleasure of getting to know is a man named Vladislav Shurin. Shurin lives in the city of Donetsk in the Ukraine. He's an English professor there at the University of Donetsk. He has impeccable language skills but he was taught the King's English so he has this quirky British accent that makes me smile every time I hear him speak.

Our guides would do whatever it took to get the job done . . . including hooking up a horse to a homemade sled to haul one of my clients around who had broken his leg a week before his expedition.
(Dmitri Sikorski photo)

Vlad and I have shared a lot of camps and a lot of laughs. He has taught me a lot about the history and culture of Russia and the Ukraine. He also told me that when his country was part of the Soviet Union, things did not go so well. "The Communist Party leaders were always telling us how much better off we were than the Americans," Vlad says disgustedly. "Now we find out we are a Third World country! We are like a poor African country. We have been lied to all of our lives. We were part of a great experiment called Communism, which failed. While the rest of the world evolved and moved forward, we stayed the same. Now we are 40 years behind America!"

Another one of my favorite interpreters is Andrey Shutov. Andrey is also from the city of Donetsk in the Ukraine. You will read more about him in an upcoming chapter.

I have discovered that the Russians, despite having lived through some tough times during the Soviet Union era, have quite a sense of humor. I'll never forget the street vendor we met on Moscow's famous Arbat Street in the early 90s.

Arbat Street is a pedestrian street that has been around since the late 15th century. Today it is lined with souvenir shops and street vendors and has become a favorite destination for tourists. In the early 90s when we were there, not many people spoke English in the shops but somehow whoever was running the shop would always find someone who did speak English so they could help you out.

Taking a tour of a small Siberian village with friend, Boris. (Denny Geurink photo)

I was looking to buy one of those Russian-style fur hats and asked the street vendor if he would take American money. He didn't know what I was talking about but told me to wait just a minute. It wasn't long before he was back with a young man, who approached me with a big grin on his face. "How can I help you, sir," he said, smiling. "Did you want to buy this hat from my friend? What were you saying to him?"

The daughter of one of our guides models beautiful Russian fur hat her father made from a red fox he trapped. (Ken Horm photo)

"I asked him if he would take U.S. dollars for this hat, and how much it would cost in American money," I replied.

"Let me see your American money," the young man said. I handed him several one- dollar bills. He looked them over carefully and then grinned.

"Your American dollar looks just like the Russian buck!" He chuckled. "Of course we will take your American dollars."

We all had a big laugh over that one. Because we were walking around without an interpreter at the time, the young man volunteered to follow us around and help us with our souvenir shopping. What a great gesture.

Today you don't even need an interpreter with you on Arbat Street as pretty much all the shop owners and vendors now have someone there who speaks English. They have picked up on our decadent capitalistic ways very quickly!

In fact, everything about Russia has changed tremendously in the past 22 years. Its capital city of Moscow has gone from being one of the poorest cities in the world to the most expensive city in the

One of our interpreters, Galina Unichanko, compares her fingernails to the claws of a bear. Not much difference!
(Steve Van Poucke photo)

world. According to Dmitri, on any given day, there are over two million foreigners in Moscow, a far cry from the "closed society" days of the Soviet era.

CHAPTER 6

THE FOOD

ONE OF FIRST THINGS I noticed when I arrived in Russia was how different their food was from ours; at least in the way they prepared it and what they considered suitable for each of the three square meals per day.

My first introduction to Russian cuisine came on that inaugural trip to Moscow back in 1991. We had just checked into our hotel and decided to go out for dinner, having no idea what a challenge "going out for dinner" would be. The first challenge we faced was just trying to find a restaurant! We drove all over town looking for a place to eat. It was still the Soviet Union back then and it soon became apparent that the communist system didn't put a whole lot of emphasis on eating out, fine dining, and fancy restaurants. Here we were in a city of over 10 million people and we couldn't find one decent restaurant! Even the little town of several thousand I was from had a couple of restaurants.

And when we did finally find a restaurant, after nearly an hour of driving around the city, I could see why it took us so long. It was in the basement of some drab-looking building, with a very small sign out front. I never would have even guessed it was a restaurant. It looked more like a small studio apartment a college student would have rented off campus. No neon sign. No brightly-painted moniker. No flashing arrows. No Open sign. Absolutely nothing that would lead you to believe someone was cooking and serving food there.

We were met at the door by a stoic-looking man who led us to a small table in an isolated corner of the restaurant. Even though the restaurant was almost empty, Dmitri told us that this was the area reserved for foreigners. He told us that foreigners and locals were usually segregated in restaurants, hotels, and other public places. They tried to keep foreigners from interacting with the local people. We first noticed this practice back at the hotel. Not only were we lodged in separate rooms but also on a separate floor. I guess they didn't want us to poison the locals with our evil capitalistic views.

And . . . as we came to find out . . . foreigners paid a different rate for their room than did the locals. Dmitri told me that he paid less than half of what we paid for our rooms. Several times on subsequent hunts, he would tell me not to speak when we went to register at a hotel. He would register me as a Russian rather than a foreigner to save money on the rooms. Anyhow, I digress. Back to the restaurant.

As we sat at the table, talking about how hungry we were and what we wanted to eat, I suddenly felt a presence behind me. I looked up and saw a young lady with a pen and pad in her hand, staring hollowly at the table.

"Hi!" I greeted her with a big smile. She nodded nonchalantly and continued to stare blankly into the smoke-filled air. She never said a word. Never cracked a smile. Didn't even look at me. Wow! In the U.S., you are greeted with a big smile and a "how are you" and a "what can I get you to drink?" I was taken aback by the complete lack of any enthusiasm. Nobody in the restaurant seemed glad that we were there, patronizing their business.

The waitress handed Dmitri a menu. Dmitri said something to her and she just shrugged her shoulders. "Sorry guys, no English menus, only Russian menus," he told us. "So tell me what you want to eat and I will order it for you."

"What do they have?" I queried. "I'm kind of hungry. I could eat a horse!"

"I'll see if they have that," Dmitri replied.

As it didn't seem like he was joking, I quickly added, "That's just an expression we use in the U.S. when we are really hungry. I really don't want to literally eat a horse."

"Well, they actually do eat horses in Russia," Dmitri quipped. "I just don't know if they serve it in this restaurant."

"I'll pass on the horse, really!" I replied.

I found out several years later, on a trip to Yakutsk, that Dmitri was right about the horse meat thing in Russia. In one of the restaurants we visited, they actually had quite a selection of tasty horse entrees. Among them were Fillet of Colt, Steak of Mare and Stallion Meatballs. You could also order a glass of warm Mare's Milk to go with your Colt Fillet! Yum! Again, I digress.

"Well, Denny, it seems they have some sort of steak on the menu." Dmitri told me. "I don't think it's probably beef as they don't have much beef in Russia. It's probably a pork steak. And they also have chicken and fish. I don't think I would order the fish, though, as we are a long way from the sea. I'm afraid it won't be very fresh. Who knows how long it took to ship the fish here and I don't know how well it was refrigerated. So . . . what do you want to order?"

I was starting to get a pretty good picture of what Dmitri thought of restaurant food. He had warned me before we started to look for a restaurant that one of the reasons Russians don't eat out is that the food in many restaurants is suspect. Whether that was the reason there weren't a lot of restaurants in Russia, or whether it was an effect, I didn't know. But, we had insisted on finding a restaurant while Dmitri had suggested that we buy food and cook it ourselves. Obviously, Russians don't know how lazy Americans are! Heck, we would rather eat out any day than cook something for ourselves!

"Tell you what, I think I'll try the steak," I finally said to Dmitri after contemplating the possibilities.

Dmitri passed my order on to the waitress in Russian. She didn't say a word, just shook her head. Dmitri said something else, and she again shook her head but this time she accompanied her head shake with some sort of explanation. Aha, she wasn't a mute after all!

"Ah, sorry, Denny they don't have any steak left," Dmitri said. "Is there anything else you would like to try?"

"OK, how about the chicken," I replied.

Again, Dmitri passed my request along to the waitress in her native tongue. And again the waitress shook her head. Dmitri spoke to her some more and she came back with a very curt reply and shook her head one more time. "Sorry, Denny, they don't have any chicken left either," he said. "Anything else you want to try?"

"How about the pork?" I replied.

One more time Dmitri relayed my request to the waitress. One more time she shook her head. Dmitri spoke to her again. There was a definite hint of disgust in his tone of voice this time. Even though he was speaking in Russian, I pretty much knew what he was saying to her.

"You don't have any freaking pork either? What kind of a lousy restaurant is this? Good grief!" is what I think he said . . . loosely translated! At least that's what I wanted to say at that point.

"They don't have any pork either, Denny," Dmitri groused. "Anything else you want to eat?"

Well, as far as I could tell, we were down to the fish! While I wasn't all that eager to eat the fish after what Dmitri told us about it earlier, I was hungry and just wanted to move this whole thing along. Obviously, we really didn't have any other options available anyway.

"I guess I'll have the fish," I told Dmitri.

Once more Dmitri relayed my food order to the waitress. She shook her head yet again. Dmitri was now definitely irritated. I was glad I didn't understand Russian! As he looked back at me and began to speak, I said: "Yeah, I know, they don't have fish either! What do they have? Do they have any freaking food here? This is a restaurant, right?"

Dmitri spoke to the waitress again. The conversation definitely got ugly as they bantered back and forth. Finally, Dmitri said: "Denny, they have hot dogs and rice. That's it! Do you want to eat hot dogs and rice? I told you we should have bought some food and cooked it ourselves! Do you want to leave? Let's just leave and get some food and cook it."

"I'll take the hot dogs and rice," I replied. If this didn't show Dmitri how much Americans detest cooking for themselves then nothing would! We would rather go to a restaurant and eat hot dogs and rice than buy food and cook it ourselves! Pretty pitiful when you think about it.

Another contributing factor with my decision to go with the Chef's Special was that I could see the poor waitress was getting pretty upset. She had a tear in the corner of her eye and I felt bad for her. It wasn't her fault that the restaurant didn't have anything but hot dogs and rice. I told Dmitri to apologize to her for our rude behavior. We understood it wasn't her fault that the place didn't have any food fit to eat. Dmitri agreed. It wasn't the waitress's fault. He conveyed our apologies.

A bit later the waitress came back to our table and presented us with our plates of hot dogs and rice. The "chef" had tried to spruce it up a little with a sprig of parsley lounging on top of the pile of cold rice. We tried not to laugh out loud! Let's have a little respect here! As hungry as I was, it actually tasted pretty good. Ah, heck. I would have eaten the horse at that point!

After the meal, still feeling a bit bad for the poor waitress, we decided to leave her a nice tip. Apparently, Russians aren't much into tipping. When she came back with the change from our bill on a small tray, I told her to keep it. She looked at me quizzically, and tried to hand the tray back to me. I don't think she was used to getting tips; she definitely was not used to getting that large of a tip.

She said something to Dmitri and tried to hand the tray to him. He said something back to her and pushed the tray away. Right then a look of complete surprise overcame her face as she put her hand to her chest. "For me?" she gasped in Russian. "All of this for me?"

"Yes, for you," Dmitri replied.

Ah, there it was! There's that smile we'd been waiting for! She said "Spaceba" several times as she walked away . . . actually, it was more like a skip! Spaceba we found out was Russian for "thank you." That was the first Russian word we ever learned.

"She will probably go home now and take the rest of the week off," Dmitri scolded. "Russians usually don't leave a tip, and when they do it's not much, maybe only five percent or less. You guys just gave her month's wages! You guys tip way too much."

Our main problem was that we didn't realize how little money these people made plus we hadn't yet fully grasped how much the Russian currency was worth. We were told the exchange rate when we traded some of our dollars for rubles but I don't think it really registered. We often referred to the rubles as "monopoly money" because it took so many rubles to make one dollar so we treated it like monopoly money. Dmitri said our waitress probably only made between $10 to $15 dollars a week. Gives you an idea of what life was like under communism way back in 1991.

This whole episode was a unique insight into the stark difference between capitalism and communism. This establishment was owned and operated by the government, not a private individual so there was no incentive to be cordial, no incentive to smile, and, as we found out, no incentive to offer a large menu of tasty entrees.

When you have private ownership of a business, the owner knows he has to do everything he can to offer the best product and the best service possible so the customer is happy and will want to come back. That's because when you own a business, the amount of money you make is based directly upon how much product or service you sell. Not so when an enterprise is government-owned and operated. These people working here couldn't care less if we never came back . . . and probably hoped we wouldn't, it would make their job a whole lot easier. They still got paid the same amount of money, no matter what. There was no way for them to make any extra money.

We would discover another big difference between restaurants in Russia and America the following year when Dmitri came over for a visit to the U.S. and I took him out to one of our restaurants. Actually, it was as much a lesson on the difference in the amount of food we have in the U.S.

as compared to the lack of food in Russia. First, Dmitri was shocked by how many people in America ate out. We were on a 30-minute waiting list! Then, as we sat in the waiting area to be seated, he kept watching all of the half-eaten plates of food being brought back into the kitchen.

"My God!" he gasped. "Americans throw away more food than we have!"

I guess I had never realized just how much food we do throw away here in the United States. As I began watching the trays of food going from the tables back to the kitchen, where they were being dumped, I actually felt a little ashamed of our country. We do throw away more food than many poor countries have! What a waste.

The next day we took Dmitri to a supermarket to buy some groceries. Again, he was flabbergasted by the quantity of food available in the U.S. compared to Russia. "Look! There is so much bread in America that it's falling off the shelves!" Dmitri quipped. "In Russia, people sometimes have to wait in line for over two hours to get a loaf of bread."

If nothing else, my first trip to the Soviet Union showed me how lucky I was to be born in America! We sometimes take this country for granted. We don't know how good we have it!

Fish Bread

One of the strangest culinary items I've encountered while in Russia was served to me by one of our camp cooks on a trip around 1995. We were staying in a small village about 400 miles east of Moscow. Our cook was a kind, grandmotherly lady named Anna. She told us that during our stay she wanted to introduce us to some of the local foods that she grew up on during the old Soviet Union days. She wanted us to try things we may not have had a chance to eat back home in the States. Being an adventurous kind of guy, I told her I was up for that. One day, however, she really pushed the envelope.

Dmitri and I were sitting at the dining room table having a cup of coffee when Anna walked in with a loaf of fresh bread she had just pulled from the oven. The warm loaf of bread looked inviting with its golden brown hue and soft texture. I was eager to try a piece. Anna said something to Dmitri as she set the loaf on the table in front of us and handed Dmitri a knife. Dmitri got a strange look on his face and turned to me with a quizzical grin. "Denny, Anna says this is 'fish bread,' whatever that is." He gave the loaf of bread the evil eye. "I've never heard of fish bread. I don't know what the heck it is. Maybe she ground up some fish and added it to the flour when she cooked it. I don't know. All I can say is that a loaf of bread that tastes like fish doesn't sound good to me."

"Can't say as though I want to eat bread that tastes fishy either," I replied, "but we don't want to offend Anna. Let's give it a shot."

Dmitri took the big sharp knife and cut the bread about a third of the way into the loaf. Oh my gosh! There, smack dab in the middle of the loaf, surrounded by baked dough, was an entire fish! Head, tail, fins, scales, and *everything!* The head was poking out of the piece Dmitri had just cut and the beast was staring up at us with a glassy eye!

Dmitri gagged and pushed the bread away from him, and cursed in Russian. I don't know exactly what he said but, believe me, he was cursing in Russian! I felt sorry for Anna as she scooped the loaf of bread off the table and rushed it out of the room. I swear the fish wagged its head and stuck out its tongue as she darted off to the kitchen.

Later that afternoon Anna returned with a fresh loaf of homemade cheese bread. Now that's more like it! A loaf of bread with cheese baked in the middle of it is a whole lot more palatable!

Denny, That's Not Pasta!

One of my most unusual encounters with Russian food occurred in one of our moose hunting camps in the mid-90s.

One of my clients had scored on a big bull moose and the guides had brought some of the meat back to camp for dinner. I was eagerly looking forward to my first taste of moose meat!

Zoya Abdilina, one of our interpreters helps prepare a meal in tent camp in Siberia. (Denny Geurink photo)

At dinner time Dmitri called us to the cook tent. We sat down around a large wooden table, flanked on each side with 2 X 8 planks of rough sawn wood which stretched from one stump to another and served as benches. The cook placed a bowl of two-to-three inch long, by half-inch wide, strips of thin white pasta in a tasty cheese sauce in front of us. I figured it was some sort of fettuccine. I ate the bowl of pasta with gusto and waited eagerly for the moose steaks to follow. As I could see the cook wasn't quite ready with the steaks, I asked Dmitri if the cook could give me another bowl of pasta while we waited.

"That's a really tasty pasta dish he whipped up," I said as I handed my bowl to the cook. "Tell the cook he did a great job!"

"What pasta?" Dmitri queried.

"The pasta we just ate," I replied.

"Denny, that's not pasta," Dmitri came back.

"It's not?" I said incredulously. "Then what the heck is it?"

"It's the sinus cavity from the moose," Dmitri said with a grin. "You want some more?"

"The sinus cavity of a moose? Aaaaaghh! Never mind, I'll pass," I replied.

"But you said it was tasty!" Dmitri said, still grinning.

"Not anymore!" I winced.

Moose Meat Surprise

A couple of years later, I was hunting moose near the city of Yakutsk with a group of clients when we were served another moose surprise dish. The guides in this camp were local native people called Eveny. While they are a very warm and friendly people, they definitely had different ideas about what parts of a moose are good to eat than we did. As we sat at the dinner table waiting to eat some of the moose one of the guys had shot a few hours earlier, I started to get an uneasy feeling. The very first thing the cook set in front of us was the same "pasta" dish I had had in the last camp. When I declined it, the interpreter, Misha, asked me what was wrong.

"I know what that stuff is," I told Misha. "It's the sinus cavity from the moose, right?"

"Yes, Denny, it is," Misha replied. "But the guides here consider it to be a delicacy. It's very tasty. You should try some."

"I have tried it before, and while it doesn't taste as bad as it sounds, I just can't eat it," I said. "I just can't get the thought of nibbling on a big snot-filled nose out of my mind!"

Misha laughed and then said, "Denny, the cook is putting some other moose dishes on the table, why don't you eat one of these?"

"Well, what exactly are they?" I replied. "I can't really say that I see anything that looks like a steak or roast. What's this one?" I said, pointing to one of the plates.

"That's moose tongue," Misha said. "It is also considered a delicacy. Do you want some?"

"No, I think I'll pass on the tongue," I replied. I didn't feel like French kissing a moose either. "What about that one? What's that?"

"That's the heart," Misha said.

"And that one?" I said, pointing to another plate.

"Those are the kidneys." Misha smiled.

"And that?"

"Those are the lungs," Misha said, chuckling.

"Oh, my God!" I gasped. "Where in the heck is the meat? This is the gut pile. What happened to the steaks and roasts?"

"These dishes are all considered delicacies." Misha smiled. "The guides don't really like the steaks and roasts as much. They will go back and get that stuff later and take it back to the village for the others to eat. They save the good stuff for themselves. Nothing will go to waste."

"I think I'll stick with the bread and cheese tonight," I told Misha.

The next day I followed one of my hunters around with my TV camera and captured his hunt on film. After the big bull was down, the first thing the guide did was go over and cut out one of the eyeballs and take a bite! There was stuff squirting everywhere! Holy crap! He then looked over at me and offered me a bite. I declined as diplomatically as I could, trying desperately to suppress my gagging reflex. The hunter also declined when he was offered a bite! We looked at each other with a silly grin of disbelief.

As the guide began field-dressing it, I paid careful attention to what he was doing. Sure enough, out came the sinus cavity. Then he pulled out the heart, lungs and kidneys . . . and some other things I don't even want to talk about. He stuffed everything in a big plastic bag and got ready to leave.

"Wait a minute!" I said to the guide. "I want the tenderloin to take back for the hunters and me. You guys can eat the guts, we want the meat."

The guide looked at me quizzically and smiled. He had no clue what I was saying. I went over to the moose carcass and pointed at the tenderloin. "Denny want tenderloin," I said, jabbing at the inside of the rib cage next to the backbone. "Tenderloin! Tenderloin! Denny want tenderloin!"

"Ah, fillet!" The guide chuckled. "Denny, fillet!"

"Yes, fillet." I smiled. "Denny want fillet."

The guide peeled both fillets off and handed them to me. I had brought along a big plastic bag of my own as I was determined to bring the tenderloins back and eat them instead of the gut pile. The things were huge! I bet they weighed at least 8 to 10 pounds each! I carried them back to camp like a bag of gold. I couldn't wait to eat some moose tenderloin for dinner.

That evening I found out just why the guides prefer the innards to the steaks. The cook pan fried the fillets into a little pile of burnt charcoal. Way overdone. They were tough and tasteless. As we chewed on the shoe leather aka tenderloin, the guides gleefully polished off the juicy gut pile.

The next day I cut off several steaks from the remaining fillets and marinated them in a mixture of coca cola, catsup, salt, pepper, mustard, and anything else that looked like a spice. The cook looked at me like I was crazy. I then found some rocks and built a fire pit. I burned wood in the fire pit all day long until I had a nice pile of red hot coals. I found a roll of old heavy wire the guides had carried in for some kind of project and made myself a grill top . . . well, something like a grill top! When the guys got back to camp, I took the homemade grill top and placed it over the fire pit. I put the steaks on the grill top and cooked them until they were medium-well done and handed them to my hunters, who were waiting with great anticipation. They were excellent!

As my clients oohed and ahhed, the guides looked on in disbelief. They were busy munching on the heart and lungs.

I walked over to one of the guides and offered him a fillet. He declined and pointed at the pile of lungs on his plate and said "Delicatessen, Delicatessen!"

While we did have some strange meals in our remote camps, most were very tasty. Even the presentation was great. (Denny Geurink photo)

It was amazing how good our meals were considering we were in the middle of nowhere and they were prepared on a small woodstove.

But I insisted. "Try it, just try it," I said, holding the plate with the fillet in front of him. Reluctantly, he grabbed the fillet in his hand and took a small bite.

"Oohh!" he exclaimed in utter shock. "Oohh! Delicatessen! Delicatessen!"

"Delicatessen?" the other guides queried.

"Da, delicatessen!" he blurted.

The other guides then all took a bite and began oohing and ahhing just like my clients. Now they knew what a fillet was supposed to taste like! The guides and my hunters had me grilling steaks the rest of the week! In subsequent years I took a grill top and marinating sauce to moose camp with me.

NOTHING GOES TO WASTE

Over the years I have eaten all sorts of what we Americans would consider strange dishes. I've tasted bear paw soup, fried moose tongue, tripe from a Maral stag, horse meat, goat meat, blood meal, mare's milk, Rocky Mountain oysters from red deer and mouflon sheep, plus a host of mystery meats that I shudder to think about. Some of it was on a "don't ask, don't tell" basis.

But, you have to remember the people we were hunting with are used to living off the land. They are modern day Jeremiah Johnsons living in the remote regions of Siberia. They ate everything. They were starving. Nothing went to waste. Actually, in reality, they aren't any different than our ancestors. I remember watching my grandpa butcher a hog once. When he had finished processing the hog, there wasn't anything left but a spot of blood on the garage floor. He could see I was surprised by how efficient the butchering process had been. That's when he looked over at me and winked. "Denny, we eat everything but the squeal!"

The people we met in Siberia over the years remind me so much of my grandfather and his generation. As I mentioned above, the guides ate everything but the grunt of a moose.

What we didn't eat in camp, they took back to their villages with them after the hunt. They considered our moose hunts to be a way for them to stock up meat for the winter, while we were looking at the hunts as a way to get a big set of antlers for the wall. This turned out to be quite a conflict of interest in those early years.

One of the contributing factors to the big difference in the perception of what a hunt consists of between us and the guides stemmed from the fact that we were actually getting moose tags reserved for the locals for subsistence hunting. When I was first contacted about setting up moose hunts in the Yakutia region of central Siberia, the outfitter told me there were only three or four moose tags set aside in his area for "foreign" or non-native hunters. Meanwhile, the native people could get approximately 18 moose tags a year to gather meat for the villages.

I told him that I couldn't come that far to set up hunts for just three people a year. It would be way too costly. That's when we began brainstorming. When he told me about the 18 tags reserved for the locals for subsistence hunting, I asked him if there was a way for him to transfer some of the local tags to foreign tags. I told him we would gladly give all the meat to the locals. My hunters were coming for the trophy, not the meat. Heck, we couldn't get that much meat back home anyway. It would cost way too much in baggage fees . . . plus the hassle we would have with the Department of Agriculture, bringing in a hoofed animal from Russia.

He was able to work out an agreement with the local authorities for a reassignment of moose tags. He and the guides were actually quite pleased with the arrangement. Not only did the natives get the meat they were after, we bought their tags, paid them to guide us, and brought the meat back to the villages for them after the hunt! It was a "win- win" situation all around.

But this arrangement led to a problem on those first few hunts. The guides were used to shooting the first thing they saw, whether it be a cow, calf, or small bull. They were not trophy hunting, they were meat hunting. Consequently, they were pushing the hunters to shoot anything they saw. My hunters, meanwhile, were here to shoot as big a moose as they could find. It took a few years for us to sort this out. The guides finally realized that we were going to wind up shooting a moose at some point in the hunt, whether it be the first one we saw or the last one we saw. They were going to get their meat regardless. That's when the guides actually got excited about trying to find the biggest bull possible.

I'll never forget when we returned to town those first few years with the helicopters loaded down with moose meat. Because we hired a chopper to fly us out and drop us off at camp, and then come back after the hunt to pick us up, it was much easier for the guides to get the meat back to the village. Normally they would have had to walk or take a horse to camp, so it would take many trips to pack a moose out. Now all the meat was coming back to town at one time. And everyone in the village knew it was coming! As soon as they heard the chopper getting close to town, they poured out of their homes with buckets, wheel barrows, axes, saws, and plastic bags. It was free moose meat day in the village!

One year the locals were waiting for us in a large field just outside of town. They had a long table all set up with an assortment of snacks and drinks. It was like a hero's welcome! As soon as we got out of the helicopter, they escorted us to the table and asked us to sit down and then waited on us like we were a bunch of dignitaries. We were a bit humbled by the whole experience.

Talk about nothing going to waste! When a bear is harvested, the Russians will even scrape the fat off from the bear's chest. They take this fat back to camp and boil it down into a thick, clear liquid and put it in a jar. They use the liquid fat for medicinal purposes. Some Russians even eat a tablespoon of fat every day for preventative maintenance, much the same way my mother used to make me take a tablespoon of cod liver oil when I was a youngster.

One year when I was sick in camp with a cold, the cook tried to get me to eat a tablespoon of the boiled fat. I wanted to but just couldn't get it past my nose. He then told me to rub it on my chest like Vick's vapor rub. I did. I smelled like a dead fish for several days but, by golly, it cleared up my head cold! A lot of these old home remedies have been handed down for generations . . . because they work!

After several years of eating a lot of strange foods on these trips, I planned a standardized menu for the camps. While we did thoroughly enjoy a lot of the Russian cuisine like borscht soup, fried cheese bread, flat chicken, and other local delicacies, there were a few things I wanted to phase out . . . like the bear paw soup. I created a full menu for the entire hunt and had the outfitter give it to all of our cooks before we arrived at the camps. It included a lot of the Russian dishes plus a few good old American favorites like eggs and bacon for breakfast!

Author's Note: As mentioned earlier in this chapter, we found it almost impossible to find a place to eat on that first trip because restaurants and eating out were not a cultural part of the Soviet Union. It's amazing how quickly this changed once the communist government fell. Once capitalism moved in, restaurants began popping up like morel mushrooms after a warm spring rain. Just one year later, in 1992, we had a wide selection of great eating places to choose from. Today you can find everything from McDonalds to TGIF Fridays to Pizza Huts and Subway shops. God bless capitalism!

CHAPTER 7

THE CULTURE

BEING A HISTORY BUFF, I was especially fascinated by the cultural and social differences between the United States and Russia on those first few trips back in the early 90s. I was intrigued by how differently our countries had evolved over the years under two drastically different forms of government. The contrast between communism and capitalism was dramatic. You could see it in many facets of the everyday lives of the Russian people; it was evident in the clothes they wore, the cars they drove, the food they ate, and the places they lived.

It was especially evident in their homes. There were very few "houses" in the cities. Everyone lived in a government-owned apartment complex. These apartment buildings were large, ugly, and run-down. Even recently-built complexes looked like they were at least 50 years old. There was absolutely no emphasis on design and beauty. Buildings and communities were basic and functional, giving the impression of a stark, cold existence.

While driving through St. Petersburg one day I commented to Dmitri about how dull and drab the outside of the apartment buildings looked. They were all in dire need of paint. The yards were messy and uninviting and there was very little grass or shrubbery to spruce them up and make them look "homey." The hallways and stairways were dark and dingy . . . almost creepy. Yet when I had a chance to visit one of our guide's and one of our cook's apartments, they were bright and cheerful on the inside.

"That's because all of these buildings are government-owned," Dmitri explained. "The people who live there aren't going to spend any of their money to fix up the outside of the building when they don't even own it. They just spend money on the inside because that's where they live. It's not like in the U.S. where you own your own home so you want it to look nice on the outside as well. You don't mind spending money on something that belongs to you. But you're not going to spend your money on something that isn't yours."

Makes a lot of sense. For me this was an eye-opening, first-hand look at one of the major differences between capitalism and communism . . . the ownership of private property.

I also learned from Dmitri that all Soviet citizens were required to have passports and personal documentation with them whenever they moved about in their own country, just like foreigners did when they came to visit. If they stayed more than three days in Moscow, they had to register with the local authorities. And if a Russian wanted to move from one city to another, he had to get permission to do so. The Soviet Union was paranoid about keeping track of it citizens. Big Brother was always watching you!

Another thing that really intrigued me in those first few years in Russia was the transportation system. Back in the States, just about everyone owns a car or pick-up truck. In Russia at that time there weren't that many people who owned a private vehicle. Mostly they walked from one place to the other or they used public transportation. That's why the underground metro system in Moscow is one of the largest and busiest in the world. And that's why above ground, the streets are choked with street cars and buses. There's not a country in the world that has more public transportation than Russia. It was one of the core principals of communism.

Most of the cars that we did see on the roads were small, plain, boxy cubicles called Ladas. The Lada is a Soviet-engineered car that was first built back in the 70s. It's a dull, drab, and purely functional vehicle designed to get people from Point A to Point B. No frills, no sport, and no speed. I didn't see any convertibles, pick-up trucks, or brightly-colored vehicles in Russia in the early 90s.

By comparison, back in the U.S. at that time, we were in love with our cars and trucks. (Still are!) Many people see their vehicle as an extension of their personality. Our cars and trucks were big, beefed-up road hogs with bucket seats, chrome wheels, and leather interiors. There was nothing even close to that in the Soviet Union back in the early 90s. To me this was another stark comparison of life under communism as opposed to life under capitalism.

Today, just 20 years later, the streets of Moscow are jam-packed with cars. In fact, traffic has become a major problem in Moscow because the road system wasn't designed to hold this many vehicles. And, just like in any other major city around the world, you will now find every make, model, and size of car for sale in Russia. We drive past a huge Ford dealership every time we go from the airport to our hotel.

Scene from Red Square. Once off limits to foreigners it is now one of the most popular tourist destinations in the world. (Denny Geurink photos)

Toilet paper can be used as another tool to compare capitalism and communism. Toilet paper? A tool? I know what you're thinking . . . this guy's missing a card! Please indulge me. I was introduced to what I call the "Toilet Paper Effect" on my very first trip to the Soviet Union back in 1991. It all started one day when I got into a rather interesting discussion about, of all things, toilet paper, with one of my interpreters. I asked him why Russian toilet paper was so coarse and rough.

Another scene from Red Square. Notice the heavy police presence right after the coup.

"Our toilet paper in the U.S. is much thicker, softer, and smoother than the brown paper bag material you guys use," I said, chuckling. "We use that kind of paper in a butcher shop to wrap meat. Heck, our toilet paper even looks and smells good."

"That's pretty easy to explain," my interpreter replied. "In the U.S. all the toilet paper companies are privately-owned. Each company tries to make its brand of toilet paper better than the other company's toilet paper, so they can sell more of their product and make more money. So your toilet paper is always getting softer and smoother. It's always improving. Here in the Soviet Union, the government owns and operates the one and only toilet paper company. There is zero competition. They don't have to bother making it any better because you can't go anywhere else to buy better toilet paper. If you want toilet paper, here it is! You use the government's toilet paper or you do without.

Changing of the guard in front of Lenin's tomb on Red Square. (Denny Geurink photo)

"In some of the villages, people use old newspapers or magazines instead of toilet paper," my interpreter chuckled, "because it's softer!"

Speaking of toilet paper . . . the toilets you throw the paper into are just as bad, if not worse, than the paper. This is especially true of the toilets found in public "restrooms." I use the term toilet and restroom here very loosely. Again, there is no emphasis on comfort and convenience in the Soviet Union. Most of the toilets found in public places are nothing more than a hole in the floor. That's right a hole in the floor! There are no "toilets" per se. No porcelain throne to sit on! There is nothing to sit on! You need to take a number two, you squat over an open pit, praying you don't lose your balance and fall into the smelly abyss. I have no idea how those little 70-year-old ladies did it. Heck, my wife has a fit when I leave the seat down!

When we had to make a pit stop while traveling down the road, we would pull into a "rest area" – again, I use the term loosely – and try to hold our breath the whole time we were in the pit area. You will find out what the definition of gag reflex is when you enter one of these facilities. Finally, we started doing the same thing most of the local Russian did; that is, we would take care of business behind the building where you could at least breathe while you relieved yourself. You could see that the locals were avoiding going into the building by all the toilet paper and "droppings" scattered around the building!

I discovered another poignant difference between capitalism and communism on that first trip back in 1991 when Dmitri and I got on the subject of productivity. Dmitri told me that the Soviet Union was talking about increasing the work day from 8 to 10 hours in its factories to boost productivity. They just weren't getting enough done in an 8-hour day.

"The people in the factories seem to be working slower and getting less done," Dmitri explained. "That's one of the problems with communism. There's no incentive to work harder and get more done so you can make more money. Everyone gets paid the same, no matter how hard they work. Why should Boris work his butt off when he gets paid the same as Anatoly who just sits around all day and does nothing? The slower Anatoly goes, the slower Boris goes. Instead of getting more done, they get less done. This kind of system just doesn't work. That's why it's collapsing."

"Communism breeds stupid, lazy people!" one of my other interpreters chimed in. "It just doesn't work. The problem is that it's taken 75 years to prove that it doesn't work. So now we are 75 years behind the rest of the world!"

This negative attitude towards communism was especially prevalent with the younger generation in Russia. I'll never forget the time we were in the town of Shushenskoye after an ibex hunt and went to visit the home where Lenin had been placed under house arrest from 1897 to 1900. He had been exiled there by the Czar for advocating the overthrow of the monarchy. His brother Alexander "Sacha" Ulyanov had been arrested on May 8, 1887 for trying to assassinate the Czar. It seems Lenin's whole family was bent on revolution.

During our sightseeing visit, the tour guide, a young man in his late 20s, put everything in perspective. "This is where Lenin worked out his Marxist ideas that led to the Bolshevik Revolution in 1917," our tour guide stated. "This is where all the bulls**t started that led this country into chaos, isolation, and poverty. If only the Czar had executed Lenin instead of putting him under house arrest, this country would have been a whole lot better off."

Whoah! Wasn't expecting that one!

As Dmitri and some of my other interpreters had so colorfully pointed out to me, their life under the communist brand of socialism was harsh. Because there was no way to earn extra money by working harder or producing more, many people at this time resorted to more "creative" ways to supplement their income. This became especially prevalent during the transitional period between the break-up of the Soviet Union and the establishment of Russia's own brand of democracy.

Back then Russia was much like the old American Wild west. It was a freewheeling time of discovery, graft, and corruption. There was pretty much an "anything goes" kind of attitude in the country until they found their way into the 21st century. During those early years, we had to regularly grease the wheels to make the system work efficiently. All of my outfitters were good at greasing the wheels; Dmitri was particularly good.

For the first few years we were in business together, Dmitri had me bring along gifts from the U.S. to give to the local officials to help speed up the customs process. These presents ranged from hard-sided gun cases, Swiss Army knives and Gerber Tools to cartons of Marlboro cigarettes. One year I brought along a fancy display of all the different kinds of rifle cartridges made in the United States . . . which had been specifically requested by one of the customs agents!

Dmitri was able to cultivate a good working relationship with many of these government officials, and my presents were part of the dynamic. If the customs officials were allowed to work at their own pace it would take many hours to clear customs but, with a little grease for the wheels, we could get it done a lot quicker.

One of the most iconic sights on Red Square is St. Basils Cathedral, built in 1555 by Czar Ivan the Terrible. (Denny Geurink photo)

But, even with grease, it took a while to get anything done in Russia. They just don't seem to know how to do anything quickly. I think it's a holdover from the old communist days when nobody was in a hurry. In the U.S. time is money. In the Soviet Union time was, well . . . just time. Because my clients were so used to the way things are done in the U.S., they had a hard time dealing with how slow things moved in Russia. I would always tell them before we left home to forget about the Western time clock. Be patient.

We have what I call the McDonald's mentality in the States. You order your food at one window, pay for it at the next window, pick it up at the next one, and are back on the road in five minutes. No such concept in Russia.

"In the U.S. we have Eastern Standard Time, Central Standard Time, Mountain Standard Time, and Pacific Standard time," I would tell my clients. "But in Russia they have just one time. I call it 'Russian Standard Time.' That means things get done when they get done. There is no set time schedule. Nobody is in a hurry. If someone tells you it will take an hour to do something, it could take 30 minutes, or two hours, or two days. There is no concept of time management."

After several years of bringing gifts to Russia and handing them directly to the customs agents, this all changed one year. As I was hauling out a present for one of the agents, Dmitri quickly pulled me aside and said: "Denny, don't give that to him. He can't accept gifts anymore. It's against the law. Give it to me and I will give it to him later."

I had to chuckle over that one. So while it was now illegal to give a gift to the agent, it still happened! Just not out in the open!

One of the most interesting . . . and hair-raising . . . episodes of greasing the wheels occurred in downtown Moscow back in the mid-90s. I sure could have used the colonel's "Get Out of Jail Free" card on this occasion but, unfortunately, I didn't have it yet!

I had just finished checking into the hotel and was getting hungry after my long flight, so I decided to grab a cab and head to a local restaurant. On the way to the restaurant, we were pulled over by a policeman. Back then the hotels would take your passport and keep it for several hours—and even overnight—to complete the registration process. I usually waited to get my passport back before leaving the hotel but forgot all about it on this occasion.

As the policeman walked up to the cab and asked the driver for his papers, I suddenly got a bad feeling in the pit of my stomach. That's when I realized I had left my passport back at the hotel registration desk. Crap! After checking the taxi driver's papers, the policeman looked in the back seat at me. "May I see your passport," he queried in pretty decent English, obviously knowing I wasn't a Russian.

"I left it at the hotel so they could register me," I replied nervously. "I can go back and get it and show you if you want."

"Big problem!" he said with a steely stare. "You need to have passport."

"I do have a passport, but they took it from me at the hotel," I replied. "I can show you if you want to follow me back to the hotel."

"Oh no, can't go to hotel," the policeman continued. "Must have a passport with you. Big problem. Please come with me back to my car. Maybe we need to go to police station."

You can only imagine the sick feeling that swept over my entire body at that moment. There's no freaking way I wanted to spend the night in a Russian jail! I thought my knees were going to buckle on the way to his cruiser. When I got into the cruiser there sat two more cops. Holy crap! This was getting worse by the second!

After I sat down in the back seat of the cruiser, the officer turned around and looked at me with a whimsical grin. "No passport is a big problem in Russia," he said for the third time. "What to do? Maybe we go to police station?"

There is no way I want to go to a Russian police station! I cringed as I quickly tried to figure out what the heck I was going to do to get out of this predicament. That's when it hit me smack between the eyes! He asked me "what to do?" He's got a silly grin on his face . . . this guy is looking for

money! Heck yeah, that's it! He wants money! I'd seen
Dmitri and Michael in this kind of a spot with cops several
times. The way out was through my wallet!

"How about this?" I said as I pulled a 50 out of my wallet
and showed it to him. "Will this solve the problem?"

Can you imagine trying this back in the States! A cop
comes up to you and says he is going to write you a ticket
and you offer him a 50! Think about it! Where would that
get you? Go directly to jail. Do not pass GO! But this was
Russia, as Michael Silin would say.

"But there are three of us," the officer came back. "Still
big problem."

I hauled out two more fifties. Heck, I'd have given him my
whole wallet to stay out of a Russian jail cell. "Here are three
fifties!" I said. "Problem solved?"

"Problem solved," the policeman replied with a big wide
grin on his face as he took the cash from my hand. "OK, you
can go back to taxi now." And then came the coup de grace.
"Have a good day!" he chirped.

You never saw a guy hop into the back seat of a taxi cab so
fast in your life. I'll guarantee you one thing; I always have
my passport with me now when I am traveling in Russia . . .
or any other country for that matter. Lesson learned

Many Russians in those early years disliked policemen
because of the kind of incident I described above. It was a
fairly common practice for policemen to pull you over, come
up with an infraction, and hint at a bribe to solve the problem.

I remember one time when Dmitri and I were with a group
of hunters and we got pulled over. We had all of our gear,
including several cases of hunting rifles and shells, in the
van with us. Dmitri was not happy! I can't print the words
he called the police officer! Needless to say, they were not
kind and endearing! While we had all the proper paperwork,
Dmitri said we were going to have a bit of a problem.

"We have enough firepower in this van to take over a small
village," Dmitri quipped. "These guys are going to freak out
when they see all these rifles and ammunition. They will try

to find something wrong. Someone may have forgotten to dot an "i" or cross a "t" on their paperwork. They will find it. They are going to want to get some money from us, but I'm not giving these *#@**# anything!"

Sure enough, the policemen got all excited when they saw that the van was full of Americans and lots of luggage . . . and firearms to boot. They began going over everything with a fine-toothed comb. First they went through all of our passports and paperwork then they had us take all the rifles out and checked the serial numbers against the paperwork we had for them. Then they started counting the shells. They said we were off by one or two. Aha! An opening! They were about to have us take all of our luggage out and open all the suitcases when Dmitri finally gave in and offered them $200 in cash. They took it and we were on our way.

I suppose I could complain about the under-the-table cash transactions we had to make over the years but I'm actually not all that upset. Some of my clients would get all bent out of shape from time to time when we had to slip someone a little cash but when I pointed out to them how much faster and smoother things were going with a little greenback grease, they usually saw the benefits of this unique modus operandi.

The beauty of this kind of system is that you could solve any kind of problem right on the spot. Like when clients gave me the wrong serial number, or the wrong make and model, or the wrong caliber for their rifle, which we then submitted for their rifle permits! Yes, believe it or not! All of these things have happened! More than once! Rather than going through some long, drawn-out procedure, we corrected the mistakes right then and there. "Just call it a fine for giving me the wrong information," I would tell them. They were happy with that.

I can tell you there was one guy we had on a stag hunt in Crimea back in 2005 who was very happy with the Russian way of doing things!

We had just finished eating in a nice restaurant and were walking out the front door and down the steps when one of my hunters, who had consumed way too much vodka, stopped and started to pee! You read that right! He started to pee on the steps in front of the restaurant! You can only imagine the shock I felt when I saw this moron urinating in public! Before we could get to him and stop him, a policeman came over, grabbed him by the arm, and hauled him off to his cruiser. Houston, we have a problem!

Dmitri quickly followed the policeman and our client to the cruiser and began talking to the police officer. Can you imagine what would have happened to this guy in the U.S. had he walked out of a Logan's Steak House and started peeing on the sidewalk? Idiot! He was going to spend the night in jail! No ifs, ands, or buts! He was in big trouble! But not so fast! This is Russia!

After a few minutes of dialog, and the exchange of some cash, Dmitri came back with one very humble, frightened client. After getting a severe tongue lashing from Dmitri and me, we stuffed the guy in our van, hauled him back to the hotel, and put him in bed. The next morning I asked him if he knew how close he was to spending the night in a Russian jail cell. He said he certainly did, and just the thought of it had scared him sober! He thanked Dmitri profusely for saving his butt.

The willingness of some Russian airline ticket agents to earn a little extra cash on the side has helped me upgrade to first class a number of times. The first time I became aware that I could get a first class upgrade simply by slipping the ticket agent a crisp Benjamin Franklin happened on a flight from Moscow to Petropavlovsk. I was at the ticket counter getting processed when the ticket agent pulled my interpreter in close and said something to him in the "Pssst, hey buddy, you want to buy a watch?" kind of voice a guy on the sidewalk in a big city would use as he rolled up his sleeve.

My interpreter then came up close to me and said in a low voice, "Denny, do you want to fly up front in first class?"

"Sounds good, but I checked out first class ticket prices before I left home," I replied. "They are double the cost of a coach class ticket, so I think I'll pass."

"No, Denny, you don't have to pay double for first class," my interpreter said. "Just give the guy a hundred bucks and he will upgrade you. He's trying to make a little extra money. His job doesn't pay much."

"A hundred bucks to upgrade to first class!" I gasped. "Heck yes, I'll pay a hundred dollars for an upgrade to first class!" I grabbed my wallet, pulled out a hundred dollar bill and was about to hand it to the ticket agent when my interpreter stopped me.

"No, Denny, no!" he whispered. "Don't hand it to him over the counter in plain sight. Put it in your passport and then hand him your passport."

I put the hundred dollar bill in my passport and handed it to the ticket agent. He lowered the passport, let the hundred dollar bill fall out into his lap, and handed me my passport back along with a first class ticket! Cool!

I tried this several other times after that. Sometimes it worked and sometimes it didn't. I have also had it work with the flight attendants. But, I wouldn't try it any more today as a whole lot has changed in Russia the past two decades. The last time I tried it back in 2005 I got the evil eye from the flight attendants!

Russia has pretty much made it through its Wild West stage and is no different today than most modern day countries. You can even buy Charmin toilet paper in the stores! A lot of the stuff we did back in the 90s wouldn't work today. Ah, I miss the good old days!

CHAPTER 8

SURROUNDED BY BEARS!

"ARE YOU SURE IT'S safe?" Tom Moore asked anxiously, the worry creeping into his voice. "I don't mind telling you, I'm a little nervous about this hunt. I'm afraid of bears. Especially grizzly bears! I think I'd rather go stag hunting. You think we can talk Dave into a stag hunt? I really don't want to hunt bears! And in Russia? That doesn't make me feel any better!"

This was the second telephone conversation I had with Tom, a Traverse City, Michigan, native. He was trying to ease some of the fear that had been preying on his mind as he got closer and closer to an upcoming grizzly bear hunt in Russia. His son, David Moore, from Illinois had booked the hunt several weeks earlier for himself and his father. From the beginning, when Dave and Tom began debating whether to go on a Russian brown bear hunt or on a Ukrainian stag hunt, Tom had made it quite clear that he was voting for the stag hunt. But, Dave wanted to do a grizz hunt and seeing he was the one paying for the hunt, by golly, they were going to go grizz hunting!

"Dad, you're going on a grizz hunt!" Dave chided his father every time the topic surfaced, "so quit making a big fuss. You'll be fine. Don't worry about it. Denny will take care of everything."

Well, I'm here to tell you Tom was plenty worried! He had a healthy respect for bears that verged on outright fear.

"You said we'll be up off the ground in a stand, right?" Tom continued over the phone. "We're not going to be down on the ground with these things, are we? How far away are the shots? We won't be too close will we? A hundred yards or so, right? The guide has a big gun for back-up, right? Has anybody ever been attacked by a bear on this hunt? I'm telling you, I'm a little nervous about this whole thing."

I assured Tom that everything would be fine and we would make sure his guide kept him safe. "Besides, you'll have a big gun with you, Tom, so don't worry about it. Just make a good shot," I assured him. And in an effort to lighten the mood, I chuckled. "We haven't lost anybody yet!"

"I don't want to be the first one!" Tom fired back. "And that's another thing . . . we're going to be out in the woods with a Russian guide? Can't we have an American guide? Can't you guide? I don't mind telling you, that makes me a little nervous too!" Tom had grown up in the Cold War era when Russia and the U.S. were thought to be mortal enemies. The new era of Glasnost and Perestroika hadn't caught up with him yet.

"The Evil Empire and all that stuff." Dave chuckled when he told me about his father's fears of going to Russia. "Throw that in there with a genuine fear of grizzly bears and you can see where my dad is coming from."

After several more telephone conversations on the same subject, it was time for the hunt. Tom and Dave arrived into St. Petersburg on August 28, 1998, with two other hunters from the States. My outfitter, Dmitri Sikorski, and I met them at the airport and escorted them to our camp in a small village about 400 miles east of Moscow. After a good night's sleep and a leisurely day in camp, it was time for the evening hunt. We sighted in the rifles and got ready to hit the bear woods.

Our Russian grizzly bear hunts are conducted much the same way a Canadian black bear hunt is run . . . that is, they are evening hunts done from a stand overlooking a food source; the big difference being our food source is a food plot rather than a bait pile. The guides plant a number of these food plots throughout their hunting areas. Most of the plots are planted with a high-protein grain like oats. The bears will hammer these food plots in the fall in preparation for the long, cold Russian winters.

Once an oat patch is established, the guides construct a small shooting platform about 15 to 20 feet off the ground overlooking the plot. The clients are taken out in the evening a few hours before dark to wait in these stands for the bears to come out and feed in the oat patches. The guides sit with the hunter on the stand to make sure the client remains safe.

Finally, it was time to go hunting. Dmitri introduced the hunters to their guides, went over the safety rules, and then addressed all the questions the hunters and guides had for each other. The hunt of a lifetime was about to begin for Dave, Tom, and the rest of the group. Well, almost . . .

"I might just stay in camp tonight," Tom mumbled as the other hunters began loading their gear into the waiting jeeps. "I'm not feeling too good. Maybe I'll skip tonight and go out tomorrow night."

"Dad!" Dave admonished, "you're going out right now! Don't give me that I'm sick stuff. You're hunting tonight. There's nothing the matter with you and you know it! You'll be fine. Quit being such a fraidy cat and get into the jeep!"

After some lively discussion, and a bit of prodding, Tom finally agreed to go hunting. He jumped into the four-wheel drive vehicle with his guide and disappeared down the road heading out of town. Dmitri and I walked back into the apartment house that served as our base camp. This was one of our nicer camps. It was a two-story structure with individual rooms for each hunter, complete with hot running water, showers and flush toilets. It also had a large dining area where we could enjoy our meals together and hang out. Dmitri and I headed to the dining area to sip on a cup of coffee while we waited for the hunters to return later that evening.

It was about 6 P.M. when the hunters left. It usually gets dark around 10 o'clock, so Dmitri and I were looking for the hunters to get back to camp at sometime between 11 P.M. and midnight. Of course, the time a hunter gets back to camp depends upon whether he shoots a bear or not. If a bear is shot, it takes longer to get back to camp because the guides usually let if lay a while before they retrieve it. By the time they find the bear, load it into the vehicle, and get back to camp, it could take a couple of more hours. So, the later a hunter gets back to camp, the better we liked it. Dmitri and I were hoping everyone got back late tonight.

You can only imagine the sick feeling in the pit of our stomachs when we heard one of the vehicles returning to camp less than two hours later. It wasn't even dark yet! I looked out from the second-story window and saw Tom get out of the jeep. "Rats!" I thought to myself. Tom chickened out!

Dmitri and I hustled down the steps and out the door to where Tom and his guide were standing. "What happened?" I queried. "Why are you back already? You're supposed to hunt until dark!"

"What happened is I shot a bear!" Tom shouted excitedly. "I shot a bear! Take a look. It's right here in back of the jeep. I shot a bear!!"

"Whoa nellie! You're kidding me!" I said. "You got one already? Wow! That didn't take long. That's great! Congratulations! See, it wasn't as bad as you thought it would be."

"Actually, it was!" Tom replied. "It was a pretty scary hunt. But I couldn't be happier right now. I actually shot a bear. I really didn't think I would get one." As we stood there admiring Tom's bear, he continued. "Denny, I have a bone to pick with you." Tom chuckled. "You told me most of the shots are from 80 to 100 yards. You said that I would be up in a stand and not on the ground with these things. Well, let me tell you what happened.

"After parking the jeep on this old logging trail, my guide and I walked for a while until we reached the edge of an oat field. As we started sneaking through the oats towards the shooting platform, the guide all of a sudden grabs my arm and whispers, 'Tom, Stop! Big bear to right.' He motions for me to get my gun up and swing right.

"I slowly brought the rifle up to my shoulder and eased right. I was looking for a bear 80 to 100 yards away. All of a sudden, I see this bear just 30 years away with his head down in the oats! Oh my God! I started shaking like a leaf as I tried to get the scope on him. About the time I'm on him, the guide grabs my arm again and says, 'Tom, Stop! Bigger bear to the left!'

"Now I'm really getting nervous! I started easing back around towards the left, again looking for a bear 80 to 100 yards out. But what do I see? Another, even bigger, bear just 35 yards away! Oh my . . . ! Now I'm starting to shake even harder as I try to bring the rifle back around to the left. Just about the time I get the gun around, the guide grabs my arm again and says, 'Tom, Stop! Biggest bear in front!'

"I looked back around towards the front and see this big bear standing up on his back legs with his nose high in the air trying to smell us. This bear was 100 yards away but . . . I lost it! We were surrounded by bears! By now I'm shaking so bad, I can't hold my rifle steady. The guide grabs my rifle, takes me by the arm, and we start sneaking towards the stand. We would wait for all three bears to put their heads down and start eating before we took several steps. We could only walk a few yards at a time. It took us 20 excruciating minutes to reach the stand. We slowly climbed up into the stand, moving only when we were sure the bears weren't looking at us.

"We were finally in the stand! We were finally off the ground! I didn't think we would ever get there! The guide leaned my rifle in the corner of the stand and started patting me on the knee and telling me to take deep breaths. He was trying to calm me down. After about five minutes, I regained my composure. The guide then motioned towards my gun and said, 'Tom OK? Shoot?'

"I slowly picked up my rifle and shot the closest bear to the stand. I didn't care which one was the biggest. I just wanted to shoot one and get it over with. The bear growled, popped his teeth, and tore off into the woods. I breathed a big sigh of relief. I was feeling pretty good until what happened next! You won't believe it!

"The guide climbs down the stand, hauls out a pistol, and runs into the woods after the bear! I'm thinking, 'You got to be kidding me!' I'm out in the middle of nowhere, in Russia, in a field surrounded by bears, and my guide just ran into the woods after a wounded bear! Oh my gosh! If he gets eaten by the bear, I have to walk back to the jeep . . . if I can find it . . . in the dark, through a woods full of hungry bears! I'm screwed!

"After a few minutes of sheer terror, my guide finally comes back out of the woods, puts his thumb in the air and yells, 'Tom, good shot!' What a relief! I was never so glad to see anybody in my life!

"And here we are."

"Now, that's a story!" I exclaimed. "Wow. It would have to happen to you. You were already a little anxious before heading out . . . to put it mildly! That's the first time anyone has had that kind of an experience. I guess the bear gods put this one together just for you."

"My guide wants me to have a toast with him." Tom laughed. "I can only imagine it has something to do with vodka! I don't know how to tell him I don't drink vodka."

"Well, maybe just have one little shot with him and switch to cola or something." I chuckled. "It's a tradition to have a shot with the guides after a successful hunt. He will feel insulted if you don't have just one small shot with him. But, of course, it's totally up to you. If you really don't want to drink any vodka, just tell him you're allergic to it or something."

"Well, maybe just one shot won't hurt," Tom replied. "I just don't like the taste of it."

So up to the dining room Tom and his guide went. Dmitri and I followed. And the toasting began! First we had a shot to toast the successful hunt. Then another shot to toast Russian and American friendship. Then one to good health. Then one for our families. Then one for love. And so it went. True Russian tradition!

Soon, Tom was feeling no pain. And as each one of the hunters came back to camp, Tom retold the story . . . a little louder! Which, of course, was followed by another round of toasts. By the time Dave got back to camp just before midnight, I had heard the story enough times to tell it myself.

Tom Moore celebrates surviving his grizzly bear experience with shot of vodka and cigar. (David Moore photo)

When Dave rolled into camp, I went down to meet him to see how his hunt had gone. When he got out of the jeep, the first thing he asked was: "Is my dad back yet? He didn't chicken out, did he?"

"Yeah, he came back early," I answered, "BUT . . . he didn't chicken out! He shot a bear! He's up in the dining room telling the story right now. By golly, he did it!"

As we unloaded Dave's gear from the jeep, he paused for a second then looked at me with a puzzled expression on his face. "Is that my dad I hear up there?" Dave grinned. "He sounds kind of loud! He hasn't been drinking, has he?"

The window to the dining room was open and you could definitely hear Tom telling his bear story. I smiled at Dave and replied, "Yes, that's your dad, and he's had a couple of shots."

"But my dad doesn't drink hard liquor," Dave replied.

"Well, he started tonight!" I laughed.

Dave and I walked up to the dining room and were met by Tom as we walked through the door. "Dave! Dave! I got one!" Tom yelled as he thrust his arm around his son and gave him a big hug. "I shot a bear! Can you believe it! I shot a grizzly bear my first night out!"

Dave looked at me with a big grin and said, "I can't believe this is my dad. I've never seen him like this. He's not a drinker. This is unbelievable. "

As Tom repeated his story one more time for his son, everyone had yet another toast. Soon Dave had caught up with the rest of the group and everyone was in a festive mood. After the victory party finally wound down in the wee hours of the morning, everyone went off to their rooms to catch a little shut eye. A few minutes later, Dave walked back into the dining area and approached me.

"Denny, I just want to tell you how happy I am right now!" Dave smiled, choking back a tear. "I can't believe my dad got a bear already. I don't even care if I get one or not. I'm just glad my dad is happy. And what's really nice is we are really bonding here. My dad and I were never real close when I was growing up. Oh, he was a great father and a great provider for the family, but we were never really close. That's why I wanted to do this hunt so bad with him. I wanted to get to know him better. And now here we are with our arms around each other, hugging each other, and telling hunting stories. This is great! This is what I came for. Thank you, Denny! Thank you!"

By the time Dave was done telling me this little story, my eyes were getting a little moist as well. Too much vodka, I told myself.

As Dave ambled back to his room, I said, "Wow! I'm happy to hear that. Glad it worked out for you and your dad. By the way . . . don't worry, Dave, you'll get something too."

And he did. Before the week was over, Dave had bagged a bear and a wild boar. While it was a great hunt, it was an even better personal journey for Tom and Dave. I know I'll never forget that camp. It brought back great memories of me and my dad and our first Canadian fishing trip together.

David Moore (center) celebrates successful hunt with Russian guides. (David Moore Photo)

CHAPTER 9

A LESSON ON FEAR

"**I** GET THIS STRANGE FEELING right in my chest," sputtered Andrew Shutov, flapping the shirt pocket over his heart for emphasis. "It is how you say, very funny feeling. Kind of tingling feeling."

"The word I believe you are looking for, Andrew, is FEAR!" I offered as we listened to our new Russian friend, Shutov, describe a close encounter with a large grizzly bear. "It's called total, absolute, unbridled fear!"

"Yes, fear!" Shutov shot back. "Very much fear."

"And how about your shorts, Andrew? Do you need clean shorts?" I chuckled.

"Yes I think clean shorts would be good." Shutov grinned. "I have very funny feeling in shorts too."

This conversation about fear and soiled shorts took place in September of 1994 at a bear hunting camp, south of St. Petersburg. Shutov was filling in as a cameraman for Bob Coker, one of three hunters who had joined me on a bruin hunting expedition to the Land of the Bear. Coker, from Eufaula, Alabama, was filming the hunt for a video he was working on. He wanted to film one of the first – if not the first – Russian bears ever shot with a bow and arrow. Shutov was supposed to have been along as an interpreter but he got a little more than he bargained for when Coker's regular cameraman was unable to make the trip.

Coker had been sitting in a tree stand overlooking a small patch of oats when the action began to heat up on Day One. Coker had positioned Shutov in a ground blind a fair distance from the tree stand, hoping to capture the action from ground level. The bears were supposed to come out into the field under the tree stand Coker was sitting in . . . a safe distance from Shutov. But, that's not the way it worked out.

As Coker watched four bears feeding in front of his stand, a fifth, very large, bear stepped out of the woods. The other bears immediately scrambled for cover. One of them almost ran over Shutov, who was so frightened that he forgot to turn on the camera!

Shutov was still recovering from this harrowing experience when a herd of 20 wild boar began moving down a trail behind him. Two very large and very ugly boars broke off from the herd and began feeding towards Shutov. As they fed closer and closer, Shutov decided to stand up and wave his arms to scare them away. Instead of running off, however, the two Russian boars charged.

Fortunately for Shutov, they broke off their charge at the last second and ran into the woods just a few yards shy of ripping him up with their huge, razor sharp tusks. That's when the "very strange feeling" in Shutov's chest became even more pronounced. Again, he was too frightened to turn on the camera, missing out on some great action footage but who could blame him?

"They were as big as the bears," Shutov later exclaimed back at camp. "They had very long and very sharp tusks. Tomorrow I sit in a tree too! No more sitting on the ground."

The next day Shutov was sitting in a tree stand next to Coker when Coker arrowed what just may be the first interior brown bear ever taken in Russia with a bow. The big bear walked right under Coker's stand. He drilled the bear at 35 yards. The guides estimated the bear to be in the 8-foot class. We are waiting for final word from Coker's taxidermist to determine the animal's actual size and where it will place in the record books. It was indeed a very nice bear.

Another person who can tell you about the meaning of fear is Tom Thompson from Danvers, Illinois. Thompson had a dangerously close encounter with a big bruin near Magadan in 2005. He wrote a story about his hunt that offers a unique

insight into what goes into one of these trips from a client's perspective. Here are some excerpts from his story.

***

Late April of 2005 found myself and my hunting partner Keith Jeffries on a Magadan Airways flight from Anchorage AK to Magadan, Russia. The purpose of the trip was a long- awaited and highly-anticipated two-week hunt for the Siberian version of *Ursus Arctos Horribilis*. We had heard stories about these bears being much more plentiful and aggressive than their Alaskan cousins, so we were extremely excited about our adventure.

After a several hour layover for customs and immigration at the Petropavlovsk airport, during which we learned what Denny meant by "Russian Standard Time," we were on our way to Magadan. There we met Mikhail, our translator, and escorted to the camp.

The camp was located at the mouth of a small river on the coast of the Sea of Okhotsk. The snow-capped mountains and rugged coastline made for some of the most beautiful scenery in the world. The only problem was that an early spring had melted much of the snow, making the use of the camp snowmobiles impossible. That meant our mode of transportation would be via LPCs, or leather personnel carriers . . . our boots! In other words we would be doing a lot of walking! Oh…and a rubber boat if the sea was calm.

I will say that the camp was impressive. The tent frames had been made from driftwood using chainsaws and hand tools; they even had hand-sawn plank floors. Wood stoves and cots made them very comfortable. Cooking and dining were done in separate tents and a sauna had been constructed for bathing.

After introductions were made, we shared a few vodka toasts with our new friends, and the adventure began.

After six days of walking mile upon mile through some of the toughest terrain on earth, and seeing close to a hundred smaller bears, the sea finally calmed and we were able to take the boat out. The camp had a 16' Zodiac boat equipped with a 30HP outboard. This greatly expanded our hunting area. The guides wrapped me in heavy rubber rain gear, life jackets, and hip boots. They then loaded me into the boat and out to sea we went.

The operator ran the boat parallel to shore, staying 100yds or so out. We saw lots of wildlife, including waterfowl, snow sheep, seals, eagles, and, of course, lots of bears. The bears had just come out of hibernation and were ravenous. They were browsing on pine seeds, last year's berries that had been uncovered by the recent snowmelt, and dead salmon if they could find them. Their favorite food, however, was kelp that had washed ashore and left on the beach during high tide. When the tide went out, the bears would head for the beach and gorge themselves on the kelp.

Using a mixture of sign language and some key words from a small Russian to English translation sheet, my guide Alexi indicated that we would beach the boat near a tall ridge that protruded out into the ocean. We would then leave the boat and use the ridge as cover, ascend the cliffs, find an elevated observation post, and glass for bears feeding on the kelp.

We found a crevice in the cliff that was full of loose shale but passable. We used this crevice to access the top of the cliffs. There the landscape opened up into miles of dwarf spruce. These are spruce bushes that had been flattened by the winter snows and were slowly straightening back up after the melt. The only way through them, or over them, is to step on the branches and ride them down while holding on to other branches, kind of like walking on springs. We had to pay close attention to our footing; one misstep would find us at the bottom of a six- to ten-foot-tall jungle of needles and branches. As we neared the top of the ridge, the spruces gave way to tundra and a beautiful view of the coastline.

We stepped out into the clearing, thankful to have a few yards of easy walking, and headed to the crest of the ridge to get a view of the beach below. Alexi motioned for me to move up ahead to the crest and peek over the edge.

I moved forward, slowly scanning the landscape ahead of me. Just as I cleared the top of the ridge, I spotted a huge bear coming up the trail on the other side. He was a mere 15 yards away and walking straight towards me! At that moment my entire body was gripped in sheer panic! I had nowhere to go! I could hear him breathing. I could see his breath! I could see his beady little eyes sizing me up! I was screwed!

Dense spruces lined both sides of the trail in front of me and behind me. I was caught out there in no man's land! The bear showed no sign of backing off. In fact, he began picking up speed as he closed in on me. Was this where my hunting career was going to end? On some remote mountain top in the middle of Siberia? There was no way I could stop this bear from getting to me, even if I shot him right through the heart. He would cover the ten yards left between us in less than a second. It was all over but the shouting!

My memories of the next second are a slow motion blur. Somehow my instincts for survival took over. I shouldered my .338 Win mag, found the base of the bear's neck in my crosshairs, and pulled the trigger. That was the only shot that would stop this grizzled blur of tooth and claw at this tiny distance. As I was chambering another round, the bear stood up on his hind legs and raised his front paw to take a swat at me. I took aim to put a second round in him before he could complete his swipe at my face but, it wasn't necessary. He fell dead with the claws of his front leg only a few inches from my boot!

My God! I had just gone toe to toe with a big Russian brown bear and survived! It was a miracle. I still can't believe I survived such a close encounter with a brown bear and lived to tell about it! It took a long time for me to stop shaking.

Alexi circled the bear carefully to make sure he was dead. When he was sure it was dead, I pulled the bolt back on my rifle to clear the chamber. It was at that point that I realized that I had already ejected a live round onto the ground. I would never have thought I would have been the type to do that!

After the adrenaline rush was over and Alexi and I shared some high-fives, we took some pictures. Then, when I finally had a chance to sit down, I tried to run through my mind what had just happened. It took me awhile to realize how lucky I was to be sitting there enjoying the view.

As it worked out, my buddy Keith also shot a really big bear only a few miles away. He was with another guide hunting a river valley. We picked them up with the boat on our way back to camp. When we both learned that we had each tagged a bear, we spent the two-hour boat ride back to camp telling and retelling our stories and high-fiving all the way back.

All four of the hunters in camp wound up tagging nice bears. The hunt was a great adventure. We had not only harvested nice bears but Keith and I also made two great new friends on that trip. We still get together with them once a year or so. The guides and the camp personnel were all great, we became friends with them and, were it not for the distance, I am sure we would see them often.

One highlight of the trip was that we had the honor of celebrating Victory Day with the guides while in camp. Victory Day is a Russian holiday to celebrate the end of World War II and to honor the memories of all the people they lost. It is the equivalent of our July 4th. We fired a 21-gun salute and toasted our countries, veterans, and each other. All in all, I can't imagine a better trip, although I am willing to try!

CHAPTER 10

AN ENCOUNTER WITH THE WWF

I KNEW IT WAS JUST a matter of time until she asked me "the question." I was on a flight from Anchorage, Alaska, in April of 2003 heading for the Kamchatka Peninsula for the start of the 2003 spring bear hunts. On board Magadan Air Flight 802 were also a number of people from the World Wildlife Fund. While not as hostile and fanatic as some of the anti-groups, I think it would be fair to say that the World Wildlife Fund is certainly not a pro-hunting organization.

I had been engaged in pleasant conversation with several members of the contingent, including Margaret Williams, who was the editor of the organization's *Russian Conservation News*, and Managing Director of the WWF's Arctic Field Program. I knew the group was excited about this field trip and were looking forward to visiting park and wilderness areas in Kamchatka, where they hoped to see some bears coming out of hibernation. Their enthusiasm was evident. They were here to save the bears! Then the question came.

"So, Denny, what are you going to do in Kamchatka?" Williams asked.

"Just the opposite of what you are going to do." I smiled, trying to introduce my profession in a lighthearted way. The smile left her face immediately.

"What do you mean?" she queried.

"I organize and lead bear hunting expeditions on the Kamchatka Peninsula," I replied, still trying to keep a smile on my face, and still trying desperately to keep the mood lighthearted and friendly. "I've been coming to Russia for 12 years now. My company is the number one brown bear outfitting service in the world. We harvest more big brown bears than any other hunting company in the world."

I don't know why I said those last three sentences. They just blurted from my mouth. Part of my sales pitch in more hunter-friendly crowds, I guess, but it was certainly not a good choice of words for the present time and present company. Heck, I didn't know what to say. I just wanted to fill in the dead silence that suddenly spread over rows one through six.

"You shoot bears?" she said as tears began to well up in her eyes. "How can you do that? There are hardly any bears left in Kamchatka. How can you be part of an activity that is wiping out the bear population in Kamchatka?"

"Well, for one thing the bears aren't almost gone in Kamchatka," I quickly interrupted. "There are more bears in Kamchatka now than there were 12 years ago when we first started hunting here. Actually, my business is saving the bears."

A look of utter disbelief slowly crept over her face. "How do you figure that?" she queried with a slight hint of disgust in her voice.

"Well, before we started bringing bear hunters over here from the U.S., the Russians were actually carrying on a sort of commercial hunting program," I explained. "The guides were shooting bears and parting them out. They were selling the hides, gall bladders, claws, meat, and teeth. In order to make enough money to feed and take care of their families, they had to shoot a lot of bears.

"For example, if a guide needed to make $5000 a year to support his family, he had to shoot four or five bears. Now I pay him over $5,000 for just one bear. And I tell him that if he shoots any more bears on his own, to make extra money, I will not come back to hunt in his camp.

I have made the bear in Kamchatka much more valuable to keep alive for my clients than to be shot on sight.

"Bears used to be shot indiscriminately. It didn't matter if they were boars, sows, or cubs. They were mowed down for their body parts. The first few years we hunted in Russia, the guides kept shooting bears on sight to make extra cash, even while we were out hunting with them. If my clients passed on a bear because it was too small, they shot it anyway. I was in one camp where the guides had nearly 40 bear hides stashed in an old out building. I was very upset.

"After I dropped several camps because of this practice, the rest really started to clean up their act. I bring in hundreds of thousands of dollars to these people every year. I told them that if they shoot the bears, there won't be any left in a few years for my clients. Their business will die. They won't make any more money from me. But, if we shoot only the surplus, we can keep hunting bears forever. It's taken them a few years to subscribe to this concept, but I have won most of them over. We have instilled in them a desire to manage their resources and not waste them."

I could see that I was starting to make some sense to the group. You could have heard a pin drop as I continued.

"It's the same thing that happened in Africa with the elephants some years back," I explained. "When several countries there passed laws to shut down elephant hunting, the elephant population took a dramatic nosedive. That's because the elephant was worth much less as a resource than it was before. And, because there was no money coming in from hunters to pay for protecting the elephants, the poachers took over.

"They began slaughtering elephants for their ivory, feet, and tails. The rest was left to rot in the sun. Many of the very same people who used to guide hunters and protect the elephants became poachers and killed them indiscriminately. Without a way to support their families on the income they made from hunting, they turned to poaching. And because the elephant was worth a lot less, they needed to kill more of them. It's a vicious cycle.

"Fortunately, the government leaders in these countries realized their mistake and re-instated hunting on a limited basis. There was again money to pay for elephant protection and the guides had a way to make enough money to feed their families again. They went back to protecting the elephant. The elephant population jumped back and now there are more elephants than when the hunts were banned.

"I know this may be hard for you to understand, but animals are a renewable resource, just like trees, corn, wheat, etc. If managed properly, they will never become extinct.

"You also need to understand there are no social 'safety net' programs in Africa and Russia like there are in the United States. There is no welfare, food stamps, aid to dependent children, unemployment benefits . . . no government hand-outs at all. These people live by the seat of their pants. If I don't pay them to guide my clients, feed my clients, buy bear tags, etc., they will shoot them anyway to just survive."

Williams looked at me in a little different way, and said, "That's a very interesting concept. I edit a magazine for the WWF here in Russia. Would you mind if I interview you for a story when we get to the hotel in Petropavlovsk?"

"No problem," I replied.

The next day we sat down in the hotel café and I explained it to her all over again. After she got up and left the table, a gentleman approached me from a nearby table and introduced himself. "Hi, my name is Andrew Meier and I'm the editor of *Outside Magazine*," he said. "I couldn't help but overhear you talking to the lady from the World Wildlife Fund. We publish a magazine about things outdoors, like hiking, camping, climbing, and so forth. While we are not pro-hunting per se, I would say we aren't as anti-hunting as the WWF might be. We do some nature-related stories and I would like to interview you as well about the brown bear here in Kamchatka. Would that be all right?"

"Have a seat," I motioned. I told my story one more time.

I don't know whether Williams ever published a story on our interview. I asked her for a copy if she did but never received one. As for Meier, I asked him the same thing with no response. I did find out later that he mentioned a little bit from our interview in a story published in the December 2004 issue of *Outside Magazine* titled "A Message In Blood," which certainly was not a pro-hunting story.

Over the years I have run into several other organizations that frown on hunting in general, and bear hunting in particular. However, after presenting them my point of view, most at least came away with a different perspective. While I'm sure I didn't convert any of them to my side of the aisle, at least they realized I had some good points.

It's a proven fact that sportsmen contribute more money and time to conservation efforts than any other group of people out there. A lot more! In fact, they are responsible for the comeback of many species of wildlife in the U.S. such as the wild turkey and pronghorn antelope. Hunters and fishermen have contributed billions of dollars to wildlife conservation programs through license fees and excise taxes on sporting goods. Without their license dollars and contributions to various wildlife programs, most of the states in this country would not have a conservation department.

The monies raised by organizations like Ducks Unlimited have bought and paid for millions of acres of wildlife habitat that support millions of animals, from ducks, geese, swans and songbirds to whitetail deer, elk, moose and wild turkeys . . . and yes, even bears!

Scenic photo of birch trees near pond in Siberia in late summer. (Denny Geurink photo)

Scenic photo of mountains in late summer. (Michael Shutt photos)

Scenic photo of horses high in mountains in Siberia in late summer.
(Michael Shutt photo)

Guide glassing mountains in Siberia in late summer.
(Michael Shutt photo)

Photo of a waterfalls found in a mountain range in Siberia
(Denny Geurink photo)"

Scenic photo of snow-covered mountain on the Kamchatka Peninsula
with a dormant volcano in background. (Mike Muster photo)

CHAPTER 11

AMERICAN HUNTER TAKEN TO POLICE STATION

"**P**LEASE TAKE CARE OF Ray and make sure he comes back OK," Norma Brenner pleaded with me as we were about to board the plane in Grand Rapids, Michigan, on September 18, 1995, for a fall stag hunt in Russia. Norma's husband, Ray Brenner from Shelbyville, was pumped up for the hunt and eager to get started. Dick Davis from Otsego; Don and Tom Mabie from Cedar Springs; and Wesley Wiggers from Hudsonville, all in Michigan were also excited and ready to hunt. Norma, not so much. Worry was written all over her face. She pulled me aside to express her concerns.

"Don't let them take Ray and put him in jail," Norma continued. "I really don't like him going over there. Are you sure it's safe?"

Ray and Norma Brenner were in their early 70s and had grown up in rural Michigan during the heart of the Cold War. They had heard all the Cold War rhetoric and some of it had definitely made an impression, especially the stuff about people the Soviet government didn't care for (like Americans?) getting arrested and thrown in a gulag. Norma was very worried Ray would wind up getting arrested and thrown in jail. Ray was also a little nervous and Norma's open fear and pleading with me wasn't helping his confidence any.

"So what does Ray plan on doing that will get him arrested?" I joked with Norma, trying to lighten the mood. "Don't worry, he'll be fine. I'll make sure he stays out of

134

trouble and get him back safely," I assured her. "We have done this many times. Don't worry about it."

It's rather amusing how many people in the early years of my tourism business were afraid to go on a trip to Russia. Their fears ranged from being afraid the guides would purposely leave them out in the woods, to traveling on broken-down airplanes and helicopters, eating unsafe food, having their guns taken away, to the fear Ray Brenner had . . . being arrested and thrown into jail because he was an American.

Once we arrived in St. Petersburg, we were met at the airport by my outfitter, Dmitri Sikorski. After clearing customs, Dmitri took us to a nice restaurant where we enjoyed a tasty meal. We then loaded our gear into a waiting van and headed for the stag hunting area. The ride to camp was uneventful. The camp itself was located on the edge of a small Russian village. It was a motel type of set-up with separate rooms for the hunters, a kitchen where the meals would be served by professional cooks, and a nice lounge area where we could kick back after a day in the woods. So far, so good. Ray was losing his fear of being in Russia.

The next morning we got up for a delicious breakfast, which included eggs, fried kielbasa, cheese, bread, and hot coffee. Like was good! Ray was feeling great about the hunt.

After breakfast Dmitri took us out to meet the guides. Each hunter would have his own guide and hunt in his own area. After the introductions, the hunters began loading their gear into the waiting jeeps and got ready to go. Dmitri and I headed back to the kitchen to get a second cup of coffee.

What Dmitri and I didn't know is that Ray had forgotten something in his room. Ray tried to explain this to his guide, telling him to wait for him, and he would be right back. By the time he got back, the rest of the group had already left for the hunt. There was one jeep left, with the driver standing outside next to it smoking a cigarette. Ray approached the driver and told him that he was ready to go. The driver seemed a bit perplexed at first but when Ray jumped in the jeep and gestured he wanted to go, the driver jumped in behind the wheel and sped away.

After about 20 minutes, the jeep rolled into a small town. Ray had been chattering away the whole time about how excited he was to be in Russia hunting stag. The driver nodded and smiled respectfully. The two seemed to be getting on splendidly. But now Ray was a bit puzzled. He figured he was heading for the forest so he was a bit surprised to be pulling into a small town. Maybe the guide, like Ray a bit earlier, had forgotten something and they were going to make a quick pit stop?

You can only imagine the weird feeling that crept over Ray's body when the jeep pulled up in front of the local police station and stopped. After turning off the engine and stepping outside, the driver motioned for Ray to get out. He started chattering at Ray in Russian. Ray was reluctant to get out and told the driver he would just as soon stay in the jeep but the driver opened the door and insisted that Ray get out. That's when Ray noticed a couple of things. First, apparently the driver didn't speak or understand any English at all! And second, that badge on the driver's shirt didn't look the same as the badges on the other guides shirts. It was a policeman's badge!

Ray's bewilderment was quickly turning into sheer panic! The driver, uh, police officer, led Ray into the station and motioned for Ray to take a seat. Ray's worst fears were coming to life! He had been arrested and taken to a Russian police station! Norma was right! He was going to be locked up in a Russian prison! He would never see his wife again! Oh my God!

It was about then that Ray got a really weird feeling. Not only was he sitting here in a Russian police station dressed in full hunting camo, but he was still carrying his rifle! What the heck was going on! Was there going to be a shootout? By now Ray was sweating profusely.

The longer he sat there the more confused he got. The police officer was chatting away with another officer and seemed in no hurry to put Ray behind bars. In fact, he was smiling and pointing around the room and didn't seem a bit concerned that Ray was sitting there holding a powerful hunting rifle in his hands. Ray kept saying to him, "What am I doing here? I want to go back to camp? Does anybody speak English?"

After about 30 minutes of total panic and confusion, a young woman walked into the police station and overheard Ray speaking English. "What is the problem?" she asked Ray in perfect English. "May I help interpret for you?"

Ray was visibly excited to finally find someone who spoke English. "Please tell them I want to go back to my camp!" he pleaded. "I don't know why they brought me here. I just want to get out of here and get back to camp!"

The lady spoke to the police officer. They both looked at Ray, pointing and chattering, and then they started laughing. The officer pointed at Ray and motioned for him to follow him outside and back to the jeep. Ray quickly jumped inside and prayed that the guy was going to take him back to camp and not off to some gulag in Siberia.

After 20 minutes, the jeep pulled back into camp. Ray scrambled out of the jeep and nearly jogged to the kitchen where Dmitri and I were just finishing up a third cup of coffee. We were surprised to see him! "Ray, what are you doing back already?" I queried. "You couldn't have shot a stag already! Did you forget something?"

"They arrested me and took me to jail!" Ray blurted. He was as pale as someone who had just seen a ghost. "I've been sitting in the police station for the last hour or so. I was scared to death! I'm just glad to be back!"

"What?" Dmitri gasped. "What the heck are you talking about?"

"My driver took me to jail," Ray replied. "I don't know what's going on!"

"What do you mean he took you to jail? Where is your driver now?" Dmitri asked.

Ray Brenner poses with stag. A much happier moment than his trip to a Russia police station. (Denny Geurink photo)

"He's outside in the parking lot," Ray answered, still visibly shaken.

Dmitri quickly got up from the table and hustled out the door. While Ray and I waited for Dmitri to come back, Ray told me the story of how he had forgotten something and went back to his room to get it and when he got back, everyone else was gone. That's when I started to think there was some sort of mix-up.

"Where were Dick and his guide when you went back out to the parking lot?" I asked Ray. "You were supposed to ride out to the hunting spot with Dick and his guide. They were going to drop you off at your spot with your guide along the way. Didn't you go with the guide Dmitri introduced you to?"

"I thought he was my guide," Ray replied. "He had the same kind of green camo shirt on as the other guides. And he had a badge like the other guides. I didn't notice until later that it was a policeman's badge."

A few minutes later, Dmitri walked into the dining area with the police officer and they were both grinning from ear to ear. "There's been a very funny mistake," Dmitri said with a laugh. "Did you know this guy is a police officer and not a guide? Didn't you notice this wasn't your guide?"

"I didn't know it until we got to the police station," Ray replied. "He is wearing the same kind of shirt and has a badge just like the other guides. I thought he was my guide."

"Well, when you came up to him and started motioning for him that you wanted to go for a ride and jumped into his jeep, he figured you wanted him to take you for a ride to town," Dmitri continued. "He didn't know that you wanted him to take you out hunting. He doesn't speak any English and he's not a guide. He figured you knew that, seeing he was wearing a police badge. And, also, by the way Ray, didn't you see the police insignia on the side of the jeep?"

"I didn't see it until we got back," Ray said sheepishly. "It looked like the insignia on some of the other jeeps."

"The badges some of the other guides were wearing were game warden badges," Dmitri explained. "And the insignia on some of the other jeeps were game warden insignias. Your guides are the local conservation officers around here. A lot of times the guides we hire in Russia to take you out hunting are the local game wardens. They are out in the woods all the time and so they know where all the game is. They make perfect guides. Here in Russia they can be hired as guides. Probably something you aren't used to in America."

Probably not!

"Anyhow, when you jumped in this man's jeep, he figured you wanted to go to town," Dmitri went on. "And seeing he is a police officer, he wanted to show you the station where he works. He was feeling pretty proud to show an American the place where he works. When you were jabbering in English at the police station, he could see you were getting nervous but he didn't understand a word you were saying. Thankfully this lady who spoke English came in and he understood you wanted to come back to the camp. So he brought you back to camp. That's it. That's what happened. You weren't arrested, Ray! You just went for a quick tour of the local police station!"

Ray looked at the police officer. Then he looked at me and Dmitri. A big grin swept over his face and he burst out laughing. We all started laughing hysterically!

"You got to be kidding," Ray said with a big grin. "I don't mind telling you I was scared. I thought sure my wife was right. I thought I would be thrown in jail and never see her again. I can't wait to tell her what happened!"

The following morning Ray stuck to the other hunters like glue. He took all his gear to breakfast with him. After breakfast he was the first one to jump into the vehicle with his guide. He was never late for another thing the rest of the hunt.

But Ray's adventures . . . er, misadventures . . . weren't quite over yet. On the way back to St. Petersburg, Ray was sitting up in the front seat of the jeep with our driver, enjoying the ride, when he noticed the cool fur hat the driver was wearing. He began pointing at the hat and jabbering to the driver, telling him how much he liked his hat.

"Denny, when we get back to town, is there a shop or something around where we can buy fur hats like the driver has?" Ray said, still pointing at the hat. "I'd love to take one of these Russian fur hats home as a souvenir."

"No problem," I replied. "There are a lot of places that sell fur hats in St. Petersburg. I'll take you out shopping when we get back to town."

All this talking and pointing didn't go unnoticed by the driver. He could see that Ray was interested in his hat. About that time the driver began eyeing the hat Ray was wearing. It was one of my logo Outdoor Adventures hats I give to my clients before each trip. It was a nice green, brushed cotton hat with my logo of a fly fisherman, pine trees, and an eagle on it. Pretty sharp hat, if I do say so myself! The driver started pointing at Ray's hat, nodding, smiling and giving the thumbs-up sign. In another words . . . he liked Ray's hat.

Ray pointed at the driver's hat and did the same; gave it the thumbs-up sign. As they both sat there admiring each other's hats, the driver motioned to Ray that they should switch hats. Ray looked at me and said, "Denny, I think this guy wants to trade hats with me. If I trade with him, will you give me another one of your hats when we get back home? I'd like to have one of your hats too."

"No problem, Ray," I responded. "I think you're right. He wants to do a hat swap with you."

Ray then motioned to the driver that he would like to swap hats. The driver grinned from ear to ear and handed Ray his fur hat. Ray took his hat off and they made the deal. I don't know who was prouder at that moment. The driver had an American outfitter's hat and Ray had a Russian fur hat. How cool was that!

After a few minutes admiring his new fur hat, Ray asked me if I knew what kind of fur it was. "It looks like fox fur," Ray said. "The fur is kind of reddish and long like a fox. Can you ask him if this is a fox hat?"

I told Ray I wasn't very fluent in Russian but I knew a few words and fox was one of them. "Lisa? Lisa?" I asked the driver as I pointed at the hat on Ray's head. "Lisa?"

Lisa is the Russian word for fox.

"Nyet," the driver answered. "Ne Lisa. Sabaca! Sabaca!"

"Sabaca?" I replied in disbelief. "Sabaca?"

"Da, sabaca!" the driver emphasized.

Sabaca is another Russian word I knew. It meant dog! Ray had the skin of a dog mounted proudly on his head.

The driver then went on to explain to me that his dog had died and he had such nice fur that he decided to make a hat from it; something I later found out wasn't all that unusual in many of the small remote villages in Siberia. If the villagers had a dog or cat with luxurious fur pass away, they would make a fur hat from their expired pet. "Nothing goes to waste in Siberia," they would tell me. "Fur is fur, right?"

"Well, is it a fox hat?" Ray queried after the driver finished explaining where the hat came from.

I didn't have the heart to tell Ray he had a dead dog curled up on the top of his head! He was sitting there all proud, like a king with a shiny new crown. His chest was puffed out like a tom turkey in full strut. Ray had just made the deal of the century, trading a ball cap for an authentic Russian fur hat! I figured he had been through enough already, with the ride to the police station and all, and I wanted to spare him further embarrassment.

"Yeah, it's a fox hat," I told Ray. "It sure is sharp hat, isn't it?"

I don't think Ray took that hat off the rest of the trip. He wore it everywhere we went, even on the airplane ride back to the States. I never saw a guy so proud of a hat! And he received a lot of compliments on that hat. Unfortunately, I made the mistake of telling one of the other hunters later that the hat was made from the guide's dog and not a fox. He kept asking me about the hat and said he knew it wasn't fox fur. I told him not to say anything to Ray. He promised me he wouldn't.

Well, he didn't say anything to Ray about what the hat was made of *but*, every once in a while, he would rub and pat the hat while saying, "Nice hat! Good hat! Good boy! That's a gooood hat!"

This perplexed Ray no end. I don't think Ray ever did find out that his hat was made from a dog hide. Well . . . up until now, that is!

When we got back to Grand Rapids, Norma was there to greet us. She came up to me and gave me a big hug for bringing Ray back safely. "Oh, Ray, I'm so glad to see you," Norma gushed. "I was so worried about you. I thought I would never see you again. I'm so happy you made it back home all right!"

"Well, let me tell you what happened," Ray said with a wry grin as he and Norma walked off towards the exit doors of the terminal. "The police took me to jail the first day I was there . . . "

"Oh My God!" Norma gasped. "I told you so! I told you that would happen, didn't I?"

Ray looked back over his shoulder and gave me a wink from under his handsome new fur hat. I have no idea what he told Norma but I'll guarantee you he made it exciting!

CHAPTER 12

THE GOOD, THE BAD, AND THE UGLY

YOU ALWAYS HEAR STORIES about bad outfitters when people start talking about booking trips with guide services and lodges. It seems like everybody knows someone who has a cousin who had a friend whose brother's best buddy had a bad experience. Someone who got screwed by an outfitter who didn't know what he was doing. Or worse, the outfitter misled them. To be sure, there are unscrupulous outfitters out there who do mess up hunts by being inept or untruthful. It certainly does happen.

Fortunately, there aren't as many bad outfitters around as there are stories about bad outfitters. That's because in this business, you live and die by your reputation. Bad outfitters come and go like bad reality shows. It's like any other business, if you make a habit of screwing your clients, believe me, you won't last long. I've run into a few of these outfitters myself. They do exist, but don't last. You can figure any outfitter who has been in the business for over 10 years is running a good operation.

Of course, even a good outfitter can have a bad hunt. Lots of factors can spoil a hunt, with weather being No. 1 on that list. It's no different than a good carpenter pounding a nail in the wrong place once in a while, or a good restaurant messing up a meal from time to time. This is not a perfect world. Everyone has a bad day. Anyone who tells you that they never had a bad day, or never messed something up, is either lying or delusional! In the 22 years I have been taking people to Russia on hunts, we have had a few bad hunts. All you can do is try to make it up to the client by replacing his bad hunt with a good hunt.

One thing that I have learned over the years in this business is that a lot of the bad outfitter stories you hear are actually the result of having a bad hunter in camp. That's right . . . a bad hunter! It's not the outfitter's fault at all! It's the hunter's fault!

A magazine called *The Hunt Club Digest* published a story by Tracy Breen back in 2006 focusing on bad hunters. It was titled "The 10 Worst Hunters To Have In Camp." It was a hard-hitting story that revealed the ugly side of the hunting profession as never shown before. Up until then, all the focus had been on bad outfitter stories. Nobody took into consideration the fact that the source of some of the bad outfitter stories was actually a bad hunter.

Ms. Breen starts out her story with this paragraph: "We all have met him in camp. The guy who thinks he is the greatest whitetail hunter since Fred Bear." She then goes on to list the 10 worst kinds of hunters: (1) The Movie Star; (2) The Drunk; (3) The Whiner; (4) The Shooter; (5) The Great White Hunter; (6) The Know-It-All; (7) The Abuser; (8) The Rhinestone Cowboy; (9) The Wanna-Be-Hunter; and (10) Mr. Tough Cookie. If you are a hunter, you can pretty much figure out what each of these individuals is like since you probably have run into them at one time or another in your camps.

At the time this article was published, I was in a transition period from being mostly a hunter who booked hunts with outfitters for myself to an agent who booked hunts with outfitters for my clients. I was now seeing both sides of the story clearly for the first time. I realized that not all the bad outfitter stories you hear were the fault of the outfitter and many were the result of a bad hunter.

During the nearly quarter of a century working on the outfitting side of the spectrum, booking over 1,000 hunters into dozens of camps, many of whom I've spent weeks with in the bush, I have had a chance to run into all of the 10 hunter types outlined in the magazine article. Some over and over again! Here are the stories of a few of them.

THE KNOW-IT-ALL

I'll never forget a spring bear hunt in the early 1990s when I traveled to one of our camps on the Kamchatka Peninsula with four guys from Michigan. We were hunting in the Milkovo region in early May, about half way up the peninsula. We arrived at camp to find that there was still almost 10 feet of snow on the ground. It was up to roof of the cabins! The guides had to dig steps down through the snow to get in the cabin door. Not good!

Our hunts are designed to coincide with the time the bears start coming out of hibernation. This occurs when spring weather arrives and the warm sun begins to melt the snow away from their den sites. During a normal year, the spring melt begins in mid-to-late-April on the southern end of the peninsula so, naturally, we hold our first hunts here in late April.

We conduct a second hunt in early May, a little farther north on the peninsula where spring arrives a little later, and the bears wake up later. And we run a third hunt even farther north where the bears come out in mid-May. It all sounds pretty cut and dried, doesn't it? It is . . . until Ma Nature throws you a curve ball!

This schedule works just fine and dandy during the course of a normal spring. Unfortunately, not all springs . . . or summers . . . or falls . . . or winters . . . are normal. We all know that. Sometimes spring comes early so the snow begins to melt several weeks ahead of schedule, causing the bears to wake up early. And sometimes spring comes late, so the snow melts several weeks later than usual, causing the bears wake up later. Obviously the arrival of spring not only has a big effect on bear hibernation, it also has a tremendous effect on the number of bears a hunter will see during his hunt.

Trying to predict when spring will be late, when spring will be early, and when spring will be normal, is a fool's game. All you can do is schedule the hunts based upon the average spring break-up over the past century. Early and late springs are aberrations you cannot predict. Most hunters are aware of this. Most hunters.

Anyway, when we got to camp and found out there was still 10 feet of snow on the ground, and the guides told us the bears were still sleeping, the hunters were a little uptight. But the guides also told us that the rapidly-warming weather should wake the bears up any day now, so we shouldn't get discouraged. I figured the clients understood all of this.

The first day the hunters went out, they didn't see a thing. Not even a track. They were understandably disappointed, but not ready to quit the hunt. That didn't happen until the third day!

After the morning hunt on the third day, all four of my clients refused to go out after lunch. Even though none of them had ever hunted brown bears in their lives, they had all suddenly become experts on brown bear behavior. If they weren't seeing any tracks that could only mean that there weren't any bears in this area. End of discussion.

"There aren't any bears around here!" they complained. "We just keep going around in circles in the same area day after day. The guides are stupid and lazy and don't know what they are doing. They are freaking lost! You took us on a freaking wild goose chase. You will be talking to our lawyers when we get home."

Ah, the gang-up-on-the-outfitter strategy! It's always a pain when one guy becomes irate on a hunt but when he talks a few others into the "let's get together and gang up on the outfitter," things go south in a hurry.

I tried to reason with them. I explained to them that this was a good camp and that there were a lot of bears around. I had been here before and knew this to be a fact. The reason they weren't seeing any bears yet was because the snow was too deep for the bears to dig out of their dens. I assured them

LAND OF THE BEAR 147

that the bears would be coming out any time now because the weather had been very warm the past few days. They would be waking up very soon.

And I explained to them that the reason the guides keep going back to the same areas over and over again is because this is where the bears are hibernating. It only makes sense to go to where the den sites are located and check for awakening bears. Right? If you were deer hunting, wouldn't you keep going back to the same spot you had been seeing that big buck all summer long? It's just common sense.

Ah, but not common sense to a guy who is bound and determined he's getting screwed by the Russians!

"And by the way," I continued, "another reason the guides keep snowmobiling around in the same area over and over again is because the noise from the snowmobiles will actually help wake the bears up. Hey guys, you're on a seven-day hunt. Don't give up after only three days!

"I can remember a number of hunts back in the States where I didn't get anything until the last day. Heck, even the last hour! You can't throw in the towel yet! You still have four days to hunt!"

Ah, but they knew it all. They were experts. I was full of crap. Even though I had been doing this for many years, they knew more about spring brown bear hunting than I did.

Thankfully, one of the hunters swallowed his pride and decided to give it another shot. He agreed that the group shouldn't give up after only three days. "I know things don't look real good up to this point," he exclaimed, "but I paid $10,000 to go bear hunting and, by golly, I'm going bear hunting! I think Denny is right. The bears will be coming out of hibernation any time now."

The other three guys were not convinced. They went back to the cabin, lay on their beds, and sulked. All they could do was piss and moan and threaten me with a lawsuit. By now the guides were also getting upset. They were upset because the hunters refused to hunt. Things were getting ugly fast. But redemption was close at hand!

Snow covers one of our camps on a 2010 trip. Notice in back ground that only the peak of cabin roof sticks above the deep snow.
(Denny Geurink photo)

Here's a photo that shows you just how much snow many areas of Siberia receive each winter. The snow on the roof of the house is taller than the house itself. (Seafriends.org photo)

Two hours later, the one remaining hunter rode back into camp, yelling and screaming at the top of his lungs. We could hear him hollering a hundred yards out.

"I shot the God Bear!" he yelled. "I shot the God Bear!

He was referring to a local legend that claims that there was a species of super-sized brown bears living in this part of Russia as recently as a couple of decades ago. Based upon skeletal remains, scientists say these bears grew from 12 to 16 feet tall. Some say they still exist in the very remote areas of Russia. The locals call them God Bears." Apparently, my hunter had read about the legend. And, apparently, he had shot a very big bear!

"You should see all of the tracks out there now!" he stammered with unbridled enthusiasm. "You know where this trail leads to camp?" he said, pointing to the snowmobile trail he had just ridden in on. "There are tracks from at least six different bears crossing the trail not 200 yards out! And out there in the lower elevations of the mountains . . . where we have been circling around for three days . . . you can see where at least two different bears dug their way out of their dens right through the snowmobile trail. Denny was right!"

Guides sometimes need to dig steps down into deep snow to reach the door of our cabins. (Mike Muster photo)

You should have seen the "I told you so" look plastered all over my face!

Naturally, the other three guys were now chomping at the bit to go out hunting. But now we had another problem. Their guides were so upset that the "spoiled American hunters" had refused to go out and hunt with them . . . calling them stupid and lazy . . . and saying that they were lost . . . that they were now refusing to hunt! It took all my diplomatic efforts to get the guides to agree to take the other three guys out the next morning.

The next day they were all back in camp by noon with bears. Moral of the story . . . Never give up!

THE LAWYER

I really don't know where a lawyer belongs on the 10 worst hunters' list referred to in the article mentioned earlier; maybe they are a compilation of all of them. Or, maybe they should be listed separately as No. 11 "The Lawyer" in a story of "The 11 Worst Hunters To Have In Camp." Ha! I'm being a little facetious here. Of course, not all lawyers are bad; many are good people and good hunters. I've had a few in camp with me that were amazing people and great hunters. But, some of them, unfortunately, contribute to the negative perception many people have of lawyers. One of the worst experiences I have ever had in a hunting camp was with a lawyer whose real name I will, of course, not mention. Let's call him Jack.

I was on a moose hunt with four guys in September in the late 90s. We were going to a very remote camp in Siberia near the Arctic Circle. It always took us at least two days just to get to this camp but the moose hunting was fabulous so it was worth the extra time and effort. One of the hunters on this trip was a lawyer who apparently had a hard time leaving the office and courtroom behind. We weren't long into the trip when I noticed he was writing everything down in a little notebook he had taken along. He noted every word

I said and every observation he made. He would ask all kinds of leading questions and jot the answers in his little book. This soon became obvious to the other hunters in the group as well.

"Denny, did you notice that Jack is writing down every word you say on this trip," one of the other hunters said to me on the second day into the expedition. "If you say someone burped and they actually belched, he is writing it down. If you say we are going to turn left and we actually veer left, he's writing it down. **#@8^* lawyer!"

"Yeah, I noticed," I said with a hint of disgust in my voice. "That's why I am saying 'I think' and 'almost and 'usually' when I answer him. This guy is a starting to become a real pain in the butt."

Well, we soon found out his ulterior motive. After we boarded the helicopter that was going to take us to camp, Jack asked me how long the helicopter flight was.

"About an hour," I replied. I hate having to watch every word I say because some guy is going to twist them around to screw me later! After about an hour, I spotted the camp site from the air. This is where we would be landing to set up the tents and do our hunting. I had been there many times before and recognized the lay of the land. "There's camp!" I announced as the helicopter pilot began to take the chopper down. "You guys ready to do some hunting?"

Everybody eagerly responded with a rousing "yes!" Except Jack.

"Denny, you said it was an hour to camp," our lawyer friend litigiously announced. "We have been in the air for only 50 minutes. I figure this helicopter can fly 125 miles an hour. So, if we have been in the air only 50 minutes, we could be 20 to 30 miles from the real camp. I think we are in the wrong spot. This helicopter pilot is lost. You took us to the wrong spot. I just want to tell you that if I don't get a moose here, I will be seeing you in court!"

My jaw dropped to my chest! So did the collective jaws of the rest of the group. "You're kidding me, right?" I said, gritting my teeth. "I said ABOUT an hour. Isn't 50 minutes about an hour?"

The only way to access most of our camps in Siberia was with a helicopter. They would often sink up to their belly in the deep snow when we landed in camp where there was snow. (Denny Geurink photo)

"No, I'm serious," Jack replied. "I think we are in the wrong spot."

Needless to say, this was not a good way to begin a hunt. The rest of the guys in camp didn't have much good to say about lawyers that week. Lots of lawyer jokes were told when Jack was out of camp. Heck, some were even told while he was sitting at the dinner table with us! The other hunters were about as happy with Jack as I was.

But that's not the whole story!

Obviously our interpreter had heard and understood everything that went on since we left Moscow. The Russians don't have much use for our legal system and lawyers anyway, so this little incident did not sit well with him. He could see the handwriting on the wall. If Jack has a bad hunt . . . he sues Denny . . . and Boris (let's call my interpreter Boris . . . not his real name) gets dragged into court along with Denny. It could cost Boris a lot of money just to get to the U.S. to defend himself. That's how the U.S. legal system works. Even if you're innocent, you spend a ton of money trying to prove it. Boris was getting upset.

He tells the guides and cook what's going on. After just one day in camp, Jack is not a very popular guy. Besides writing down everything that happens in camp, including whether the soup is hot or cold, he asks the guides a lot of questions through the interpreter. And . . . he tries to question them on his own. Things like: "Is this the camp we are supposed to be in?" "Are you sure?" "Where are we going?" "How far do we have to walk today?" "What is the terrain like?" "Have you ever seen any moose there?" "Is this area over-hunted?" "Have you really been here before?" "Why this camp?" and on and on and on.

Some of these are legitimate questions when asked by a respectable hunter without an ulterior motive but, in Jack's case, he was just trying to trip up the guides. And they soon figured him out. When he asked how far they would walk today, and the guides said five miles, but they walked six, it meant that the guides didn't know where they were going and were lost. The amazing thing is Jack figured he could understand Russian after just a couple days in camp and was telling me what the guides were telling him! Of course, it was different than what I had told him!

In reality, Jack had no clue what they were saying. When Jack yammered at the guides, they just yammered back. There was no real communication going on but that didn't stop Jack from interrogating the guides, the cook, and the interpreter every chance he got. And he wrote everything down.

After about the third day, the crap hit the fan. One of the guides and the interpreter approached me and took me aside. "Denny, these guides, the cook, and I don't like this idiot lawyer you brought to camp," Boris whispered in a low voice. "He is nothing but trouble. He's a first class jerk! It could cost us all a lot of money if he takes you and me to court. The guide proposes that he takes Jack very far away from camp and leaves him in the forest. What do you think?"

Just like Jack was serious about taking me to court if he didn't shoot a moose, this guy was dead serious about leaving our good friend Jack in the forest! We were in BFE Russia! This was Siberia, not some wood lot in Michigan. Lots of people had disappeared here during the Czar and communist periods of this country. I was hunting with indigenous people who live by the seat of their pants. They live by their own set of rules. They don't much care for some spoiled, rich American who disrespects them every chance he gets. When you see the phrase "Ugly American" in the dictionary, you see Jack's photo next to it.

Wow! All I had to do was give the word. As tempting as it was (not really!), I told the guide we can't do that kind of stuff. Please take good care of Jack. I need to get him home safely or I will have even more problems than someone not shooting a moose. I was shaking like a leaf. I kept thinking of those "immortal" words Dorothy uttered in the *Wizard of Oz*, "Toto, I have a feeling we're not in Kansas anymore!"

Bottom line . . . the lawyer shot a big moose and I never heard from him again. As we boarded the plane back to the U.S., one of the other hunters came up to me and quipped: "Denny, I hope you learned a lesson from all of this!"

"What's that?" I queried.

"Never take a lawyer hunting!"

THE WHINER

This is probably one of the most common types of "bad hunters" you will run across in a hunting camp. You know, the guy who complains about everything. Problem is, these guys can ruin a camp in a big hurry with all their whining and negativity. What usually happens is that they turn the whole mood of the camp sour. Negativity spreads like a disease. It's the "one bad apple spoils the barrel" syndrome. Pretty soon everyone is whining and complaining.

Fortunately, sometimes when you get a whiner in the camp, the other hunters see him for what he is and actually help you try to get the whiner under control. I had this happen in one of my moose camps a few years ago.

The expedition started out in Chicago, where we all met at the airport and caught a plane heading for Moscow. One of the hunters began complaining as soon as he got on the plane. Let's call him Bill. The seats were uncomfortable, the food was cold, the service was bad, the ride was rough, the plane was old, and on and on and on.

When we got to Moscow, the taxi ride to the hotel was too long, the people at the hotel desk were too slow, the room was too small, the bed was too hard, the shower was too small, blah, blah, blah. Bill's glass was always half empty . . . never half full. Bill was one of those guys that, no matter what you do to make his stay pleasant, he is determined to be unhappy.

It didn't stop once we got to camp. The soup was cold, the bed was uncomfortable, the food was awful, the guides were stupid, he had to walk too far, yada, yada, yada.

On the second day of the hunt, one of the other guys came up to me – let's call him Jim – and asked if it would be all right if he had a word with "The Complainer," as the other hunters had by now nicknamed Bill.

"Denny, this guy is ruining my hunt!" Jim said disgustedly. "I paid a lot of money to come on this hunt and want to have some fun, but Bill is always complaining and whining and it's driving me and the other guys crazy. I know you have been talking to him and trying to get him to stop complaining but, it isn't working. Maybe if I had a talk with him it might help."

"Have at it," I told Jim. "Maybe if it comes from one of the other hunters instead of me it might help. He's driving me nuts too!"

I had no idea what Jim was going to say. He had been rather quiet and shy up to this point, so I was wondering just how he was going to talk with Bill, who was loud and verbose. I just hoped it would help. By the way, Jim was about 6 foot 5 inches and weighed about 250. Bill was about 5 foot 9 and weighed around 175 pounds.

When Bill walked into the cook tent that evening, Jim asked him if he would step outside the tent for a minute so he could talk to him. The rest of us all craned our necks and peered out the tent door to see what Jim was going to say. Our jaws dropped to our chest when Jim took the pointy finger of his big club of a hand and thrust it into Bill's chest, knocking him backwards.

"Listen, you whiney, complaining son of a bitch!" Jim growled in a low, gruff voice, "I paid a lot of money to come on this hunt. I came here to have a good time and you are ruining my trip with all your whining and complaining. I'm sick of it. You complain one more time and you will be breathing out of the back of your head because that's where your nose is going to be. Got it?"

"Ggggg got it!" Bill stammered, quite taken aback with the current state of affairs. He had no doubt that Jim would make good on his promise. Jim was one tough, bronc-bustin' son-of-a-gun from Nebraska. One crashing blow from his big right hand would send Bill to the Promised Land . . . to paraphrase Jimmy Dean's "Big John" song. That song came immediately to my mind when I witnessed what had just happened outside that small cook tent in the middle of Siberia.

Needless to say, there was no more complaining in that camp.

Mr. Tough Cookie

Once in a while you will get a guy on a hunt who thinks he can bully and boss his way through the trip because he has a lot of money. This kind of guy is used to getting his way and doesn't mind bulldozing everyone else over to get what he wants. He is going to tell you what to do because, by golly, he paid good money for this hunt. Because he gave you money, he owns you, and you need to do what he says. He will order you around like one of his hired hands. I call it the "Daddy Warbucks" syndrome.

When I am along on a trip, I try to make sure everyone has a good time. I try to keep these guys happy, as long as they don't get too obnoxious. Well, on a bear hunt a few years ago, I had one of these guys start to get on my nerves. Let's call him Frank. One day as I was coming into the bunk house, Frank yells out: "Denny, bring me a Coke!"

The soft drinks are often stored in a snow bank just outside the bunk house to keep them cold so it was no problem for me to step back out the door and grab a Coke for Frank.

"You mean, Denny, please get me a Coke," I said, chuckling as I handed the bottle to Frank. I was hoping he would get the hint. He didn't.

This happened to me a few more times over the course of the next several days. I was starting to get a little irritated but I bit my tongue and remained civil. It wasn't long before Frank began ordering a few of the other guys around as well. "Hey, Steve, bring me a Coke!" "Hey, Bill, bring me a Coke!" And so on.

"Ah, I can't wait until he tells Nick to bring him a Coke!" I thought. "Then we are going to see some fireworks fly because you don't order Nick around!"

Nick had hunted with me several times before. He is a really nice guy and would give you the shirt off his back if you asked him nice, BUT . . . you don't tell Nick what to do! Maybe with a please he would do it, but not a direct order. I soon found myself hoping he would bark an order at Nick. I knew he would sooner a later. Then it happened!

"Hey, Nick, get me a Coke!" Frank barked one evening. YES! I whispered to myself! Here it comes!

"Get your own @#**%#@ing Coke!" Nick shot back. "You got a **@#**@ broken leg? You bring *me* a Coke you (bleeping) lazy SOB! I've got more money than you do. Get me a (bleeping) Coke @**%@*!"

You could have cut the thick, blue air in the cabin with a knife! Frank was dumbfounded. His face turned a bright pink as he stared at Nick. I knew he wasn't going to mess with Nick because Nick was a burly construction worker with sledgehammer fists. Frank just stared for a second and then began spitting and sputtering. "Hey, Nick, I apologize for my behavior," Frank began. "In fact, I apologize to all of you guys. I know I'm in a camp with my peers. It's just that I'm so used to barking orders at work that I sometimes forget where I am. I'm really sorry I've been acting like a butthole. Sorry guys!"

Well, you have to give Frank his kudus. He learned a lesson and he apologized. That's more than some guys do. Frank was a great guy the rest of the trip . . . and on several other trips after that. He never ordered anyone around after that. At least not in camp!

The Good!

I guess I kind of mixed the order around of "the Good, the Bad and the Ugly" theme of this chapter. I started out with the Bad and the Ugly. I don't want this chapter to sound like most of my clients have been jerks, as that couldn't be further from the truth. In reality, most of them have been great people and a lot of fun to be around. Over 95 percent of my clients have been wonderful people. Only about five percent fall into "The 10 Worst Hunters" category. It's just that these five percent make for such interesting story material!

Quite a few of the people I took to Russia on these hunts as clients came back home with me as friends. You've read about a few of them already in previous chapters and will read about others in subsequent chapters like Nick Jorae, Jim McDivitt and Earl O'Loughlin. All of these guys went on more than one hunt with me; Jorae has been on at least seven or eight hunts. There have been many other people who started out as clients and later became friends.

Another client who became a good friend is Chris Fuller from Jackson, Michigan. Chris went on six or seven hunts with me and so we got to know each other very well. Fuller was a real upbeat guy who's favorite saying is "Life is too short to spend it worrying and complaining!" Ain't it the truth! I wouldn't have a chapter titled "The Good, The Bad, And The Ugly" if everyone subscribed to Fuller's philosophy on life.

Dale Fulkerson from Livonia, Michigan is another former client who has become a lifelong friend. Dale wound up buying into my business back in the late 90s and was helping me take clients to Russia for several years until he contracted Lyme's disease. The weird thing is he had survived all kinds of wild and wooly experiences in Siberia only to contract this debilitating disease while mowing grass in his back yard! Go figure! He is one of the most upbeat, fun-loving guys you will ever meet. My clients and I really miss having him along him on our expeditions.

A couple of real characters I met along the way were Fred Lemmon from Georgia and Ken Horm from Ohio. Both became good friends with whom I have spent time with back home in the States. Like Fulkerson, Don Nixon from Luther, Michigan is a former client who later bought into my business and helped me escort trips for many years. He remains a good friend to this day and we still see each other on a regular basis.

Michael Elmore, who now owns and operates Outdoor Adventures, was also a former client who became a good friend. He had gone on a number of trips with me and fell in love with Russia like I did back in the early 90s. He enjoyed going there so much he wound up buying my business from me in 2011, giving me a chance to retire and write this book.

Another client who became a very close friend was Lynn Hunt from Edmore, Michigan. He and his wife, Mary Jo, have been to both the Ukraine and Africa with me several times. Shortly after their first expedition with me back in 2004, Lynn invited me to come up and hunt turkeys with him on his farm. We had been talking about turkey and deer hunting in camp and he knew I was an avid gobbler chaser.

Lynn wound up filming me for an episode on my TV show. He later invited me up on a deer hunt. And so began a long and wonderful friendship.

We became such good friends over the years that I wound up buying a house and 40 acres right across the road from him. I bought it from Mary Jo's daughter, Sandy. We spent ten great years hunting and fishing and hanging out with Lynn and Mary Jo. They were the best neighbors a guy could ask for. Sadly, Lynn passed away in February of 2013. This has left a big hole in my life. I will really miss him. He was one of the kindest and gentlest persons I have ever met.

One of the most emotional trips I ever set up for a client happened about ten years ago when I got a call from a guy named Robert (Bob) Killion, from Monrovia, Maryland. Killion called one evening in January or February, just before our spring bear hunts, to ask about our Russian adventures. "Hey, Denny I saw your ad on TV about bear hunting in Russia," Bob said excitedly. "I've wanted to go on a big brown bear hunt all my life but kept putting it off for one reason or another. It's been a dream of mine for a long time. Well, I can't put if off any longer. I have terminal cancer. My doctor says I have only six months to maybe two years to live."

"Oh, man, I'm sorry to hear that," I said, startled by Bob's sad revelation. "I'd like to help you make that dream come true."

"I really probably shouldn't be doing this because of the shape I'm in but my wife says I need to go and fulfill this dream so I really want to go on this hunt," Bob continued.

"Well, what kind of shape are you in?" I asked. "Can you ride around on a snowmobile? Could you make a short stalk if the guides got you close to a bear?"

"Yeah, I think I could do that all right," Bob said. "I've been through some pretty intensive chemo and lost a lot of weight and all of my hair, and I'm pretty weak and have a hard time keeping food down, but I'm determined to do this. Will you take me? I heard that all of your hunters always get a bear. I really want to get a bear. You think you could get a person in my condition a bear?"

"I'll try my best!" I replied. "I'll talk to the outfitter and the guides and tell them to get you as close as they can to a bear so you don't have to walk too far. When I tell them your story, they will do everything in their power to make your dream come true. They are good people!"

"OK, sign me up!" Bob enthused. "I'm really looking forward to this. Just one more thing, if I don't make it long enough to go on the hunt, what happens to my money?"

"I'll tell the outfitter not to pay any of the food, lodging, and guide fees up front," I replied. "But I do need to get you a license, rifle permit, and a CITES permit so you will just be out the deposit."

"Sounds good!" Bob said. "I'll see you in a couple of months!"

Wow. I never had a guy tell me he might not live long enough to go on a hunt with me! I was a little shook up after our conversation. Well, Bob made it to Kamchatka in the spring. He was thin and weak but determined to make his dream come true! I was proud of the other hunters in camp who went out of their way to help Bob haul his luggage around and try to make him as comfortable as possible . . . especially Denis McClure, who shared a camp with Bob. I was proud of the guides who bent over backwards to get him out into the field. I was proud of the cook who tried to prepare meals he could keep down. And I was especially proud of Bob who, despite being in obvious pain and distress, lived his dream! Bob was the epitome of true grit!

Bob wound up taking a big brown in the 9-foot class. You never saw a guy so happy in his life. He had tears in his eyes when he told me the story of his hunt. When he was finished, I had a tear in my eye.

Less than two years later, Bob's wife called me one afternoon to tell me that Bob had passed away. She wanted to thank me for helping him make his final wish come true. "He talked about that trip just about every day for the rest of his life," she said, her voice cracking. "He was so happy that he could do this before he died."

So was I.

I've told Bob's story quite a few times. And I always finish the story with the lesson Bob taught me. "Denny, you tell people not to keep putting off things they really want to do," Bob explained to me one day. "You tell them to follow their dreams while they can because you never know when your time is up. Your whole world can turn upside down in an instant. Don't keep saying you're going to do something next year, because next year may never come. Do it now!"

Something to remember.

One of my favorite hunters is a guy named Jeff Gorski. Jeff lives in Texas and has a heart as big as Pecos County. Jeff has been on a number of hunts with me. He's a plain, down- to-earth guy who loves to hunt and have a good time. Jeff calls himself "a redneck with money." One of his favorite expressions is "Go Big or Go Home!" Jeff loves to go big.

I'll never forget one hunt when flew back to Moscow to spend the night before returning to the States. As we left the airport in a van to go to our hotel, Jeff asked me if we were staying in the same hotel we had stayed in before the hunt. I told him we were.

"Hey, Denny, that hotel wasn't bad but I prefer to stay in something a little nicer," Jeff said. "Do they have any nicer hotels here in Moscow?"

"Yes, they do have some pretty nice ones like the Sheraton, the Hilton and the Marriott but they're very expensive," I replied. "That's why we stay at the Izmailovo. It's only about 150 bucks a night."

"Do they have a Ritz Carlton in Moscow?" Jeff continued. "I always like to stay at the Ritz when I travel."

"They just built a new Ritz Carlton near Red Square," I answered, "but I hear it's very expensive. If you want to stay there, go ahead. We can meet you in the morning. I can't afford to stay there."

"Don't worry about it, I'm buying," Jeff came back.

"But there are five of us," I said with a bit of hesitation. "That's going to cost way too much. We'll just go to the Izmailovo and meet you in the morning."

"No problem," Jeff countered. "I insist. It's on me."

Jeff got on his cell phone and called his American Express hotline number where he has access to a 24-hour concierge. He told the lady to book five rooms at the Ritz and cancel the five rooms at the Izmailovo. We were all a little shell shocked. I had never been to a Ritz Carlton but knew of the reputation it had. This was going to be an experience!

OK. Picture this. We had just spent a week in the bush hunting moose and sheep. We were dirty, sweaty, grubby, and dressed in camo from head to toe. Throw in a week's worth of stubby whiskers and muddy hunting boots, and you can only imagine the look on the receptionist's face when we walked through the front door and up to the counter at the Ritz. Oh, ya, and we were toting aluminum gun cases and moose horns!!!

"Can I help you?" she said in shock as she backed away from the desk. We must have looked like a commando unit fresh off a Special Forces operation. I felt sorry for the poor girl. She was about to have a heart attack!

"Yes, you can," Jeff said as he walked up to the desk and plopped his American Express card down. "My name is Jeff Gorski and my concierge just called and made reservations for us."

"Oh, Mr. Gorski!" the receptionist exclaimed as she quickly stepped back to the counter, the color returning to her face. "Yes, we have your reservations right here." Apparently, the American Express platinum membership thing made quite an impression on her. After getting all the registration paperwork filled out with our information, the receptionist looked at up at us and queried, "And how will all of you be paying for this?" she said. "With credit card or cash?"

"I'm paying for all the rooms," Jeff said.

"All of them?" the receptionist gasped in a bit of shock. The rooms cost $956 a pop!

"Yes, all of them," Jeff smiled.

"All of them?" the receptionist came back. "Are you sure, Mr. Gorski? All of them?"

"Yes, all of them," Jeff said again with a chuckle.

When I got up to my room, I couldn't believe the decadence! There must have been 10 pillows on my bed. There were chocolates scattered all around the room. The shower and tub had more lotions and soaps than a pharmacy aisle. And there were robes and slippers everywhere. Incredible!

After taking a shower, I went back down to the lobby. I was the first one down so I found a comfortable-looking couch in the lobby and waited for the other guys to show up. As I sat there listening to a man in a tux tickling the keys of a grand piano, a young lady dressed in evening wear came up to me and asked me if I cared for a cup of tea. I told her that sounded good! Heck, we, er, Jeff, just paid $956 for the room; they should give us a cup of tea!

A few minutes later, she returned with a silver teapot on a silver tray with a porcelain tea cup and some crumpets. Pretty fancy, I thought, as she set it on a mahogany table in front of me. Then she smiled, dropped a piece of paper on the tray, and walked away. Hmm, wonder what this is, I puzzled as I picked up the piece of paper. Looks like a bill. It is! Yikes! This cup of tea just cost me $28 dollars! I've stayed in a Motel 6 back in the U.S. for what one cup of tea cost here at the Ritz! Good grief!

I drank the tea and then went back to my room to get more money. I figured I would need it! In the few minutes I was gone, someone had come into the room and remade the bed, re-supplied the chocolates, cleaned out the shower, and replaced the wet towels with dry ones. This place was off the hook! I could go on and on about the meal we had later and the wine we drank but you get the picture!

Well, that's one of my Jeff Gorski stories. In some of the subsequent chapters, you will read about some of the other clients I have had the pleasure of meeting.

CHAPTER 13

TALES FROM GRIZZLY CAMP

SOME OF THE MOST exciting and enjoyable camps in Siberia the past two decades have been our grizzly bear camps. These camps were especially memorable in those early years when I was taking people to Russia who had grown up during the Cold War. My clients didn't know what to expect when they got to Russia. They had a lot of misconceptions on how they would be treated, what the camps would be like, and, of course, wondered if they would even get back home! Remember, this was the "Evil Empire." There were plenty of horror stories going around.

Many of my clients would only go to Russia if I went with them! That's why I started personally escorting the trips. Over 90 percent of my clients back then would not have gone without me.

That's because these hunts were a whole lot different than anything they had ever done before. It wasn't like going to Colorado or Wyoming where you just hop in your pick-up truck and take off cross country. You were traveling to a strange new world full of boogeymen and mystery. The hunters who went those first few years were brave souls who conquered their fears for the sake of knowledge and adventure. They were thrill seekers with open minds who were anxious to see a land shrouded in mystery; a country which had been cut off from the rest of the world for over half a century. While it's fairly easy to go to Russia now, it wasn't way back when.

Let's take a look at what some of my clients thought and what their impressions were on their adventures to

"The Final Frontier." Here are a few excerpts from my newspaper columns, which were written at the time of the trips.

Big Bear, Beautiful Birdies Impress Group on Trip to Russia

"I'd like to propose a toast," Mike Morey Sr. said, as he stood at the table surrounded by his son and hunting buddies in September of 1997. "I would like to toast the many good people I've met on this trip. I've been fortunate enough to hunt all over the world. I've been to Africa, I've been to Alaska and Canada, and I've hunted out west in the United States. I can honestly say I've never been treated so well, never hunted with better guides, never saw more game, and never had a better time than I did this week in Russia. I want to thank everybody for making this a trip of a lifetime."

"Here, here!" the others chimed in as they rose to their feet and clicked their champagne glasses together. "I'll toast to that!"

We were in Vologda, a fair-sized city about 400 miles east of Moscow. We had just finished another successful week of bear hunting and had stopped at the house of one our guides for dinner before heading back to Moscow to do some touring. Mike Morey, of Mt. Pleasant, Michigan had taken his son, Mike Jr., to the Land of the Bear to pursue grizzlies. They were joined by friends Steve Lambert from Clare, Michigan; Bill Gehoski, from Remus, Michigan; John Seibt, of Clare, Michigan; and Charlie Momber of Grand Rapids, Michigan.

The action started a little slow the first night with several sightings and a couple of misses. It was raining fairly hard and threatened to continue to rain all week. Fortunately, the soggy, wet weather didn't spoil the bears' appetite as they continued to come out into the oat patches in front of the hunters' blinds each evening. Mike Jr. and Seibt were the first to score. Seibt's bruin was huge.

"I had been seeing bears every night," said Seibt, "but this was by far the biggest of the bunch."

Seibt's bear was a dandy, estimated to be over 16 years old by the guides who scored it as a Gold Medal animal. Seibt is going to have it scored by SCI when he gets back to Michigan. It should place high in the record books.

Mike Jr's bear was an average one so, a few nights later, he went out and tagged an even bigger one, this one estimated to be 9 years old. He also shot a big wild boar.

It's funny how some guys seem to have all the luck. It's like ice fishing. You can be fishing in one hole, using the same bait, the same tear drop, and fishing the depth, and not catch anything, while the guy next to you catches his limit not two feet from your hole!

Well, the same type of thing happened on this trip. It seemed like every time Seibt and Mike Jr. went out, they were covered up by bears and boar. Seibt even took his video camera out one day and just filmed the bears in front of his stand. Both he and Mike Jr. had numerous opportunities to shoot bear, while Lambert and Momber had only one shot each, which they, unfortunately, missed.

"Hey, I had my chance," Lambert said. "That's all you can ask for."

Gehoski and Mike Sr., fortunately, got a second chance. They each downed a bear after missing their first few opportunities. They didn't see nearly as many as Seibt and Junior, but the bruins they got were nice.

One of the highlights of this trip was playing a round of golf at the posh Moscow Country Club after the hunt. The Moscow Country Club was the only golf course in Russia at the time. Mike Morey, Sr. had been doing some research on Russia before his hunt and learned that Moscow had just constructed this new golf course. Being an avid golfer who has traveled to a number of countries just to golf, he was especially eager to get a chance to golf while in Moscow. "Denny, is there any chance we could play a round of golf at the Moscow Country Club while we are in Russia?" Morey queried one evening via a late night telephone call. "That would really put the icing on the cake for me and my friends on this trip."

"I didn't even know they had a golf course in Moscow," I replied, a bit surprised by his request. "Let me talk to Dmitri and see if he can find anything out about this course. It does sound like fun. I wouldn't mind trying it myself."

I found out from Dmitri that Morey was correct; there was a new golf course in Moscow. Construction on the course began in 1988 and was just completed in 1994. Problem was, according to Dmitri, the Moscow Country Club is an exclusive course for members only. And the membership fee is $100,000! A little steep for somebody who wants to play one round of golf while on vacation!

"But when I told them that there were some Americans who wanted to play a round of golf while they were traveling through Moscow, they said they would waive the membership fee for you and let you guys play one round for $125," Dmitri said. "You will be some of the first Americans ever to golf at that country club! What do you think? Is it worth $125?"

When I passed this news on to Morey, he was ecstatic. "Heck yes, we will pay the $125 green fees!" Morey gushed. "I'd have paid a lot more than that!"

And so we played a round of golf at the Moscow Country Club! It was a blast! We probably wound up spending more in the club house buying logo T-shirts, golf balls, tees, and all manner of trinkets and souvenirs than we did for the green fees. Needless to say, the people working there were glad we came!

Bears and birdies in the same week. Not a bad trip.

By the way, anyone can play a round of golf at the Moscow Country Club today. In fact, a resort has been built on site where you can book a room at the 5-star hotel and golf to your heart's content. Several major golfing events, including The Russian Open, are held at the club each year as it is one of the stops on the European PGA tour. A round of golf there today will cost you $250 on weekdays and up to $400 on the weekends.

MICHIGAN MAN IS LOCAL HERO IN RUSSIA

When veteran hunting guides in Russia sit around a wilderness campfire at night swapping bear hunting stories under a bright, star-filled sky, the name of one Michigan man will be spoken during these highly-animated conversations. The name of that man is Nicholas "Five Bears" Jorae. That's the new name the local guides in this part of Siberia gave Jorae around the campfire one starlit evening. The ceremony was accompanied, of course, by shots of vodka and some other traditional rituals. Jorae had been inducted into the local Bear Hunters Hall of Fame. The 53-year-old contractor from Laingsburg, Michigan was on his fifth trip to Russia, in April of 2001. Three of these trips were in quest of giant brown bears. As Jorae has learned in recent years, they don't call Russia the "Land of the Bear" for nothing.

"I just love to hunt bears," says Jorae. "And if you want to hunt big bears, this is the best place in the world to do it. Some people like to hunt African game; some like to hunt deer and elk; some like small game. Me, I like the big bears. That's why I keep coming back."

On each of his previous two bear hunting trips to Russia, Jorae had tagged two brown bears. On his most recent trip, he shot number five, thus earning the colorful nickname of "Five Bears." This nickname may have to be changed to "Six Bears" this fall after Jorae returns from a giant moose/brown bear combo hunt scheduled for the Kamchatka Peninsula in August.

"That might be my last bear hunt for a while," says Jorae. "I want to keep coming back to Russia to hunt but I think I'll start going after some other animals. But, who knows. I wouldn't mind going back on that interior grizzly hunt again. I really enjoyed that hunt. It was one of my favorites. I'll probably do that again in the near future."

"You will be back to hunt bears." The guides chuckled as they lift their glasses to toast Jorae's accomplishments. "You're a bear hunter and you can't get the bear out of your soul. You and the bear are one."

Jorae loves hunting in Russia not only because of the abundance of big brown bears found there but also because he enjoys the land, the people, and the culture.

Nick "Six Bears" Jorae shows off some of the hides the guides trapped in the area where he harvested one of his bears. (Denny Geurink photo)

"Over the years I've met a lot of good people over here," says Jorae as we swapped stories with the guides into the wee hours of the morning. "The guides are among the best in the world. I've made a lot of friends over here and I like coming back to see them. These people are genuine and real."

The friendship Jorae has cultivated with the guides over the years was highlighted on one trip when his guide, Victor, actually invited Jorae to his son's wedding. Victor's son was getting married in the middle of one of our trips so he took the night off from guiding Jorae and, instead of taking him out to the woods, he took him to his son's wedding! It was quite a thrill for Jorae.

"I was treated like royalty!" Jorae enthused. "Victor took me around and introduced me to all his friends and then toasted me at the reception. I can tell you one thing; these people really know how to celebrate a wedding! They were up dancing and drinking vodka toasts all night long! All the old ladies kept trying to haul me out on the dance floor. I told them I didn't know how to dance but that made no difference. They treated me like a long lost friend. These Russian villagers are really nice, kind people; some of the nicest people I've ever met."

Grizzly Bear Hunt Gets Heart Pounding

"I don't know if my heart has ever beat that hard," John Fiddelke, aka Hugo, enthused as he relived his bear-hunting adventure back at camp in September of 1995. "It felt like I had two hearts in my chest. I didn't know I could get that excited."

I guess you couldn't blame Fiddelke for getting all geeked. This was his first ever bear hunt. He, Gary Athey, and Dan Martin had joined me on a Russian grizzly bear-hunting expedition a few weeks back. The three were accompanied by their wives, who came along to tour St. Petersburg while their husbands chased the big bruins. It all happened pretty fast for Fiddelke.

"I really don't know what to compare it to," Fiddelke said, chuckling. "I've only hunted bears now for an hour and a half in my entire life! My guide had pointed at his watch and indicated to me that the bears would start coming out at 8 o'clock. He then pointed to the different directions where they might come from. Sure enough, at three minutes to eight, we heard a bear coming out of the woods and into the apple orchard we were hunting.

"The first thing I heard was a twig snapping. Then we heard another twig snap. Suddenly, I caught some movement in the grass. Then I could make out the form of a bear as it approached one of the apple trees. That's when my heart really started to pound. I only had a small opening to shoot through so I waited for the bear to step into it. He began picking up apples and eating them as he walked. When he stepped into the opening, I squeezed the trigger. He ran only 30 yards before dropping. My hands are still shaking."

Fiddelke's trophy measured seven feet and sported a thick, dark fur, a beautiful inland grizzly.

While the men enjoyed their time in the woods (Martin also scored on a nice grizzly), the women enjoyed their personal tour of St. Petersburg. This was the first time taking wives along one of our trips. Judging from the reactions we got, it won't be the last.

"It was first class all the way," said Jean Bonnaci. "The city was beautiful. I found the people to be quite friendly. The entertainment was wonderful and varied from the museums to the ballet and opera. I was a little afraid at the thought of going over there but when I got there, I didn't feel that way at all. In fact, I felt a lot safer there than in the streets of most cities in the United States. The whole experience was heartwarming."

Gina Athey agreed. "I enjoyed it immensely. I learned a lot about the people and culture. Having a personal tour guide was great. We got to visit places in town you normally wouldn't see. I got a real feel for the city. I especially enjoyed the entertainment. The visit to camp where the guys were hunting was a great experience. It was a wonderful trip, a lot more than I expected."

Why Do You Want to Go to Russia?

"I bet I had at least five guys in the last month ask me, 'Why do you want to go to Russia?' like it was some kind of awful place to be," mused Ron Shoemaker from Wayland, Michigan, as we chatted near Vologda, Russia in September of 1996. "I told them I was going because I wanted to shoot a grizzly bear, and I figured this was the place where I'd have my best chance to get one. I was right!"

Shoemaker was exactly right. There are more bears in Russia than anywhere else in the world! He had just downed a large grizzly with one shot his second night out to prove the point. "This is a great place to be," continued Shoemaker as we toasted his good fortune. "The people here are great; they treat you great. The guides are excellent, some of the best I've ever hunted with. I can honestly say I don't know when I've had a better time!"

Like so many other hunters from around the country who have gone to Russia to experience first-hand the hunting and hospitality, Shoemaker found that the pre-conceived notions many people have about Russia are way off base.

Some of the nicest people we have met in Russia over the years were the ones who were living out in the remote villages of Siberia. Because there aren't any motels or lodges in these small villages, our outfitter, Dmitri Sikorski, would often arrange for us to stay with someone who had a house big enough to accommodate a group of four or five American tourists. These people opened their home to us and treated us like good friends. They cooked for us, cleaned for us, and even wash our dirty laundry! That's what happened on this trip.

We were staying in the home of a couple in their mid-60s named Michael and Anna. They were one of the sweetest couples I have ever met. They were so accommodating that they even gave up their bed and slept on the floor so there would be enough places for all the hunters to sleep! When I found out that they were going to sleep on the floor, I protested and offered to sleep on the floor myself. So did Dmitri. But Michael and Anna would hear nothing of it. They insisted that we were guests in their home and there was no way a guest of theirs was going to sleep on the floor so they slept on the floor for an entire week.

I don't know how those poor old souls got up off the floor in the morning. They weren't sleeping on a big fluffy bed mattress . . . not even an air mattress! They were lying on a hard wooden floor with just a thick blanket underneath them. Heck, I'm stiff and sore after sleeping on a real mattress all night!

Then Anna would get up and cook us breakfast before we went out into the field each day. When we returned at lunch time, and again in the evening, she had a hot meal waiting for us along with a homemade pie, or cake, or cookies, or some other treat. All of this she prepared on a wood stove! Michael kept busy all day cutting wood for the stove and the sauna, which was ready for us every night.

"This trip has been a whole lot more than I expected," said Rick Buist from Palatine, Illinois, as he proposed a toast at the dinner table one evening. Buist was with his father, Don Buist, of Grand Rapids, Michigan. "You told me it would be a great hunt, but it was a whole lot more than that. I can hardly describe what a great time I've had. I can't believe all the bears this place has; and the wild boar! Living with Russian people in their homes was a real treat. Anna and Michael opened up their home to us. They slept on the floor so we could use their beds. I don't know of any place in the world where you can find hospitality like that."

Young Buist tagged two bears and a wild boar on the trip. His first bear came after only five minutes on the stand his first night out. "I sat down in the middle of the field with Yuri and looked at my watch," recalls Buist. "I remember thinking to myself 'This will never work. I'm going to sit here for hours and never see a thing. What am I doing here?' Then I looked up and there was a bear standing right in front of me. I couldn't believe my eyes! I took a deep breath to calm my nerves and squeezed the trigger. It was all over in 10 minutes. I still can't believe it."

Father, Don Buist, was having a hard time believing what was happening as well. It took him a grand total of 20 minutes on the stand his first night out to pull the trigger on a grizzly. "This is incredible!" says the elder Buist. "Ten years ago I never thought I would be standing in a garage in Russia with my son watching five Russians skin a bear we just shot. What an experience!"

One day at lunch time we looked out the window and saw three people walking across a field towards the house. They came up to the door and knocked. Michael and Dmitri went to the door. After a short conversation, they ushered the three men into the house. They took off their hats and stood looking at us with a big smile on their face.

"These guys just walked over here from a nearby village a couple of hours away," Dmitri said. "They heard that there were going to be some Americans over here and wanted to meet you and welcome you to Russia. You are the first Americans to ever visit this part of Russia and they wanted to make sure you knew that you are welcome here."

Incredible! They walked two hours to come and shake our hands and welcome us to Russia. Let that sink on for a few minutes!

We shook their hands and chatted with them for a few minutes. Anna offered them a bite to eat, and they were on their way back across the field. That's the definition of hospitality!

During the course of the week, we all became very good friends with Michael and Anna. We ate our meals with them and talked with them (via Dmitri of course) each evening, telling jokes and talking about our families and so forth. At the end of the week, when it was time to leave, both Michael and Anna had tears in their eyes.

"We know we will probably never see you again," Anna said in a soft voice. "We just want you to know how much we enjoyed having you stay with us in our home. You are always welcome here. We do hope you will come back. We think of you as our good friends."

There were a few tears on our side of the fence as well.

CHAPTER 14

IF IT WEREN'T FOR BAD LUCK, I'D HAVE NO LUCK AT ALL!

IN THE LAST CHAPTER you read about the good time my clients were having on their Russian trips. A lot of the success on those trips was because I personally escorted them to make sure everything went smoothly. There was too much red tape and too many things that could go wrong in those early years. You really needed someone right there to take care of issues as they cropped up. Most of the other outfitters who tried to set up hunts in Russia did not escort their hunts. They simply booked the hunts with a Russian guide and sent their clients over to Siberia, scared and alone. These outfitters didn't last long.

I've been on a number of flights to Russia where I ran into hunters who were on their own. They were totally unprepared for their trips. They didn't know who they were meeting, where they were going, and didn't know how to fill out the necessary paperwork to get into and out of Russia.

I remember more than one group arriving into Russia without the proper paperwork. As soon as they got to Russia, they had their rifles confiscated, along with the bag they were carrying their shells in. They wound up spending a week in a hotel living out of their back packs while waiting for the next flight home.

Because of all the horror stories I began hearing from people who tried to book directly with a Russian, or with outfitters who didn't escort their hunts, I placed a warning on our web site, advising people not to arrange trips on their own. Even when you go with an established outfitter or agent, things may not go totally smoothly. Russia was . . . and still is, to a certain extent . . . a wild and untamed place. But at least with an established outfitter, you have a layer of protection. You will generally enjoy better accommodations, better food, and better service because the Russians want to keep selling trips to an established outfitter or agent. They won't "cheap out" on the hunt to increase their profit margin like they would with a person they think they'll never see again. This translates into a better trip for the client.

I say all of this as a lead up to a story one of my former clients, Bob Coker from Eufaula, Alabama, sent me. Coker went on a grizzly hunt with me in 1994 (see Chapter 9), which went very well but two years later in August of 1996, he went back on a trip he booked on his own directly with the Russians that didn't go so well. Not all of his problems occurred in Russia, however. He had plenty of them in the U.S. as well. I believe the phrase "If it weren't for bad luck, I'd have no luck at all!" was coined shortly after this trip! Here's his story.

***

After many faxes and phone calls to Russia, all the plans were made and our invitations were received for a 1996 brown bear hunt in Siberia. I had been working on this trip for two years, now all I needed was our visas. It seemed like all the government departments in Russia were almost non-existent. The Russian Consulate never answered any of my calls on any of the five numbers I had. I overnighted our forms requesting visas along with a copy of our invitations. I also included a fee and a self-addressed pre-paid overnight envelope. I continued to phone the Russian Consultant every day with no luck. I was getting really worried. Things were not looking good. Then, finally, our visas arrived at the last minute.

I began to tune the two bows I planned to take and in the process I cracked a knuckle to the bone and needed about five stitches. Being the stubborn person that I am, I cleaned the wound and closed the gash with a tightly-pulled bandage. After a week of doctoring, I gave in and went to the doctor.

My hand was swollen to twice its normal size and ached terribly. The doctor said I had cracked the same knuckle that I had cracked as a teenager and it was dangerously infected. After trying to talk me out of going to the remote outback of Russia, he decided to prescribe some very potent antibiotics and began to explain how important it was to soak the knuckle in hot salt water three times a day. He succeeded in convincing me how dangerous it was and impressed me with the importance of keeping it cleaned, soaked, and covered with Neosporin.

Unfortunately, my hands were so swollen and sore that I could no longer grip my release and pull back my bow, let alone shoot it accurately. I bought a release and rigged one of my bows a different way that required less of a fist grip than my normal way of shooting. This new way still hurt but it was tolerable enough to pull back my bow and shoot it accurately. After all, if you are going to throw an arrow at a brown bear, it better be accurately thrown.

After tuning two different bows, I began to run out of time so I decided to set my pins after I got to Russia. I packed my bags and was off to Atlanta, where I caught my flight. I was reminded once I got to the airport that the Olympics were still in town as it took an hour to get to the terminal after I got to the airport. A police officer directed me over to get curb-side baggage care.

I noticed in retrospect that a line of five tow trucks were parked to the side in parallel to the line of taxis. As I was asked the normal questions, did you pack your own bags, did anyone ask you to carry their bags for them, can I see your passport, etc., my car was being towed with three of my bags still in it! One of which had all my money in it!

The police told me to go to the police office of the airport for instructions on how to get my vehicle back. There they gave me a copy of instructions on how to get to the towing company so I could get all my registrations out of the glove box of my car so I could go back to the airport police station to pay my fine. I took a cab uptown to my car, broke into it to get my bags, money, and car registrations. I then took a cab back to the airport just in time to make my flight. There wasn't time to pay the parking ticket, nor to move the car to a proper parking spot, so I left it.

Back at the airport I went to finish checking in. Buzz Howell, one of my hunting partners, met me at the gate. Noel Feather, the other partner, was meeting us in Anchorage, AK. The flight through Seattle to Anchorage was uneventful, except for a bomb threat at the Seattle airport, which threw all flights about one hour off schedule.

We had an overnight layover in Anchorage so we got about five hours of sleep. I realized I hadn't packed my quiver, so we went to Brown Bear Archery on our way to the airport in Anchorage to buy one. The quiver mounts on both my bows were for a quiver the archery shop did not have. I went ahead and bought a PSE quiver but I had to figure a way of mounting it to my bow.

The limo driver was very nice but he let us off at the International Terminal in Anchorage since, after all, we were flying to Russia. After he left and we made several trips form the curb to the terminal with all our bags, we found that since we were flying on Alaskan Air, we should have gone to the domestic terminal. Go figure.

We caught another shuttle bus and finally got to the right terminal, only to find a very long line at Alaskan Air. Buzz talked to all the people ahead of us and got their permission to get ahead of them.

We checked our bags, and were charged for excess, and then found out that the flight had been delayed for at least an hour. Finally, my luck had changed for the better, so I thought. The one-hour delay turned into two and, before we knew it, our connecting flight in Khabarovsk, Russia to Okhotsk was in jeopardy.

I had decided to wear my yellow pants and green deer shirt. I call it that because it has a deer embroidered over the left pocket. Less than one hour into this eight-hour flight, a man hit my arm while I was drinking a cup of coffee. The coffee went all over the left side of my light yellow pants. The stewardess got me some club soda and a cloth napkin and for over an hour, I worked on my pants. Heck, it gave me something to do to pass the time.

This flight had one stop in Magadan before we reached Khabarovsk. We decided to deplane for this brief layover so Buzz and Noel could get a quick sneak-peak of what we were in for while we were in Russia. We rode in a very cold, noisy truck from the plane to the airport building and back. The airport was just like all the other Russian airports I had been to; old looking buildings and wrecked planes and helicopters everywhere. We were all thankful for the Alaskan airplane we were traveling on, even if it was small.

One hour after take-off, the stewardess brought me some more club soda to get the coffee stain—left by another spill—off the left leg of my pants. It became a big joke on the plane about how everything served to me ended up in my lap. I wasn't about to tell anyone how I had earlier spilled the hot salt water on my lap while I was soaking my knuckle.

As predicted our plane was two and a half hours late landing in Khabarovsk. After the traditional hassle through baggage search, we missed the last two planes. We had to spend the night and catch the next plane out, which left at 12 noon the next day.

We'd finally made it through Russian baggage security when Buzz realized he had forgotten to get his passport and visa back from the hotel front desk where they had taken it to register him. Obviously, he couldn't board the plane without it!

Dmitri, our interpreter, phoned the hotel and, for $20, they sent a man to bring Buzz his documents. Because we were so late, we had to load our own baggage on the plane! Finally, we were aboard!

We finally arrived in Okhotsk but not a moment too soon. After several trips from the plane to the truck with our baggage, we were off to get on a boat that would take us on the next leg of the journey. So far, to get to this spot on a small island in the Middle of Nowhere, Siberia, we had taken a commercial jet and two puddle-jumper planes. Now we were about to board a hovercraft water-taxi. It had hundreds of people aboard. It would take us to an even smaller island where a tug boat with four jet boats roped to it, awaited.

It had taken us two and a half days to get to the tug boat. Just to make sure we didn't get stranded, there were several 55-gallon drums filled with diesel fuel on board. At the half way point of this part of our journey, in the middle of the night (3 A.M.) while still on the boat, I found out why the crew took shifts staying awake. We had several 55-gallon drums of diesel fuel on board so we could get back to civilization. In Russia, heck anywhere in the world, but especially in Russia, this was worth a lot of money.

While we were asleep under the bow of the boat in rope hammocks, in the pitch dark of the night, some Russian pirates tried to board our boat by quietly paddling to it as we were anchored for the night. The night crewman was up in the crow's nest, on guard with his AR 15. The captain was asleep in the cabin of the boat where the steering wheel was. I am sure there's a name for that compartment but, not being a sailor, I haven't a clue as to what that name is.

Anyway, the crewman had dozed off and had no clue that the pirates had boarded the ship. They went into the captain's cabin, held a gun to his head, and made him walk outside. We were all asleep in the bow of the boat when suddenly we were abruptly awakened by the sounds of rapid rifle fire!

Dmitri ran up top to see what the heck was going on. He told us to stay put. After what seemed like an eternity, he came back down to say all was safe. When we all came top side, there was no sign of the pirates. All there was left was some blood on the deck, which the crewman had missed when he was washing it before we were allowed to surface.

It took two days by tug boat and, when the water got too shallow for the tug boat, another half day by jet boats, to get to the pristine camp that wasn't set until we got there to set it. The guides did most of the work putting up camp while we put our bows together and fine-tuned our sights.

By the time we had finished with our bows and opened all of our bags to organize our gear, the guides had a late lunch prepared for us. It consisted of boiled fish and whole potatoes in the form of a soup. After lunch we prepared our gear and loaded up for the first hunt.

My guide, Nickoli, and I drove by boat for about 45 minutes to where the lake got very shallow. Nickoli got out of the boat and pulled it, with me in it, for over 1,000 yards until we came to the mouth of a small stream, about 6" deep and full of salmon. There were several sets of moose tracks going to and from the lake out of the forest but more impressive than that were the six sets of bear tracks, two of them which looked to be monsters, probably made by the same bear. We sat down on the ground, behind some grass, 15 yards from the mouth of the stream.

It was 6:00 P.M. when we finally got set up. By 10:00 P.M. it was too dark to see. We had seen the backs of several salmon as they tried to swim further upstream but no other game. I had gotten some dirt in my right eye at 5:30 P.M. and by now I had a tremendous headache. When we got back to camp, I ate supper—noodles and hash—and went straight to bed.

My bed consisted of a homemade sleeping bag on top of a bed of crushed rocks! The tent was homemade from scrap bed spreads. I was hoping it didn't rain! The mosquitoes in Russia must wear goose-down jumpsuits because it got close to freezing that night but they still bombarded the three of us all night long.

The next morning we had hash and rice for breakfast! But the coffee was good, and I don't like coffee.

On the second evening's hunt, my guide built an elevated stand about 10 feet off the ground. At 7:15 P.M., my guide decided I needed more cover. He got down and sawed some trees and brush and began putting it around me. At 7:30 P.M., while he was still working on hiding me, I heard a bear grunting. I looked behind me to see a 150-pound cub running in the opposite direction, about 30 yards away. The cub had spotted Nickoli and spooked off. We didn't see anything else that evening.

When we got back to camp, Noel had an interesting story. They had been stalking a bear when a sow and cub came out within 60 yards of them. The sow saw them and stood on her hind legs to get a better look. Noel's guide began shooting his rifle, which just about caused Noel to jump out of his skin. After three or more shots, the sow was dead and Noel was dumbfounded. Noel had no clue as to what had just happened! He told our interpreter, Dmitri, who scolded the guide. Buzz hadn't seen any bears but he did see a roe deer.

Several days went by without seeing any more game at all. We had been eating fish, potatoes or rice—or noodles—at every meal. We also had hot tea and coffee or vodka at every meal. On the 6th day, Buzz killed a goose with his bow, so had some goose soup that night. At least it was something different!

The next day I accidentally dry-fired my bow which sent my peep sight into never-never land. I made a replacement one from the cap of my pen. It looked great but didn't work well at all. I couldn't get it to stay in the string.

I think our camp cook was the Russian version of Bubba in the *Forest Gump* movie, except his thing was fish instead of shrimp. We'd had fish three times a day, every day, since we'd been here, in some form or fashion.

That next day, my guide and I tried hunting in a new area. In this new location, we were stalking through a creek most of the day. The creek was 10 yards wide and at times plum up to the top of our hip waders. The creek wound around and around in both directions. Salmon were everywhere. It gave the effect of a topless tunnel. It was very eerie, especially when rounding a bend.

When it got too dark to see, we decided to head back. While we were wading back, just as we got to the deepest part of the creek, my guide startled a large salmon that jumped out of the water and caught me in the crouch. It knocked me on my back and under the water. After I pulled myself out of the creek and got out of my wet clothes, my pants had an extra pleat in it, right in the butt area. That felt real good on the walk back to camp! Unfortunately, during the entire stalk, we didn't see any game.

That night we decided to try a morning hunt the next day. We talked about how we could get to where I wanted to hunt before daylight, without disturbing the bears. My guide said he had a plan! He decided we should hike to the location now, spend the night at the stand, and be in position at day light! Great plan! As fate would have it, it rained most of the night. We didn't see anything during the night, or on the morning hunt, so we decided to scout and stalk the rest of the day.

The next day I decided to move my tree stand about 1,000 yards from its original spot to a spot I found while stalking the creek. It had a better vantage point and it had some trails close by, with half-eaten salmon in them every 100 yards or so.

On that evening's hunt, I saw a 150-pound cub. According to my range finder, he was 123 yards away and back into the woods. I saw him about 40 minutes before pitch dark. I was hunting this stand alone. My guide was waiting for me back at the boat. I had to wade down the creek for two or three miles to get back to the lake where the guide was waiting for me. It was a very exhilarating feeling, to say the least, to wade a thigh-deep creek, in the dark, with spawning salmon constantly jumping and swimming into your body. And all the while you know that there are bears in the creek too, looking to kill and eat these salmon! Maybe exhilarating isn't the right word! Maybe a word like "terrifying" better describes the feeling!

Picture in your mind a winding stream with 8 to 10 feet deep banks, with another six feet of grass and shrubs all along the banks, visible only by the light of a mini-mag flashlight gripped between your teeth. You're alone and in brown bear country! The adrenaline is flowing into every nerve of your body until it tingles and twitches uncontrollably.

You're aware of every sound, every splash, and every movement. You try to keep your wits and not panic. It definitely seems as though it is taking much longer to wade back than it did to wade in while it was light. In fact, when it seems like you've walked twice as far as you did when you came in, you begin to wonder if you started upstream instead of downstream. If you don't stop and think and check the direction of the water flow, you might turn around and start back tracking.

Panic will try to overwhelm you. Just before it does, you see an opening ahead! You're breathing very heavily by now and you begin wading much faster as hope begins to rise from the pit of your stomach. Another 100 yards and you're into the opening! Then another 1,000 yards along the shore of the lake and you finally reach the boat! You're alive! You made it! As you tell the guide about the cub bear you saw, you make sure you don't mention the strange feelings you had while walking back because you don't want to look like a wimp!

Back in camp, spirits were getting low. No one was seeing any game. There was talk of moving camp to another spot about three hours away, or just calling it quits and going home. That night the guides shot a cow moose. Hopefully no more fish soup! Buzz, Noel, and I explained how we wanted the next meal to be moose tenderloin, battered and fried. The cook's feelings were hurt but I will not soon forget that meal!

By the end of the seventh day of the hunt, Buzz had seen three roe deer, Noel had seen the sow cub and I had seen the same cub twice. The guide had killed a cow moose for camp meat and that was the extent of the game seen while on our hunt. We decided to pick up camp and move to another place. It took all day but we lived through it.

Two hours before dark on the eighth day, the new camp was ready. After another welcome meal of moose meat, we took off for the hunt. I didn't know it was going to be and didn't prepare for an all-nighter, but that's what it was! We got back to camp right at daylight and met Noel and his guide as we arrived.

Buzz was already asleep in the tent. No one had seen anything. We were all frustrated and decided to call it quits. On the 9th day of the hunt, the 14th day after we had left Alabama, I knew things were looking up! I finally had my first semi-solid stool since arriving in Russia! By 1:00 P.M. we had finally convinced Dmitri, our interpreter, to tell the guides we were ready to leave. We debated for hours with him while he tried to change our minds but our minds were made up and finally he was convinced.

We had already packed 99% of our gear so by 1:45 P.M., we were completely packed and ready to go. Two guides stayed behind to finish breaking up camp. We were loaded into three small boats with jet engines. We decided to take these boats to the closest village, Tearz, and then catch a hydro boat to Nickolias.

On the way to Tearz, one of the small boats quit working. After we spent about 45 minutes trying to fix it, we loaded all the gear out of the broken boat into the remaining two boats and continued to Tearz, leaving a guide with the broken boat. That left two guides to help us load our gear, Nickoli and Valari.

We caught the hydroplane to Tearz. While waiting for the boat, we ran into a group of students who were also waiting for the boat. These students were fascinated to meet Americans and to hear us talk. They crowded around Buzz, Noel, and I for over an hour, listening to us talk and practicing their English.

On our boat, I befriended a 13-year-old boy named Vladimir, and his 13-year-old girlfriend named Nina. I taught them to say, "What is your name?" and "What time is it now?" They had a blast and so did I. The two and a half hour boat ride flew by. When we got to Nickolias, we went to the only hotel in town. It was not fit to sleep in.

We decided, instead, to stay at Valari's apartment for the night. His wife cooked us dinner and breakfast. Dinner wasn't much but breakfast was a complete bacon omelet with fresh veggies. After eating mostly fish for eight days, both meals were delicious! Buzz and Noel said that while I was still the fly egg king, now I could add mosquito king to my resume. (Inside joke having to do with flies and mosquitoes landing in my bowl of fish soup every day. (Long story.)

On Thursday morning (8/15/96), Dmitri, our interpreter, had to go to the airport to arrange our early flight out of Russia. They wouldn't allow us to do this over the phone due to terrorist security. It took Dmitri three hours to arrange everything. Valari's daughter, Lonari, sang and played the piano for us while we waited. She was actually pretty good! At 3:30 P.M. we caught a flight from Nickolia to Khabarovsk. Once in Khabarovsk, we checked on flights to Anchorage.

We had arrived on Thursday and we found out that Alaskan Air only flew from Khabarovsk to Anchorage on Friday and Wednesday. We couldn't arrange this flight change at the airport in Khabarovsk, however, because Alaskan Air only had employees working on days they had flights, and then only during the hours of service.

I called my wife, Tami, only to find out that it was 2 A.M. in Alabama. The local time was 6 A.M. in Khabarovsk. I asked her to arrange the change of all our tickets and I told her I would call her in eight hours. We were very lucky to get seats on Friday's flight! Then began our taxi ordeal.

All the taxis at the airport were small compact cars. The drivers wanted us to load all of our bags in one car and then have all of us get into another car to go to the hotel. Violent arguments began, in Russian of course, between our interpreter and the cab drivers. After a lengthy, heated discussion, Dmitri began to look for an independent driver who had a van.

In Russia it is very common for individuals to pick up people, just like cab drivers do, and take them wherever they want to go for a normal fee. Dmitri found a person with a large new van who agreed to take us to the hotel. As we were loading our bags into his van, five or six taxi drivers came over and began to yell loudly at the van driver and Dmitri. The van driver quickly unloaded the two bags we had managed to load into the van and he drove off.

Dmitri began his discussion again with the cab drivers. After about 45 minutes, it was settled. Three-fourths of our bags and Dmitri would ride in one car, and the rest of our bags, Noel, Buzz, and I would ride in another.

Dmitri later explained how the taxi drivers were trying to scam us and he wouldn't let them. When they refused to take bags and passengers both in two cars, he found an independent driver. He explained how, as we were loading the bags into the van, the taxi drivers began to threaten the van driver and threatened to puncture his tires. The van driver unloaded the two bags and fled, prior to any tire puncturing.

By the time we got checked into the hotel and loaded all our bags into the room, it was 9:15 P.M. We caught a ride by an independent driver for $4 to a restaurant that Dmitri had eaten at before. The meat was very good but the proportions weren't very large. By the time we got back to the hotel, it was 12:30 A.M. I called Tami at 2 A.M. our time to get our flight arrangements.

Dmitri and I were sharing a room and there was no air conditioning. After my telephone conversation with Tami, Dmitri talked to his wife four different times, trying to set up business meetings in Moscow. I am not sure of the exact arrangements because they were speaking in Russian.

Finally, Dmitri began to pack and rearrange his bags. I tried to sleep but the lights and television was on, so I couldn't. At 4:15 A.M., he finally finished. All too soon, the

7 A.M. alarm was ringing. I called Buzz and Noel and woke them and then took a shower. By the time we got all the bags loaded and to the airport, it was 10:30 A.M.

Alaskan Air had no record of the flight changes that Tami had made. Fortunately, there were plenty of seats available, except for the Seattle-to-Atlanta leg, for which they put us on stand-by. They charged us $125 to change the tickets and $108 for each excess bag.

As we tried to go through customs, we found out that there was a $30 fee to use the airport facilities. We waited in line to pay this service fee only to find out that they wouldn't accept US dollars. We had to wait in line at the foreign exchange center to get rubles then back to the airport facilities service fees line, long before the standard hassle through customs.

Now Buzz and Noel realized why I had insisted on leaving the hotel three and a half hours before departure time, even though the airport was only 10 minutes away. We made the flight with 10 minutes to spare. We had a very quick cup of coffee to keep us awake. During the seven- hour flight to Anchorage, which included a short stop, we had a snack and a meal. Both of these meals, even though they were your typical airplane meals, were better than any meal we had had since landing in Khabarovsk two weeks earlier. It sure felt good to be on our way home!

The customs in Anchorage took longer than usual, which caused us to miss our connection. They re-routed us on stand-by through Seattle, where we got bumped and I was re-routed to Salt Lake, again, on stand-by. Buzz was re-routed to Cincinnati. In Salt Lake, I got bumped and put on another stand-by flight and finally confirmed a seat on a much later flight, which I finally caught to Atlanta.

My bags had made it to Atlanta 24 hours ahead of me so it took me over an hour to locate them at the Delta Baggage area. Now I had to deal with my car issue and the towing. I had called my brother the day we arrived in Russia and asked him to pay my fine and do all the paperwork, and try to get my car out of the impound lot. I told him if he was successful to park my car in a secret location, which I explained to him. I could tell you where that was but then I would have to shoot you.

He and I had not spoken since, so I wasn't sure if the car was going to be there or not. I hoped my brother had been able to get it from the impound lot. Thank God, the car was right where I had asked him to park it! I made the three-hour drive home in the rain, believe it or not, without another incident. Boy, was it good to be home! I love America. God Bless America!!!!!

CHAPTER 15

RUSSIAN BEAR STALKS
U.S. ASTRONAUT

THIS TRIP HAD ADVENTURE and suspense written all over it right from the get go. It was destined to be one of the most interesting journeys we would ever take to Russia just because of who the participants were – Apollo astronaut Jim McDivitt and Earl O'Loughlin, a retired four-star general with the United States Air Force. You can't find two more high-profile men in the world than these two guys. O'Loughlin would be a particularly interesting person to take along to Russia because of what he did while he was in the Air Force. In fact, when I found out exactly who he was, and what he did, I couldn't believe he even wanted to go to Russia!

It all started over a year ago when O'Loughlin called me one evening and started asking questions about going to Russia. "Hey Denny, this is Earl O'Loughlin from East Tawas, Michigan. My buddy Jim McDivitt and I are thinking about going to Russia on a brown bear hunt with you next spring," O'Loughlin began. "But before we get too far into this, I need to talk to you about a few things. If we go to Russia, will we ever get back out?"

"Everybody is always worried about that," I said, chuckling. "Sure you'll get back out. We haven't lost anybody yet!"

"Well, it might be a little different for Jim and me," O'Loughlin replied. "You see, I am a retired four-star Air Force general who used to work for SAC (the Strategic Air Command). I flew RB-47 spy plane missions over Russia back in the '50s. Remember Gary Powers, the guy that got shot down by the Russians in 1960? That's what I did. He was shot down in a U-2 spy plane. The U-2 is the plane that replaced the RB-47. They know who I am. I'm in their data base."

Holy Crap!!

"Wow! That does put a little different twist on things, doesn't it?" I stuttered.

"And that's not all," O'Loughlin continued. "My buddy Jim is an Apollo astronaut who's been to the moon and back. Now he'd like to get to Russia . . . and back! I've seen the area where you hunt bears from the air quite a few times. I'd like to see it from the ground. I've always wanted to go over there for a visit."

Double Holy Crap!

"Let me make a few calls to some of my contacts over there and see what they say," I responded nervously. "We have taken some pretty high-profile people over there without a problem, but nothing like this. I don't want to be responsible for any problems we might run into. I'll get back to you in a few days."

"OK. I'll wait to hear back from you," O'Loughlin replied.

Whoa! A four-star general! RB-47 pilot! SAC! Spy! How's this ever going to fly! No pun intended. Well . . . maybe just a little one!

I made a call to one of my outfitters, Michael Silin. He had some serious contacts with a number of high government officials. He himself was a big shot in the former Soviet Union and was once prominent in the Communist Party. If anybody could find out if this was going to work, he could. I asked him to check with all his contacts. After he had checked, I asked him to check again. This was some pretty serious stuff. Each time the answer was the same.

"No problem, Denny," Silin assured me. "That was the Soviet Union. This is Russia. They are both welcome to come over. Don't worry about it!"

That's like telling a sheep herder not to worry about the mountain lion hanging around the stock pen. I guess I would have to do the worrying for both of us! I gave O'Loughlin a call and conveyed to him what Silin had told me. "We have the green light!"

O'Loughlin and McDivitt sent me deposits and we began to plan the hunt. Even though we had the green light from the Russian government, I was still a little nervous. I made sure everything on their visa applications was filled out properly, especially the general in the Air Force stuff! I didn't want any surprises! Should have known better.

When we landed in Magadan at 10:30 A.M. on May 14, 2005, I noticed something was different from the other times I had flown there. What was different is that there were two guys in suits and ties with brief cases standing near the baggage claim area! Crap! KGB! By now I could spot these guys a mile away.

Sure enough, as soon as we cleared passport control, the two guys walked right up to us. I was imagining the worst! I had led O'Loughlin and McDivitt right in to some sort of morbid trap. The plot for a future James Bond movie was unfolding right before my eyes; and it was a sure bet that I wasn't going to be cast in the part of 007. "Which one of you is the astronaut, McDivitt?" one of the suits asked in an interrogative tone.

"That would be me," McDivitt said coolly. I'm glad he was cool. I wasn't cool at all!

"Which one of you is the General, O'Loughlin?" the KGB official continued.

Oh, crap! Here it comes! I could see the headlines dancing through my head: "Former CIA spy and four-star general arrested in Russia." I was feeling ill!

"That would be me," O'Loughlin answered. Also cool as a cucumber, I might add.

Then, complete shock . . . at least to me! The two suit-and-ties stuck out their hands and said: "Welcome to Russia!"

Whoa! A welcoming committee! Not only did these guys welcome McDivitt and O'Loughlin, they wanted their pictures taken with them, and their autographs! And so it was. Everywhere we went, everyone knew that "the General and the Astronaut" were coming! And everyone wanted pictures and autographs.

Apollo Astronaut, Jim McDivitt (left), and RB-47 spy plane pilot, Earl O'Loughlin (right), pose with photo of fellow Cold War era personality Communist Party Boss, Leonid Brezhnev, on a building in Magadan. (Denny Geurink photo)

Apollo Astronaut Jim McDivitt takes a rubber raft out into the Sea of Okhotsk in search of bears feeding along the shoreline. (Michael Silin photo)

Once we arrived in camp, things didn't get any duller. My Russian outfitter, Michael Silin, promptly informed me that there were so many bears around camp that the guides were afraid to go to sleep in their tents at night without their rifles at their side! (Read full story in Chapter 16.) Their two male Laikas were kept busy throughout the night barking at hungry bears and chasing them away from camp.

As soon as we got off the helicopter that carried us to the camp, I knew why the guides were sleeping with their rifles! The cook tent was erected smack dab in the middle of a well-used bear trail! That trail led off a small rise right to the door of the tent. "What the heck?" I wondered, half-aloud. "Why did the guides set the cook tent up in such a precarious spot?"

After a quick look around the camp, I got the answer to that question. It would be impossible to set up the camp without a bear trail leading into one tent or another. The entire area was covered with bear trails. I guess it was better to have one of the trails leading into the cook tent than leading to the door of my sleeping quarters! Still, it didn't make me feel a whole lot better.

The reason the camp site was covered up with bear trails is because it was set up along the mouth of a cold, clear mountain stream where it spilled into the Sea of Okhotsk. The stream hosted heavy salmon runs from mid-summer through early fall, attracting bears from many miles around. Not a very good place to pitch a tent but . . . the perfect spot for a bear camp!

Along with me on this hunt, besides McDivitt and Earl O'Loughlin, were Anthony Nakroshis from Homer Glen, Illinois, and Richard Frye from Middleville, Michigan.

Now 75 years old and certainly not as spry as he was during his Apollo days, McDivitt still got around well for his age and he still loved the thrill of high adventure. Since he had retired from his astronaut duties, he now gets this thrill—with both feet on the ground—from wilderness hunting and fishing adventures. And O'Loughlin, who is 74, is cut from the same piece of leather.

"I really wanted to see this place from the ground someday," O'Loughlin said, chuckling as we stored our gear in the tents, "so it's a thrill just to be here. I can't believe I'm really here. Some of these guys probably chased me around in a Mig back in the 1950s."

How prophetic these words would turn out to be.

I had been hunting in the same area with eight other clients for two weeks before McDivitt and O'Loughlin arrived in camp. While I stayed in a different camp with four clients, four of the other hunters had been in the same camp McDivitt and O'Loughlin were in now. They had related some exciting tales. Besides having bears in camp nearly every night, they had watched a huge, white-winged sea eagle pick up one of the camp dogs and fly off with it. (Read full story in Chapter 16.) The guides told us that these gigantic eagles regularly prey on young snow sheep, plucking them off the cliffs near the camp. We were in a wild, rugged area, to say the least.

The four hunters in camp prior to McDivitt and O'Loughlin's arrival were in pretty good shape. Besides covering lot of ground during their stay, they had hit the spring migration of bears to the sea right on the nose. The four of them counted 270 bears during their two-week stay. That's more bears than we have ever seen on one of our spring hunts in the 15 years we have been coming to Russia. I guess you can say we aren't putting much of a dent in the bear population there!

While we normally used snowmobiles to help us get around in the spring, there wasn't any snow this year. This was the first time in 15 years of hunting in Russia that we didn't have enough snow on the ground to use snowmobiles. Winter had arrived very early last fall, and now it had left very early this spring.

I knew we would be in trouble with the snow pack when I arrived in Anchorage on the 27th of April. It was 70 degrees and there wasn't a flake of snow left on the ground. This left 75-year-old McDivitt and his 74-year-old hunting buddy,

O'Loughlin, on foot much of the time. They also spent some time in a small rubber raft they nicknamed the zodiac.

One evening, just before dark, the camp radio crackled to life. McDivitt's guide, Alexiy Skorobrekha, was on the other end. He and McDivitt were sitting along a well-used bear trail near the coast about a half-mile from camp. "We have a bear stalking us," Skorobrekha whispered. "There's a bear after Jim and me! It's circling around us through the bush, trying to get behind us. I don't know how big it is yet, but it's getting closer. Wait. Wait. It's here! It's right behind us!"

Suddenly, the camp radio fell silent. We waited to hear shots ring out from the hillside about a half-mile from camp but all was quiet. Then, the camp radio crackled back to life. "We chased the bear away," Skorobrekha chuckled. "We threw rocks at it. It was too small to shoot. Maybe only a 7- to 8-footer. Wait. It's coming back!"

Again, the radio fell silent. Back in camp we are thinking . . . only a 7- to 8-footer? Yikes! That's a pretty big bear to have sneaking up on you in the bush! Again we waited to hear shots. Nothing. Several minutes later the camp radio buzzed one more time. "It's gone," the guide whispered. That was the last we heard about the bear stalk until McDivitt got back to camp several hours later. Then the whole story unfolded.

"The bear got pretty close to us the first time before Alexiy got up and threw rocks at it," explained McDivitt. "I was waiting for him to tell me to shoot. I thought it was a pretty good bear but Alexiy said 'Small bear. Small bear,' so I didn't shoot. Then, when it came back the second time, he pointed at the camera I had around my neck, gesturing for me to take pictures of the bear. In the excitement, I had forgotten all about the camera.

"It was starting to get dark so my flash was going off every time I took a picture. I couldn't believe it! It didn't seem to faze the bear at all! He just kept coming closer and closer. It got pretty exciting there for a minute. I guess I must have looked like a pretty good meal to him!

"He got real close before Alexiy stood up again and started throwing rocks at him. I had my gun ready to shoot if the rocks didn't work. I thought for sure we were going to have to shoot him. He finally ran off for good. But, believe me, I kept looking over my shoulder the rest of the night!"

McDivitt wasn't the only hunter who had a bear after him. Tony Nakroshis had two bruins stalk him while he and his guide were skinning a bear. Nakroshis had to watch the guide's back with his rifle at the ready as the hungry bruins jockeyed for position. Brown bears are cannibalistic and will eagerly kill and eat young bear cubs or devour a bear carcass.

Apollo Astronaut, Jim McDivitt, snapped this photo of a bear which stalked him along the Sea of Okhotsk. (Jim McDivitt photo)

O'Loughlin found this out first-hand when he had a trio of bears eat his bear before he could recover it.

The next day we spotted a bear bed down in some bushes on a mountainside just above camp. Richard Frye's guide motioned for Frye to grab his rifle and follow him. We watched from camp as Frye and his guide snuck up the mountain and inched closer and closer to where the bear was sleeping in the bushes. Suddenly the bear stood up and sniffed the air! Then it looked directly at Frye.

All of us in camp felt the hair on the backs of our necks stand erect as Frye pulled up his rifle. This was the moment a bear hunter lives for! Frye made a good shot and put the bear down. He fulfilled a lifelong dream, harvesting a magnificent brown bear with long thick hair.

That evening the excitement in camp got even more intense when O'Loughlin started telling "war stories." We had just finished having dinner with the guides, and doing the mandatory vodka toasts, when O'Loughlin started talking about his RB-47 spy plane days. Our outfitter/interpreter Silin translated everything O'Loughlin was saying to the guides.

"I flew over this area in my RB-47 a number of times back in the 50s," O'Loughlin began. "We got chased by MiGs a few times and one of the RB-47s was shot down not too far from here back in 1960. But the MiGs were a lot heavier and slower than our planes so we could usually outmaneuver them."

I remember thinking to myself: "Interesting stuff, Earl, but I don't know if I would be telling these guys such stories as all of them are former military, and proud of it." But O'Loughlin continued and Silin kept interpreting.

"We flew quite a few missions over North Korea and China too," O'Loughlin explained. "The Russians were pretty sensitive about all of this and shot down a South Korean passenger plane in 1983, thinking it was a spy plane."

About that time one of the guides began saying something in Russian. Silin listened intently. "Really!" Silin exclaimed. The guide continued. "Really!" Silin exclaimed again.

"What's he saying?" O'Loughlin asked.

"Well, this guy says he was a MiG fighter pilot and he chased you a few times when you flew over here."

Whoa, Nellie! I don't know whether the guy was really a MiG pilot or not but it sure made for one of the most interesting moments I have ever had in a Russian hunting camp! Everybody started laughing, including the MiG pilot and the rest of the guides.

"Tell him to come over here," O'Loughlin chuckled to Silin. The guide came and stood next to O'Loughlin. They raised their shot glasses and toasted each other. Several more toasts to both Russian and American military men ensued. Then came a moment that will be forever etched in my mind! As O'Loughlin raised his glass with his arm still around the MiG pilot, he looked over at me and winked, "Denny, the Cold War is over!" How historic is that!

CHAPTER 16

EXCITEMENT IN CAMP

SIBERIA IS A WILD and wooly place. Besides being primitive and remote, it's one of the most geologically-active places in the world. The Kamchatka Peninsula, for example, is covered with volcanoes, geysers and hot springs. There are 160 volcanoes on the peninsula, 29 of which are still active. One of them is visible from the hotel we stay in while in Petropavlovsk. You can see smoke wisping from this volcano on a daily basis. And, of course, where you have active volcanoes and geysers, you have earthquakes. On more than one occasion while staying at the Hotel Petropavlovsk after a trip, an earthquake has rattled the pictures on the wall and shook the glass in the windows. Another time a volcano had erupted near one of our camps and covered it with ash just two weeks before we were scheduled to arrive.

Over the past two decades, there have been a number of years when I spent a month in the spring and two or three months in the fall near the Arctic Circle, under the stars, in a tent or trapper's cabin. Obviously, when you spend that much time in the Siberian wilderness, in addition to the geological phenomena, you are bound to experience many exciting, and even hair-raising, moments in camp. From almost being struck by lightning while riding a Mongolian pony through the mountains of Tyva to chasing a bear out of camp with a frying pan, I've pretty much seen it all.

These remote wilderness camps have been visited by bears, wolves, wolverines, and an assortment of other creatures during that time. I could write a whole book on

201

just these wild encounters but for now, let's take a quick look at some of the most memorable ones.

Bear In The Creek

When you hunt, fish, and camp in bear country, you are going to have a close encounter with a bear at some point. It's only a matter of time. I don't mind a close encounter when I have a rifle in my hand; it's the close encounters when I am unarmed that scare the heck out of me.

Early on in my expeditions to Russia, I carried a high-powered rifle with me because I was also hunting. But, after a few years, I had pretty much harvested all the game animals I wanted to pursue so I left my rifle home. It was a whole lot easier to travel that way. There were a number of times, however, when I wish I had taken my rife with me. Like the time when our cook, Natasha, came running back to the cabin yelling, "Bear! Bear!" with a big bruin tagging along behind her!

We were on a spring brown bear hunt in Kamchatka in early May near Petropavlovsk. We had just finished eating lunch and I had gone back to my cabin to read. Natasha, our cook, had gone down to a small creek about 75 yards from the cabin to wash the dishes, as she usually did at this time of day. The hunters were still out in the woods with their guides, so it was just me, Natasha, and our interpreter left in camp. The interpreter had gone back to his cabin to take a nap. There were no rifles in camp.

As Natasha came running up the hill towards the cook shack yelling and screaming, I stepped outside of my cabin to see what all the commotion was about. She had a look of terror splattered all over her face as if she had seen a zombie! However, I quickly realized that it wasn't a zombie but something just as terrifying . . . a huge brown bear in the 10-foot class! While it's quite unusual to have bears come into camp during the middle of the day, it does occasionally happen, especially in the spring right after they come out of hibernation. At this time of year, some bears are driven more by hunger than fear of man.

I had played out this exact scenario in my mind many times before. It always made me a little jittery to be in a camp that was emanating all kinds of food odors, from fried bacon to smoked fish, surrounded by starving bruins, and without a gun, so I had hatched a plan to deal with just this kind situation should it ever arise. Somewhere way back when, I had read that the best way to scare a bear away from camp was by making a lot of noise. The story suggested getting a couple of frying pans and clanging them together. I always told myself that's exactly what I was going to do if ever I was without a rifle and confronted by a bear. I was just hoping I would never have to find out if this really worked or not! Well, it was show time!

I ran into the cook shack right behind Natasha, hoping and praying I could lay my hands on a couple of frying pans in a big hurry. Bawanna! I saw two big cast iron pans hanging on nails near the wood stove. I snatched them up in flash and began banging them together as hard and as loud as I could. I walked towards the door, hammering the pans to make sure the bear could hear all the noise. To my utter joy and amazement, I watched the big brown stop halfway up the hill, whirl around, and gallop off into the woods. It worked! By gadfry, it worked!!!

After making sure Natasha was all right, I went back to my cabin and changed my shorts!

That evening, when we told the other hunters and the guides about what happened, the head guide came up to me and handed me a shotgun he had taken to camp with him to shoot grouse and hares for camp meat. "Here, Denny, next time you shoot bear instead of hitting it with frying pan!" he laughed.

Bear In Camp

Unlike the camp mentioned in the story above, a lot of the bear camps we've stayed in over the years were guarded by dogs. The guides took the dogs, usually a breed of dog known as a Laika, along for both companionship and protection. Laikas are medium-sized dogs that look a lot like a husky, with a tail that curls up over its back side like a fish hook. They are a fearless breed, originating from aboriginal dogs found in Siberia many centuries ago. They are often used by the guides to hunt and track wounded bears. When confronted by a bear, they don't back down. That's why I always tried to make friends with the camp dog!

Because most of the time I didn't have a hunting rifle with me, my modus operandi would be to squirrel a few scraps of meat from the dinner table – much to the consternation of the cook – then use them as treats for the camp dog, hoping to keep it near my tent at night when dangerous animals were on the prowl. Every time I woke up during the night, I tossed a scrap piece of meat outside the tent door. It didn't take the dogs long to figure out the routine. I usually had them sleeping right next to the tent by the second day in camp . . . which turned out to be perfect timing one spring in Magadan.

We were bivouacked in a tent camp in early May along the Sea of Okhotsk. Along with me on this trip were Apollo 9 astronaut, Jim McDivitt, and Earl O'Loughlin, a retired four-star Air Force general. (You read about their story in Chapter 14.) I knew I had to work the dog – actually, there were two dogs in this camp – into my corner as quickly as possible because I noticed when we arrived at the camp that our tents were pitched along a salmon stream crisscrossed with bear trails. And I also noticed that the guides were sleeping with a loaded rifle next to them in their beds! I was bunking with them in a large tent along with our outfitter/interpreter, Michael Silin. Our clients were in a separate tent. We told them to sleep with their rifles at the ready also.

The guides were amused by how the dogs followed me around in camp, sniffing at my coat pocket. (This is where I hid the table scraps I snuck out of the cook shack.) Those dogs had a great nose! They always knew when there was something in there for them; and I made sure there was something there for them when we hit the sack at night!

One night as we lay sound asleep, I was awakened at about 3 A.M. by a low guttural growling just outside the tent door. At first I thought it was a bear and my heart stopped beating for a second then I realized it was one of the dogs. The growling became deeper and louder by the second. Then the other dog chimed in. Soon, everyone in the tent was wide awake and sitting straight up in bed like fence posts. The guides began whispering among themselves and then one of them blurted, "Bear!"

"Denny, there's a bear in camp," Silin whispered. "The dogs are growling at a bear."

Suddenly flashlights began popping on all over in the tent . . . accompanied by the distinct sound of rifle bolts slamming cartridges home! About that time the dogs tore off towards the cook tent, barking and growling like enraged banshees! At the same moment, the head guide whipped open the tent door and pointed a powerful flashlight beam towards the cook tent. Sure enough, there stood a huge brown bear, sniffing at our food supply. But he didn't get to sniff long; the dogs were on him like flies on a garbage pail.

The big brown whirled and ran out of camp as fast as he could go, with the dogs right on his tail. We sat there and listened to the barking and growling for several minutes until it slowly faded off into the inky darkness. Then everything went silent. The dogs were out of hearing range, a long way from camp. "The guides said the dogs may chase the bear all night," Silin finally whispered. "We might as well go back to sleep."

I tried to get back to sleep but there wasn't any sleep left in me. I was too pumped full of adrenaline. I heard the dogs wander back into camp about three hours later, huffing and panting like marathon runners.

They eagerly gobbled up the little treats I had waiting for them outside the tent door!

BABY SNATCHERS

One year on a spring hunt in Kamchatka, the head guide took a mother Laika and several of her five-week-old puppies to camp with him. The young puppies were a big hit with the hunters. As with all puppies, they were playful and mischievous, providing us with a lot of entertainment when we weren't out in the field.

One day, while the hunters were out chasing bears, a red fox came into camp. That in itself was not unusual because we have had fox check out our camps before. Usually they are just curious to see what's going on in their back yard. They are also intrigued by the scent of camp food. A visiting fox will generally come in, do a quick inspection, and leave. But this one was different. It was a little bolder than most and didn't seem all that afraid of us . . . "us" being the interpreter, camp cook, and me. We watched it meander in and out of the woods several times before finally walking off. After it finally disappeared, we went back to drinking coffee and chatting, forgetting about the intruder.

About an hour later, we heard one of the puppies making a fuss. We looked outside the cook tent just in time to see the fox trotting off into the woods with a puppy in her mouth. Apparently she was looking to "adopt" the puppy as she carried it in her mouth the same way a dog or cat carries its young from one hiding spot to another. We quickly scampered out the tent and followed the fox into the woods. The fox gently dropped the squirming puppy near a pile of brush . . . right next to one of the other puppies! She had already carried off another puppy, without us even knowing it. We quickly ran the fox off and retrieved the two bewildered puppies.

We assumed this was an adoption procedure by the fox, and not an attempt to kill and eat the puppies, because she had not harmed them. She could have easily killed them if she wanted to, especially the first one, which we hadn't seen her steal, but the fox had carefully picked the puppies up by the scruff of the neck and carted them off into the woods. Of course, this would not have happened had the mother dog been in camp but she had followed her master into the woods that day and apparently had left us in charge of her puppies. We nearly blew our babysitting assignment!

A few years later we had another incident with puppies in camp that didn't go as well. We were hunting bears along the Sea of Okhotsk near Magadan. One of the guides had a small trapper's cabin up on a big hill overlooking the sea. Like the other guide mentioned above, he had brought a couple of his small puppies to the cabin with him. Two of my clients stayed in this cabin with the guide and a cook for several days. It was a spike camp. I was in the main camp, another small cabin a few miles away, with the interpreter and another cook.

The area where we were hunting along the Sea of Okhotsk is home to a very large species of eagle the locals call a "Sea Eagle." It's scientifically known as the Steller's Sea Eagle. This large predatory bird is quite a bit bigger than our bald eagles here in the States. In fact, it is the heaviest eagle in the world, weighing in at between 15 and 20 pounds, with a wing span of around eight feet. By comparison, the average weight of a bald eagle is a little over 10 pounds, about half the size of a sea eagle. While in camp we watched a number of these giant eagles patrolling the coastline, amazed by their size and agility. You probably know where this is going!

One day, while the guides and hunters were out chasing bears, the puppies strayed a little too far from the cabin. The cook was aroused by the squealing of one of the young dogs and ran outside just in time to see a giant sea eagle swoop down, snatch one of the puppies, and fly off with it in its long, deadly talons. Unlike the fox, this was not an adoption procedure. There was nothing the cook could do but yell and curse at the eagle as it winged off towards the mountains. It was a sad evening in camp.

Enough about puppies.

Here's a look at a typical Siberian hunting camp. (Denny Geurink photo)

The guides would often bring along a dog to ward off bears prowling around camp at night. The dogs are a fearless Russian breed known as Liakas. (Ken Horm photo)

Fire In My Tent

As mentioned earlier, I have spent an awful lot of time in wilderness tent camps the past two decades. Most of these tents were heated with wood stoves of varying degrees of size and thickness. Many were homemade by the guides, who used scrap metal and a welding torch to fashion these primitive heat sources. There were also some that were produced commercially, just for tents and cabins. While these stoves are surprisingly warm and efficient, they would probably not be OSHA-approved. They are not like the heavy, thick, cast iron wood stoves we use here in the States. I've seen stoves made out of such thin metal that they eventually burn through the sides and have to be discarded after just a few years.

These primitive stoves have caused many a tent and cabin fire in the Russian wilderness over the years; we have had a few fires in camp ourselves. Thankfully, the tents we lost burned down while the hunters were out in the woods, and not at night with the hunters inside. We did, however, almost have one burn down with someone inside . . . me!

We were hunting the Milkovo region in north-central Kamchatka in the mid-90s. I was in the tent with one other hunter and just before we went to sleep, I filled the stove with wood and "put the can on the door." The wood stoves have a soup can-sized hole cut in the door, which is framed with a circular piece of metal that sticks out the front about six inches. This circular frame has holes cut in it. A soup can fits perfectly over the extension and is used to restrict the air flow once the fire is going. We always tell guys in camp to make sure they "put the can on" at night before they go to sleep so that the fire doesn't burn too hot.

The reason these fires can get so hot is because the wood we use in our camps is birch, the only kind of wood available this far north. Birch burns hot and fast. You need to really restrict the air flow to the fire once it gets going. I've seen stove pipes get so hot they turn cherry red. Not a good thing . . . especially in a tent!

Because the wood is often wet with snow or rain, we generally bring some inside and set it near the stove to dry off. That way when we need to put more wood on the fire, we have some dry stuff available. We had done that on this particular night.

Somewhere in the middle of the night, one of these pieces of wood rolled off the pile and landed up against the stove. I don't know how long the piece of birch lay against the hot stove but it's a good thing my cot was near the stove. I was awakened by the smell of smoke. I quickly sat up in bed to see what was going on. Just as I sat up, the log burst into flames! My cot and the tent would catch on fire in a matter of seconds!

I usually have a bottle of water near my bed so if I wake up during the night thirsty, I can take a drink. On this particular night, I had just filled an empty two-liter Coke bottle with water I had pumped through my water filter from a nearby creek. I quickly grabbed the bottle of water and poured it over the burning log. Thank goodness I had it! It was just enough to put out the blazing log!

All the commotion woke the other hunter. "What the heck is going on?" he gasped, choking on the smoky air that filled the tent.

"Well, I just saved your life, and mine," I gasped. I was pretty shaken by the whole episode. I'll guarantee you one thing . . . I always make sure now that there aren't any pieces of wood close to the stove before I go to sleep!

THE RUSSIAN WAY OF DEALING WITH POACHERS

Many times the guides who take our clients out into the field are the local game wardens in charge of looking after the animals in their region. They conduct population surveys, monitor the health and welfare of the animals under their charge, and keep an eye out for poachers. And, because they are also working as local guides who depend upon high game populations to attract hunters to their area, they take poaching seriously. Very seriously!

Here in the U.S., when someone gets caught poaching, they pay a fine and wind up losing their hunting privileges for a couple of years. In certain areas of Siberia that are a long way from big cities and courtrooms where fines can be paid, poachers can lose a lot more than their hunting privileges!

I was out one evening with one of the guides, checking on his food plots out in the middle of nowhere, when we heard a shot ring out in the forest. I thought maybe there was someone else out in the woods hunting besides us. You should have seen the look on my guide's face! He was hot! This was his piece of ground and nobody else belonged out here.

He motioned for me to get back into the jeep. As soon as my butt hit the seat, we tore down a muddy trail towards the sound of the shot. I was afraid that we were going to either get stuck in a big mud hole or crash into a tree. It was like being in the General Lee on the set of the *Dukes of Hazard*! I had a white-knuckle death grip on the dash as we careened through the forest.

Suddenly, there on the trail in front of us, was another jeep. About the time we came flying up to the vehicle, we saw a guy coming out of the woods towards us with a rifle in his hands. I don't mind telling you I was a bit on edge right then! I was thinking about all the bad ways this could end! We were about to go toe to toe with another guy with a loaded gun!

My guide motioned for me to stay in the jeep. He jumped out, grabbed his rifle, and pulled out his game warden badge. He walked up to the man, yelling and screaming at him. The man, much to my relief, handed his rifle to the guide. After some more yelling and gesturing, the guy hauled the keys to his jeep from his pocket and handed them to the guide. He then began walking down the muddy old logging trail into the darkness, while my guide continued to yell at him. While I couldn't understand exactly what they were saying, I got the drift. I actually felt a little sorry for the man at that point. We were a heck of a long way from the village and it was getting dark . . . and there were a lot of bears in the woods!

When we got back to camp, I asked my interpreter to talk to my guide and find out exactly what just happened. I was still a little rattled. After questioning the guide, he told me that the guy we had confronted in the forest wasn't just another hunter, he was a poacher. He was not licensed to be out hunting and didn't have permission to hunt this area; it was leased to the guide.

"Denny, your guide told the poacher he was confiscating his rifle and his jeep and would give them back to him when he got back to town," my interpreter said. "He should make it back here in a day or two. He also told the poacher that if he ever catches him back out there in the woods, his family would never see him again."

"Are you serious?" I stammered.

"Yes, that's how it works out here," my interpreter replied. "Most poachers around here reform very quickly or they disappear. It's just the way it is. This is Russia."

CHAPTER 17

BIG STAGS ON THE BLACK SEA

ONE OF THE THINGS I was always proud of during my outfitting days in Russia was that I made my trips available to women as well as men. This was no small accomplishment in a country that for a long time regarded women as second-class citizens. Some of the guides on those early expeditions were surprised that I was taking women on a hunting trip. Others were more than surprised . . . they were annoyed and upset that I had taken ladies into their male- dominated world.

My wife, Connie, ran into her fair share of resentment on those early trips and later on, when I had her escort a few trips for me, the resentment ratcheted up a few notches! Some of the guides didn't want to have a woman telling them what to do in camp. They tried ignoring her but she wouldn't be ignored! Besides hunting and escorting trips to Russia, Connie has written a few stories about her journeys for my weekly newspaper columns. Here's one she wrote back in 1998, shortly after returning from her first trip to Crimea to hunt red stags.

***

"Oh, my gosh! That thing is huge. It looks like a tree!" exclaimed the pretty Continental airline representative behind the service counter, referring to the set of antlers perched atop our luggage cart. "Where did you get that monster!" she continued, directing the question to my husband, Denny.

"In Crimea," Denny replied, and proudly pointed to me. "It's my wife's, not mine."

She stared at me open-mouthed for a few seconds then exclaimed, "Way to go! I'm so proud of you!"

I've heard comments like that before. A lot of people still find it hard to believe that women like to hunt and a lot of people don't think I look "tough" enough to be a hunter. But the reality is that you don't have to look tough, and you don't have to be a man to love hunting.

Denny and I were on our way back to Allendale, Michigan, after a very successful red stag hunt on the coast of the Black Sea in the Ukraine. This trip was, to date, the highlight of my hunting career, and I dare say not many men have done better.

We had left Allendale ten days earlier, flown to Kiev, Ukraine, boarded an overnight train and traveled to Crimea. After a two-hour van ride, we finally arrived at the hunting camp. We were escorted to a surprisingly comfortable cottage surrounded by olive trees and enclosed within a weathered picket fence. The sound of the Black Sea just 500 yards away, and the roar of rutting stags, invaded the otherwise quiet serenity. The sun was shining, the air crisp, and everyone was filled with excitement and anticipation.

This was Denny's ninth trip to the camp; it was my first. Our company, Outdoor Adventures, books hunting trips to the Crimea. With us on this trip were Sarah and Terry Snowday from Traverse City, Michigan; Gary "Hoss" Bentley from Stockbridge, Michigan; Stuart Williams from Seattle, Washington; and Dmitri and Irena Sikorski, our Russian outfitters.

This trip was unique in that we had Sarah Fisher Snowday, the granddaughter of the Fisher Body family who started General Motors (GM), and Gary Bently, a high-low driver at GM, in the same camp. Talk about opposite ends of the spectrum! But the big gap in socioeconomic status didn't keep Sarah and Gary from becoming very good friends on this trip! Making the trip even more interesting was the fact we had Stuart Williams along. Stuart is a staff writer for the *Hunting Report*, a popular magazine back in the States. He wanted to do a story on our stag hunts.

Meanwhile, Denny intended to film the women hunting for his *"Outdoor Adventures"* TV show. I wanted to take a very big stag to impress the Russian guides, who are not used to seeing women hunt.

The very first afternoon we all piled into the back of a big, four-wheel-drive truck and were driven out into the bush. The terrain resembles the African veldt, with small scrubby trees and bushes, and lots of large grassy areas. We could hear roaring stags all around us. Unlike the high-pitched bugle of an American elk, the European elk, or stag, they sound more like they are complaining of a bellyache! They begin with a long, loud um-um-umph sound, immediately followed by several short umph, umph, umph bellows. The sound makes the hair stand up on the back of your neck!

Stags were roaring all around us. With our field glasses we spotted a number of bulls with their harems at different locations in the distance. We also saw fallow deer, mouflon sheep, quail, ringneck pheasants, ducks, red fox, and many species of hawks and birds. On one occasion, we watched an albino fallow deer buck and doe until they walked out of sight. That first afternoon "Hoss" shot a very nice bull after a short stalk in the tall grass.

The second morning Terry Snowday shot a nice bull, and later in the afternoon, Stuart Williams filled his tag. We celebrated with stag tenderloin for dinner, along with a bottle of excellent Ukrainian red wine. The guides skin and butcher the animals, clean the antlers for transport, and distribute the meat to their townspeople, who need it far more than we do. Of course, we ate our share during our stay in camp.

The next morning, it was Sarah's hunt, her first hunt ever! She had never even hunted rabbits before! She had a brand new gun, a custom-made hunting knife, and was going to be filmed for a TV show! Sarah was, to say the least, under a lot of pressure or, as she put it, she "had a monkey on her back."

Dmitri was Sarah's guide, Denny followed with the camera. They spotted a large stag in the distance and first walked then crawled through the tall grass to within 45 yards of the animal. Sarah set up her shooting stick, got her gun situated, and waited for the stag to move into position for the perfect shot. More than anything, she did not want to wound an animal. She waited. And waited. The stag was chasing first one cow then another, performing the age-old mating rites, roaring loudly with triumph then continuing the performance; but never standing still. Finally, the pressure was too much. Sarah took a quick shot but missed, and the startled animals bounded away.

The above scene was repeated two more times. Husband Terry tagged along on one stalk. Later, Sarah asked Irena and me to go along for moral support. The men didn't quite understand how she felt, and what inexperience can do to your self-confidence. We were happy to oblige. I couldn't wait to see one of these magnificent animals up close. (I was the outfitter's wife, so I had to wait until all our clients had filled their tags before I was allowed to hunt.) Irena wasn't going to hunt on this trip, just tag along to see what all the excitement was about.

Denny and Dmitri were horrified! They looked at each other as if to say, "This will never work, no way can we get close enough for a shot with a train of five people and a TV camera!" I must confess I too had my doubts but I was certainly not going to volunteer to stay behind.

Off we went, Dmitri in the lead, then Sarah, me, Irena, and Denny with the camera bringing up the rear. Dmitri soon spotted the huge rack of a stag above the tall grass in the distance and we headed in that direction.

We walked for what seemed like hours, crossing a large open area dotted with small bushes, crawling quickly, one at a time, from bush to bush. Suddenly, two cows started across the opening from the opposite direction, spotted us, and stopped to stare. We were strung out across the clearing, about three or four feet apart, in varying degrees of a crawl, frozen in place. If the cows spooked, they would alert any other animals in the area.

They walked closer, stopped, and stared; then they walked still closer and stared some more. Frozen in a half crouch, my right leg began to burn and tingle. The lead cow sniffed the air but we were downwind. She moved off slowly, looking back every other step. The smaller cow followed. Finally, the cows walked into a grassy swale out of sight. Whew! That was interesting! We began to move again.

We belly-crawled to the top of a small sandy rise on the other side of the clearing then, when the big stag lowered his head to graze, quickly scooted over the top and down the other side. Dmitri and Sarah scooted into position behind a small tree surrounded by scrub brush. I followed. Sarah set up her shooting stick, slid the gun into position, and sat there on one knee, panting, trying to calm her pounding heart and slow her breathing.

"OK, Sarah, remember, concentrate on your rifle position. Hold the stock tight against your shoulder. Just pick your target, aim, then think about how you're holding the rifle, concentrate hard on that," I said, coaching her.

She did just that. With a "whack" the shot caught the stag right behind the shoulder; he jumped, ran about 40 yards, and dropped. Sarah leapt to her feet. She had done it! The biggest stag taken this week! It sported a mammoth 8X9 rack. The "monkey" was off her back!

Back at camp, after a delicious dinner of freshly-caught fish, recounts of the day's hunts and much camaraderie and laughter, some of us went for a walk on the starlit beach and collected shells from the Black Sea but not for long; it had been a full and exhausting day.

On the final day of our stay at camp, I finally got my chance to hunt. The day dawned thick with fog. My heart sank. I had come a long way and waited patiently for all our clients to fill their tags. This was my only chance at one of those huge bulls.

We had a leisurely breakfast and waited for the fog to lift. Finally, at around 11 A.M., we climbed aboard the truck and headed out in search of my trophy. It had to be a very big one because we needed a good representative of the stags to present at seminars and sports shows back in the U.S. In addition, I was being filmed for television. Oh, boy! Sarah had passed the "monkey" to my back!

We arrived at an area where the guides had spotted some pretty decent stags the day before. Today, Dmitri was taking Stuart, who had decided to tag a second animal, out for the hunt. My guide was a very pleasant gentleman named Vitali. He had a warm smile that revealed several gold-capped teeth. I asked Sarah if she would like to come along. She seemed to attract the biggest animals wherever she went and I wanted every advantage.

Off we went through the thinning fog. I was not very optimistic but Vitali seemed confident. We hadn't gone very far when he spotted a pretty nice set of antlers turning in the tall reeds. We hunched over and crept closer and closer. It became obvious that the stag was bedded down. Very slowly we inched closer until we were almost 15 yards from the animal. Vitali signaled that I should get ready to shoot. Suddenly, the stag turned his head, caught our scent, jumped to his feet, and ran straight away from us. By the time I got him in my sights and fired, he had disappeared into the tall reeds. Oh, well, I didn't really want to shoot him in the rear anyway.

We regrouped and continued on our way, the fog lifting more and more. Suddenly Vitali stopped, brought up his binoculars, and scanned the horizon then he handed them to me and pointed. I scanned in that direction and held my breath! On the horizon, about a mile away, was the "Hartford" stag, with a TREE on his head! My pulse quickened. Oh my gosh, this was it! We had some walking to do.

We headed in the general direction of the stag, zigzagging to stay behind various bits of cover. At last we were getting within range. Vitali crept on his hands and knees to the edge of a grassy swale and signaled for me to follow. There was the stag, only 50 yards away, and he had only one cow with him. He was even bigger than I expected! I got into position and was ready to fire when the stag moved. He had his rear pointing towards me then he slowly began to move further away into taller grass. I couldn't get a shot!

Vitali signaled for Denny and Sarah to stay behind and motioned for me to follow him. He belly-crawled about 50 yards to the edge of the clearing and then crept along the edge, with me panting and puffing behind. Then we were looking out at the massive animal. He was slowly grazing, broadside to us, about 35 yards away! My heart threatened to jump out of my chest! I had to take several deep breaths to steady myself. Again, I set up the shooting stick, slid the rifle into position, and located the target area behind the bull's right shoulder. I drew a breath, held it, and pulled the trigger. The stag jumped, ran about 30 yards, and fell.

Denny let out a yelp and ran whooping from cover, along with Sarah. He had captured the whole thing on film! That's when I began yelling and pumping my fist into the air! Vitali gave me the universal high-five. I couldn't believe it! A dream come true! I had taken the perfect rack, a stag with antlers which were topped with crowns on both sides, massive and perfectly symmetrical. I couldn't even get my hands around the base of the antlers! You can be sure of one thing; I'll be back next year. You men aren't having all the fun!

Sarah Fisher Snowday, granddaughter of the GM Fisher Body family, poses with stag she harvested in 1998 (Denny Geurink photo)

CHAPTER 18

LADY AND THE BULL

"**I**GUESS IT JUST WASN'T meant to be," Linda Klass said dejectedly as we sat in the cook tent waiting for the helicopter to pick us up and take us back to town. "I've been dreaming about this hunt for a long time. I've always wanted to shoot a big moose. But, that's hunting. It just wasn't in the cards. But I had a great time anyway. It's been a great trip. You don't have to shoot something to have a good time. It's just the icing on the cake."

Linda and her husband, Ken Klass, from Ottawa, Ohio, had joined me and four other hunters on our annual fall moose hunt in Russia, just north of the Arctic Circle. All of the other hunters had filled their tags by the second or third day in camp, including West Michigan native, Michael Timmerman, from Kalamazoo, who had downed a huge bull destined for the record books. Only Linda was still looking for a moose.

Linda and Ken had come on the trip together to share the wilderness experience but only Linda had planned to hunt. The couple had purchased just one moose tag between the two of them. Linda was to be the hunter and Ken the observer; just the opposite of what usually happens when a husband and wife come on a hunt together. Unfortunately, the first day out, Linda had twisted her knee and was unable to do much walking after that so her husband took her rifle and proceeded to pick up where Linda left off.

As luck would have it, each day while Ken was out beating the bush, Linda would watch moose file through camp. At least one bull would walk through the drainage in front of the tents every day. It got to be quite humorous. Each day Ken would come back to camp exhausted after a long day of walking through the bush only to hear Linda talk about the nice bull that ambled through camp. If she hadn't taken a video camera along and filmed the moose, he would have thought he was getting his leg pulled!

One of our clients was renowned wildlife artist, Cynthie Fisher, who created an original oil painting of my wife, Connie's, stag based upon photos of her stag and seeing animals in the setting where the stag was taken. (Denny Geurink)

"Sure, you saw 10 moose today," Ken blustered the first day after he took up the hunt. "Thanks for trying to make me feel bad. I've been walking my tail off all day and haven't been able to get into rifle range of anything, and you tell me they are walking right through camp. Sure, Linda."

"I've got proof!" Linda chuckled as she hauled out her video camera and showed Ken the film she had taken. "Take a look at this."

Photo of moose camp in Siberia. (Linda Klass photo)

"What the heck am I doing out there wearing the soles off my boots?" he mumbled in disbelief as he watched several nice bulls saunter on past the camp. "I'm staying here tomorrow."

Each day, when Ken heard about the moose activity in camp and watched the video, he thought about staying in camp to hunt the next day rather than heading out into the woods again but each time the guides talked him into going out again, telling him that the chances of another nice bull walking through camp were slim.

Well, the same scenario kept repeating itself. Ken would go out and hunt hard all day while Linda stayed in camp, drinking tea and videotaping moose. Finally, it got down to the last day and we decided that if another bull came through camp, Linda would borrow a rifle from one of the other hunters and shoot it. To keep from having both Linda and Ken shoot a moose, it was agreed that Ken and his guide would stay within hearing distance of camp so that if they heard Linda shoot, they would not shoot. And if Linda heard Ken shoot, she would not pull the trigger on a bull.

Of course, now that we had a plan and were ready for a nice bull to visit camp, none came. The helicopter was supposed to come in at 2 P.M. and take us back to town. As we watched the time slowly tick away, Linda began to feel a little dejected. "Wouldn't you know it," she mused. "Now that I am ready to shoot a moose they don't come into the camp. It's like they know what's going on."

Soon it was nine o'clock. Then ten o'clock. Then eleven. Then twelve. Two hours from helicopter time. Nothing. Not even a cow. "Well, it's not over until the fat lady sings," I said, chuckling, trying to keep her spirits up. "But I do think I hear her clearing her throat."

Just then one of the other hunters, Rell Spears from Louisville, Kentucky, burst into the cook tent. "Moose! Moose! A big bull is heading for the camp! Hurry, Linda, you can use my gun." We all bailed out of the cook tent and scurried to catch a glimpse of the bull.

"Whoa, wait a minute," I stammered. "There are two of them. Look, there's another one coming out of the trees right behind the first one! They are both nice bulls!"

The moose were heading into the open drainage in front of the camp. They looked like a pair of Volkswagen buses plowing through the trees. Each sported massive headgear with wide palms and long points. As the bulls entered the drainage, Linda was so excited and so nervous that she had a hard time holding the gun. "Here," I said, as I grabbed the rifle, "you just follow the guide and I will carry the gun. I'll be right behind you."

We crouched down as low as we could and scurried single file into the drainage. First Radian, our guide, then Linda, and then me. Radian began to call like a lovesick cow as we entered the drainage. The two giant bulls stopped and stared in our direction then they began to walk slowly on an angle, closer to our position.

As the bulls closed to within 80 yards, Radian jumped up and jammed a shooting stick into the dirt. I handed Linda the rifle. She placed it on the shooting stick. She was as nervous as a mouse in a room full of cats. "OK, take the safety off and put the crosshairs right behind the shoulder," I whispered, trying to calm her down. I knew I would have to walk her through this as she was too nervous to think straight. "Put the crosshairs right behind the shoulder and squeeze. OK, squeeze the trigger."

The big gun roared and the moose staggered. "One more, right behind the shoulders," I barked. The big gun roared again. The moose fell into the grass, less than 150 yards from the cook tent.

Linda threw her hands into the air and screamed in delight, "I did it! I did it! I shot a moose! I can't believe it! I shot a moose!" Big alligator tears rolled down her cheek as we walked over to the giant beast.

"Was there ever a doubt?" I chuckled as I gave her a big hug. "By the way, is that the fat lady I hear singing?"

Linda Klass poses with big bull she bagged on the last day, the last hour right next to camp. (Linda Klass photo)

MORE MOOSE TALES FROM SIBERIA

"There must be a log, a dead tree, or something in back of him," I whispered to Maurice "Mo" White as I glassed the big bull moose standing in a small drainage about 400 yards away. "That can't be all antlers. It can't be that big. It is a nice bull, though."

It was September of 2002 and I was hunting in Siberia above the Arctic Circle with White, a Traverse City, Michigan, native. We were on our annual fall moose hunts and had just spotted a nice bull off in the distance. Problem was, the trees and bushes were still fully leafed out, as this part of the world hadn't seen a hard frost yet, which was weird because it was already well into September. Later I was to learn that it was still very warm back home in Michigan, too.

White had spotted a cow in the drainage a few minutes earlier. As we watched her munching on grass, a small bull stepped out to feed with her, probably last year's calf. A few minutes later, a bigger bull emerged from the brush. This is the bull we were presently sizing up, trying to determine whether it was big enough to go after. Finally, it stepped out into an opening. "Good grief!" I gasped. "That is all antler! He's a monster! Sixty plus inches for sure."

"Sixty plus?" Mo stuttered. "You think it'll go 60 or more?"

"For sure," I replied. "It's an absolute monster." Our guide, Ferda, was also getting excited. I pointed towards the bull and said, "Let's go." He agreed. The hunt was on.

As we made our way down the hillside towards the moose, the cover began to swallow us up but our experienced guide kept us right on course as he led us through the bush. After about 20 minutes, Ferda slowed to a snail's pace and then suddenly stopped. We all froze like statues and stared into the bush ahead of us. There, partially hidden in the brush, was the cow, not 30 yards from us. She finally moved off towards our left. We snuck to a small rise in the brush and waited. The wind was perfect, blowing right in our faces.

After a few more minutes, the small bull stepped out of the brush. We froze in our tracks as it stared right at us. Several more minutes passed and it too moved off to our left. Then we heard the unmistakable low grunting of a bull in rut moving in from our right. Suddenly there it was! It looked like a bus with a huge white rack sliding through the brush right at us.

"Oh, my . . ." Mo whispered softly, "look at the size of that rack!"

"Get ready," I whispered back. "Take him right behind the shoulder when he steps out." But he didn't step out. The big bull just stood there for several minutes and then stepped back into the brush and disappeared. Did he spot us? Did he smell us? What happened? All these questions raced through our heads as we stared in disbelief into the bush.

"Now what do we do?" Mo whispered. "Shall we go after him?"

"I think he's still real close," I replied. "I don't think he's going anywhere. He's not going to leave the cow. Just keep your eyes peeled. He's going to follow the cow sooner or later. If we go into the brush, we'll spook him." I sure hoped I knew what I was talking about!

Seconds dragged on into minutes. The guide, Ferda, who was a good foot, or more, shorter than we were, hadn't even seen the rack. He didn't even know the bull was in front of us and was now wondering why we didn't move forward. He wanted to keep moving. I kept motioning to him that the bull was right there in front of us. He was beginning to think I was crazy.

Then, suddenly, the big bull pushed out of the brush just across the drainage. His huge rack twisted and turned as he made his way through the brush and up the other side. I raised my TV camera and hit the 'on' switch. Mo clicked the safety off again and fired. The big bull staggered. Mo fired another round and he fell. Mo was in a daze. "I can't believe it! It all worked out perfectly," Mo stammered. "He came right in front of us."

"That is one monster bull!" I exclaimed as we walked towards the fallen beast. "It's bigger than I thought it was. I'm even thinking 70 inches. It's the biggest bull moose I've ever seen!"

"It's the biggest rack ever taken from this region!" our head guide told us back at camp. "I have never seen such a moose!"

All of this excitement got us to thinking—how high up into the record books will this thing go? We got that answer when we arrived back into the States.

"Just got a call from my taxidermist," Mo told me over the phone a few days after we got back home. "He scored my rack and said if it's a Yakut moose, it's a new world record. It completely blows away the old world record. It's just over 72 inches wide! The only thing we have to do is find out exactly where our camp was so we can determine what species of moose it is."

There are three main species of moose in Russia: the European moose, the Yakut moose, and the Chukotka moose. The European moose is similar to a Canadian moose. The Yakut moose and the Chukotka moose are similar to the Yukon/Alaskan moose, with the Yakut moose being a little smaller. Mo shot his moose very close to the dividing line between the Yakut and Chukotka moose territories. If his moose was a Yakut moose, it's a new world record. If it was a Chukotka moose, it would be number six in the world for that species. We are waiting for an official ruling.

In addition to Mo's moose, we shot another 10 moose this fall both in the Yakut and Chukotka regions. If Mo's moose is the number one Yakut moose, then we also have number 2 and 3 in the world for that subspecies as two of our hunters took moose in the 65-inch class in the same area.

The week after Mo shot his moose, we moved further east and shot six moose in the Chukotka region, one that measured 77 ½ inches in width! We are presently having that one scored as the possible new world record for the Chukotka species! But that's a whole new story. Bottom line? It looks like we may have harvested the No. 1, 2, and 3 world record Yakut moose and the No. 1 Chukotka moose last month. Not a bad hunt!

Authors Note: This story was written in October of 2002. We later found out that White's moose would be classified as a Chukotka Moose and was listed as No. 7 in the world record books. The 77 ½ moose we took the following week went into the record books as the No. 2 moose in the Chukotka category. It was taken by Wayne Wilde, from Shevlin, Minnesota. The following year we took over the Top 3 spots in the Yakut Moose category.

THE COMMANDER

They called him the Commander. And rightly so.

The giant moose did indeed command attention, especially from any other moose in the area that might have a notion to try and steal one of his girlfriends. While the other moose gave him a wide berth, my hunters and guides tried to get close to him. It was October of 2004 and we were again chasing moose in Russia's vast Siberian wilderness.

The Commander came from good stock. His father and grandfather had certainly commanded respect as well because the gene pool for trophy moose in this area is phenomenal. The new SCI record book will show that a lot of record moose came from this region, including Wayne Wilde's 77-incher and Maurice White's 72-incher.

The big bull was hanging out with several cows quite a way from camp. The hunters had seen his tracks in the snow and knew he was a keeper. After a few days of walking back and forth from camp to his stomping grounds, the hunters decided to set up a spike camp in the Commander's back yard.

It was cold and there was nearly a foot of snow on the ground during the mid-October hunt; quite unusual for this time of year. In fact, just two years ago, when White shot his monster bull from the same camp, the temperature had climbed to 70 degrees. This group of hunters, however, was happy to see the snow as it made the animals much more visible and easy to track.

"I had already seen six nice moose up to this point," says Doug Murray, from Silver City, Iowa. "This region has the largest number of moose in the world. They also have unbelievably big moose – the biggest in the world. The hunting here is incredible."

On the fourth day into the hunt, Murray and his guide came across the Commander's tracks again. This time they were still smoking. "My guide showed me where the moose were busy feeding on the brush," said Murray, "so we knew the animals were poking along and probably still close by. We saw where the tracks went into the woods so we made a big circle around the woods to see if they had come back out. They hadn't.

"We started making smaller and smaller circles when the guide suddenly spotted a cow standing and feeding. We knew the big bull had to be close by. We stood still and watched for about 20 minutes, looking for the bull. Finally we saw his enormous rack sticking out of the brush. He was lying down.

"All of a sudden the bull sensed our presence and stood up and began to trot off into the woods. I couldn't believe the size of his rack. Holy cow! I tried to get him in my scope but it was so thick I couldn't shoot for about 20 or 30 seconds," said Murray. "I just followed him through the woods and finally, at about 125 yards, I fired off the first shot. I knew I had hit him but he kept on going so I threw more lead.

"After he went down, we began to walk over towards him. I couldn't believe how big he was. He was enormous! The rack was absolutely phenomenal." Later, when they were able to put a tape measure to the rack, they found out just how phenomenal the bull was. It measured nearly 72 inches across.

Another bull for the books!

CHAPTER 19

THE CAPERCAILLIE TWO-STEP

I T'S 2 A.M., APRIL 29, 1997, and I'm stretched out on a bench of freshly-cut pine boughs deep in the boreal forest of Mother Russia. Our guide, Alexi Trapezikov, has just fashioned this primitive bed with an ax and a pocket full of nails. Next to me is a crackling fire with a boiling pot of tea broadcasting the sweet scent of jasmine and lemon through the inky black night which had swallowed us up several hours earlier. We were about a quarter of a mile from a capercaillie lek, waiting for daylight to arrive. This had all the trappings of a good, old-fashioned, American snipe hunt! All that was missing was a flashlight and burlap bag! But, we were a long way from America. We were in the middle of BFE Russia in search of bird almost as elusive as a snipe. The Russians call it "glukhar."

This latest Russian adventure began with a phone call from fellow writer and friend, Tom Huggler, in August of 1996. Tom, who lives near Lansing, Michigan, had just finished watching a TV show I had filmed in Russia featuring the holy grail of grouse hunting . . . the capercaillie. I didn't realize what a prized game bird this large grouse was until I began talking to Tom and other hard-core bird hunters who began calling and writing me after this episode of *"Denny Geurink's Outdoor Adventures"* aired on the Fox network. Ironically, the capercaillie hunt I had filmed was more of an afterthought than the primary focus of the show but, my perception of this highly-coveted game bird was about to change.

"Denny, why don't you organize a bird hunt in Russia?" Tom queried. "I'd love to hunt the capercaillie and a few of the other species of grouse they have over there, like the European black grouse and the hazel grouse. The grouse found in Russia are about the only ones I haven't taken yet. It would help me finish my Grand Slam of grouse."

"Do you think you can get a group of guys together who want to go and do a hunt like this?" I replied. "I've had quite a few people ask about going over there to hunt the capercaillie but they can't find anyone else to go with them. The Russians won't open up a camp, hire guides, cooks and interpreters to take one person out. We need a group of hunters to make it happen. I wouldn't mind trying it. Sounds like a lot of fun."

"I think I can," Tom answered. "I know quite a few guys who might be interested in something like this. Let me make a few calls and get back to you."

I figured if anybody could find a group of hunters interested in chasing birds in Russia, Tom could. Besides being on the editorial staff at *Outdoor Life*, Tom is one of the most avid bird hunters in the country. He has written dozens of stories – and several books – on game bird hunting. He has a lot of contacts in this arena.

The capercaillie, or "glukhar" as the Russians call it, is the largest species of grouse in the world. It's about the size of a chicken and can weigh over seven pounds. It is also one of the most difficult game birds in the world to collect because in most countries they have been pushed to the brink of extinction due to habitat loss. These birds need huge tracts of mature, diverse conifer forests to thrive. Unfortunately, these diverse habitats have been cut down and replaced with smaller, single-species plantations in most European countries. In addition to not providing the kind habitat the capercaillie needs to thrive, these smaller, single-species wood lots have also become havens for all of the glukhar's natural enemies like fox, hawks, owls, eagles, and a host of other predators.

Only in the remote regions of northern Russia can you still find the extensive taiga forests that sustain the habitat these magnificent Old World game birds require. In countries like Germany and Scotland, where there used to be a lot of capercaillie, they haven't been allowed to hunt them in over 30 years. Aggressive programs to bring the birds back have failed due to the lack of the specific habitat they require.

I was first introduced to the capercaillie back in 1991 when we chased them to fill in the time between our bear and moose hunts. Back then, we weren't pursuing them as a game bird but as table fare. Little did I know they were so highly revered in the bird hunting world!

The European black grouse and the hazel grouse that Tom also wanted to hunt are fairly widespread across Europe but, again, much more abundant in Russia's dense boreal forests. The black grouse, or "tetera" as the Russians call them, is a little bigger than our ruffed grouse and can weigh over three pounds. The hazel grouse, or "ryabchik" in Russian, is a little bigger than our bobwhite quail. They are one of the smallest species of grouse in the world. While the capercaillie would be our main target, I told my outfitter, Dmitri Sikorski, we also wanted to try for these birds as well. He said he would arrange everything.

It didn't take Tom long to round up a group of guys eager to chase these unique game birds. The hunt was on! As soon as I got off the phone with Tom, I began putting all the pieces together. A few months later, here I am lying on a bed of pine boughs at 2 o'clock in the morning, trying to get some sleep before our glukhar hunt begins. But I am too excited to sleep!

Earlier that day, Tom, Dmitri, and I had taken a two-hour drive in Alexi's little Lada from the village of Cmetahno, where we were staying, down a maze of bumpy roads and muddy two- tracks. Several times we had to get out of the tiny little sardine can and push it out of a mud hole. Actually, it's quite amazing what these little cars will go through. I would never even attempt to go down some of these trails with my Chevy; my four-wheel-drive pick-up maybe, but never my car.

We ended up parking the Lada along the edge of a large farm field that bumped up against a thick, mature forest of tall conifers and hardwoods. It was early May and there was still a lot of snow on the ground in the heavily-shaded forest. In some places it was waist deep. This made the three-hour hike into the bowels of the forest quite an adventure. The forest was thick and heavy, and closed in around us like dense fog. We were exhausted by the time we reached our destination, a small bump on the forest floor, just a quarter mile from an active glukhar lek.

A lek, for those who are not hard-core grouse hunters, is a specific area in a field or forest where male grouse get together to sing and dance to impress the ladies. The females are attracted to the lek in search of a mate. These age-old mating rituals usually occur in the same spot year after year. Capercaillie leks are secretive sites located deep within a mature conifer forest. Finding an active capercaillie lek is like finding a pot of gold at the end of a rainbow.

After reaching our destination about an hour before dark, Alexi built a little bench of pine boughs for both Tom and me and told us we should try to get some sleep. That wasn't going to happen! The crackling campfire bounced eerie shadows off the dense canopy of pine branches enveloping us; shadows of people, a tea pot, an ax, and long-barreled shotguns. The scene reminded me of a Hollywood film set for a werewolf movie. We wound up sipping tea and telling hunting stories into the wee hours of the morning.

At 2:30 A.M., Alexi said it was time to go. We snuck our way under cover of darkness into the legendary mating arena of the glukhar and waited for dawn and the games to begin. Dawn comes early in this part of northern Russia. Real early! We weren't that far from the Arctic Circle!

And then it happened! We heard the first "click-click-click" call of the male bird tuning up for his signature song. I'm going to let Tom tell the story of his exciting hunt: *"At 3 A.M. we began our first single-file stalk on a male that had suddenly opened up in full song,"* Tom explains. *"First Alexi, then me and then Denny, who was toting his video camera. It was hard going in the snow, trying to step in unison like a camo-colored ballet trio, copying Alexi's start-and-stop tactics. We got to within 50 yards of the bird, which suddenly bolted from his perch and roared over us at 25 yards. He was the size of a gigantic crane I had noticed the day before. I pulled up my 12-gauge shotgun but Alexi brought down the barrel. "Nyet!" he hissed, apparently not wanting me to miss or, worse yet, possibly cripple one of these majestic birds."*

After stalking that first bird, Tom and I began whispering and chuckling about how funny the three of us looked sneaking up on the big male perched high atop the conifer tree. Alexi had told us before the stalk began that we must follow exactly in his footsteps and move at exactly the same time he did . . . and stop moving when he did. It was kind of like a game of Simon Says.

This kind of stalking tactic is necessary to close the distance between you and the bird so you can get into shotgun range. When you first begin the stalk, you have no idea which tree the bird is even sitting in because the forest is so dense. All you can do is hear him call. But, as you get closer to where you might be able to spot him, the advantage goes to the bird because of his high lookout point. You must only move when he is at the end of his three-part song.

The song begins with a "click-click-click" noise that sounds like someone tapping a pencil on a wooden table. It then moves on to a guttural "whooshing" sound, followed by a "rasping" sound that resembles someone raking a metal file over a piece of wood. During this last sequence, the bird stretches his neck straight up and lifts his head high into the air. This final note lasts about two seconds. While he stretches his head to the sky, a thin translucent membrane covers his eye. This blurs his vision and gives you about two seconds to move in on him. During these two seconds, you can take two giant steps.

When the song is over, the male looks around to see if any females heard his beautiful serenade. You can't move a muscle at this time because he will spot you. You must wait until he starts his song all over again and gets to the last raspy part before you can take two more steps. It's like a game. You have to listen very carefully to the song and only move during the last note. It's very exciting and nerve-wracking at the same time.

So it's take two steps and stop. Take two steps and stop. Kind of like a simplified version of the Texas Two-Step . . . which led to Tom and I calling this dance of the glukhar hunter the "The Capercaillie Two-Step!" It wasn't long before we were two-stepping again.

"Soon our guide focused on another singing male, perhaps 200 yards away," Tom continues the story of his hunt. "Progress was good; within five minutes we had halved the distance. Then I stood unbalanced, legs spread, snow over my knees, water seeping into one boot. The capercaillie stopped singing. We stood still for five minutes, eight minutes, while my foot went numb with cold. The male began to call again then flushed when my trapped boot made a loud sucking sound in the snow.

"During a third stalk, we moved to within 50 yards of a huge male, plainly back-lighted from gathering light in the east. I wanted to take him and felt that I could, having shot wild turkeys at that range before. Alexi said no. Like the others, the bird blew out, leaving me disheartened. Then, without warning, another male – no doubt a subdominant – flew to a branch about 40 yards away. "Da?" Alexi asked. I nodded and began my stalk. I shot him at 20 yards. He weighed a tad over 7 pounds."

For some reason the long bumpy ride back to the village didn't seem to take near as long as the ride out. Back at Alexi's house, we met up with the other members of our intrepid group of Russian bird hunters. Tom had brought with him Joe Zikewich from Lake Orion, Michigan; Jim Gilsdorf from Ann Arbor, Michigan; J.D McDonald from Chicago, Illinois; and Joe Scillierri from Jamesburg, New Jersey. Also with us was John Baker from Walker, Michigan. John worked with me on my TV show as a cameraman/salesman.

McDonald had come along on the trip to collect a capercaillie for the Chicago Museum of Natural History. And Zikewich had come along to collect one for the Drayton Plains Nature Center in Michigan. The rest of us wanted to add one of these rare birds to our own collections.

Out of the seven of us, four guys had already collected a capercaillie the first morning out! John, J.D., and Joe Scillierri had all scored, in addition to Tom. Not a bad way to start a hunt. The following day, Jim, Joe Zikewich, and I all scored. The capercaillie portion of the hunt was over. It was time to move on to the European black grouse or "tetera". But, before we did, the guides told us it was time to celebrate the success we had experienced up to this point of the expedition. You know what that means!

Dmitri makes tea over open fire while I sit on bench our guide built with his hatchet deep in Capercaillie forest. (Tom Huggler photo)

"I'm not used to drinking vodka at ten in the morning," Tom said, chuckling as a vodka bottle appeared like magic on the breakfast table. "But who could resist the day's first toast by our co-host, novelist Sergei Alexeyev, whose last spy thriller sold 4 ½ million copies!"

"To the hunt," Sergei beamed while Dmitri interpreted, "the ancestral bond that brings all men together regardless of nationality, regardless of custom. Long live the hunt!'"

We all lifted out glasses and heartily cheered this insightful toast. Alexeyev is a well-known Russian author who loves to retreat to the forest to relax and recharge his batteries. We were surprised and honored to share our camp with him.

"I've often thought there would be no wars if hunters and anglers, and not neurotic politicians, decided world affairs," Tom mused.

Can I hear an Amen to that?

Here you can see the stark contrast between the male (left) and female (right) Capercaillie. (Denny Geurink photo)

We spent the next few days hunting black grouse in open farm fields from little huts the guides constructed from pieces of wood and straw. Unlike the glukhar, the tetera carries on its mating rituals in the middle of a field, next to the forest, rather deep in the forest itself. The guides set out taxidermy mounts as decoys and then called to the birds to bring them close. It was a totally new experience for me and one I thoroughly enjoyed!

Somewhere about this time we found out that the season on hazel grouse is only open in the fall. The season is closed in the spring because the males and females are indistinguishable and game biologists don't want people shooting the hens during the mating and nesting season. This was a big disappointment to Tom, who really needed the hazel grouse to fill in his World Slam of grouse.

JD McDonald poses with a European Blackcock and a Capercaillie he collected for the Chicago Museum of Natural History. That's Tom Huggler from Outdoor Life on the right and Denny on the left.
(Dmitri Sikorski photo)

J.D. McDonald (center) shows off Hazel Grouse and European Black Cock collected for Chicago Museum of Natural history. On left is, Alexi Trapezikov, our guide and on the right is famous Russian novelist, Sergei Alexeyev. (Tom Huggler photo)

When Alexi, who was also a local game warden in addition to being a guide, and Sergey, one of Russia's most prominent novelists, found out how disappointed Tom was they made a few phone calls. Apparently they were good friends with one of the directors of the regional game department in St. Petersburg. A couple of days later, a courier arrived at camp with a small legal document that proclaimed a special spring season for hazel grouse had been set. The season would be open for one day, with a bag limit of one grouse.

Wow! Think about it! Can you imagine something like this happening in the States? Not gonna happen! The Russians set a one-day season with a bag limit of one hazel grouse just so Tom—an American and former Cold War enemy—could take one of these birds home with him! What a class act! It's one of the most remarkable moments in a remarkable outfitting career in Russia.

When talking to Tom later, besides this generous gesture, one of the special memories he has of this trip was the warm hospitality of the Russian people he encountered along the way. This is elegantly reflected in the opening paragraph of a story he wrote when he got back home.

"It is two o'clock in the morning, and I am sipping honeyed tea in the home of Yuri, my local guide, waiting for the rain to stop sliding down the blackened window," writes Tom. (Yuri was another one of our guides along with Alexi, who you read about earlier.) "Yuri's mother, a farm wife who appears to be about 80 – my own mother's age – enters the yellow pool of light that defines her kitchen. 'Chea?' she gestures with the teapot. I smile back, folding my hands under an ear to make a pillow. I wonder if Yuri's mother will go back to bed. 'Nyet.' She grins broadly as though her life's purpose – to be routed in the middle of the night to play hostess to a visitor from America – has now been achieved. We are unable to converse further, but I see the history of twentieth-century Russia in her tired, proud face. Imagine a life that began under the last czar. Picture the many upheavals: the Bolshevik Revolution, the Great Patriotic War, the purges of Stalin, the dissolution of the Soviet Union, and now the new democracy that brings a Cold War enemy to her kitchen on a rainy night in early May."

Tom was so impressed with his hunt and the warmth of the people, he later wrote me: "Denny this trip is up there with the best of any trip I've ever taken. The hunt was great! I'm going back!"

He came back that fall to hunt the European woodcock and European quail. But that's another story for another time.

CHAPTER 20

ECOUNTER WITH A
RUT-CRAZED BULL MOOSE

EVERYONE HAS HEARD THE stories about bellicose bull moose squaring off with approaching trains and 18-wheelers during the rut. The blind rage of a rutting bull is legendary. They say that when a bull moose gets caught up in the rut, he gets pretty stupid. He has a one-track mind. All he can think about is hooking up with a lovely cow moose. A lovesick bull will wallow in the mud, pee on himself, and moan like a drunk with a toothache. During his non-stop search for a date, he will fight with anyone or anything that gets in it way. That's what they say. Well, you can put me in the "they" crowd.

I've witnessed some of this weird behavior first-hand while chasing these one-ton beasts near the Arctic Circle in Siberia. And I've also heard some pretty exciting "crazy moose" stories from my hunters.

When we shoot a moose a long way from camp, we generally bring the cape and antlers back to camp with us, along with a tenderloin for dinner. We leave the rest of the carcass out in the bush to retrieve the next day. The meat is piled up on the skin and covered with cheese cloth or a tarp. Then the guide will poke a stick into the ground over the carcass and hang a coat or shirt over the meat pile to ward off wolves and grizzly bears. The human scent on the article of clothing usually discourages predators from the kill for at least a couple of days. Usually . . . but not always!

After the meat is secured for recovery the next day, the guides load the cape and antlers onto a pack frame and head back to camp. This trek back to camp can get pretty hairy at times. Besides being followed by grizzlies, I've had several clients and their guides charged by other bulls while they are walking through the bush back to camp. You know these bulls are pretty cranked up on hormones if they can't tell the difference between a real bull and a guy carrying a moose rack! It's like they are in a drug-induced stupor.

Generally, the guide and the hunter are able to scare the bull off before anyone gets hurt. Usually the charging bull comes to his senses when he get close enough to see the men and hear them yelling. But not always. My guides have told me several stories about how they, or their friends, have been knocked over and seriously injured by rut-crazed bulls. They try not to shoot a testy bull if it's too small, they would rather scare it off, but sometimes they have to shoot it to keep from being killed. The guides consider a bull in the rut to be just as dangerous as a bear.

This opinion is backed up by scientists and researchers who report that moose attack more people than bears and wolves combined. According to Wikipedia, the online encyclopedia, in the Americas, moose injure more people than any other wild mammal and, worldwide, only hippopotamuses injure more people.

I'll never forget the time when I was out with one of my hunters and a guide named Ferda. My client had downed a giant bull and we had just spent an hour or more caping it and getting ready for the trek back to camp. We helped Ferda tie the rack and cape to his pack frame and hoist it up on his back. The antlers stuck up over his shoulders and head by at least two feet. We were making jokes about how we hoped another hunter wouldn't see us coming through the woods because, from a distance, Ferda looked a lot like a moose slipping through the trees and tall grass. From a distance you would only see the giant rack protruding high over his head.

After walking for about 15 minutes, we suddenly spotted a small bull heading our way across a large clearing. I don't know if it had seen us or was just walking in our direction. Ferda made a few lovesick bull sounds and then started laughing when the young bull began wagging his head from side to side. The bull let out a sound I can only describe as somewhere between a groan and a roar. It had definitely seen us!

The way I figured it, once the bull saw the size of the rack Ferda was carrying, it would hightail it into the woods and we would all laugh about the good joke we had pulled on him. The rack on Ferda's shoulders was at least 65 inches across, with huge, massive paddles. The young bull was barely 45 inches across. But the smaller bull wasn't in a joking mood.

To our surprise, the young bull lowered its head and started trotting towards us. While Ferda still thought it was funny, I couldn't see as much humor in the situation as I had a few minutes earlier. The bull paused on the way in to whack its antlers against a small tree and paw in the mud. It let out a few more "umps." Ferda continued to call to the bull while my client and I looked for a big tree to climb!

The young bull rolled his eyes back in his head and shook his head again and kept coming towards us. As the bull closed to 30 yards, Ferda didn't think it was quite as funny anymore either. He began yelling at the bull. It paid no attention to him. By now my skin was crawling and my bladder was weakening! When the bull got to 15 yards, Ferda began firing shots into the air from his SKS rifle. This brought the animal to a stop. His eyes rolled back to the front of his head and he stared intently at us for a good 10 seconds. After taking a few more stiff-legged steps towards us, it finally realized there were three people standing in front of him and not another bull. He slowly turned and headed back towards the woods. We all breathed a giant sigh of relief. That was as close to a rut-crazed bull as I ever want to get!

This bull had walked to within 10 yards of us before finally turning around and leaving. That would have seemed like a mile to Michael Pilarski from Romeo, Michigan. Pilarski had one of the closest calls ever with a rut-crazed bull back in September of 2002. He got about as close to a rampaging bull as a person can get without being killed or seriously injured. I'll let him tell the story.

***

Two of the greatest moments in my hunting career happened on a Russian moose hunt with Denny Geurink from Outdoor Adventures. The wildest one started on day two of the hunt, about seven miles out of camp.

My guide and I were working up the side of a small mountain when we cut some moose tracks in the muddy snow. The guide pointed at the scattered tracks, which seemed to indicate that a group of five to seven moose had just passed through the area; most likely a good bull with some cows. We followed the trail slowly and quietly. About one-hundred yards further up the mountain, the guide stepped on a small twig. It made a loud snap. We stopped to listen. After a slight pause we continued. After a few more steps, my ears picked up a small snap about 60 yards to the right. I stopped the guide with a quieting "Wiss, wiss" sound. He looked at me and I pointed to my ear then to the direction of the snap. We both paused.

Then it happened! The action was about to begin! We heard a "Whau, whau" sound coming from the brush. A bull moose had pinpointed us and he was coming in for a fight. At 40 yards we could see the beast rocking back and forth with his eyes rolling back in his head and his massive antlers swaying from side to side. What a breath-taking sight! Within 30 yards we decided this was not a shooter.

His spread was about 54 to 58 inches. He would have been a trophy in most places but not in this area. I eased the barrel of my rifle up and rested the stock on my knee. I was fascinated by the fearless challenge that the bull was putting on. Then it hit me! He wasn't stopping! My heart

really started pounding as we tried to back up. My left hand
on the guide's shoulder, holding him in front of me, I started
glancing over my shoulder, looking for any kind of cover
to run behind if the bull decided to charge. My heart really
started to race when I realized I was screwed.

This mountain side was all skinny re-growth, mostly tall
pine about three to five inches in diameter, all the kind of
trees I would get hung up on or bounce off if I tried to run
but nothing for an eighteen-hundred pound bull to plow over.
At that moment the bull closed to within ten feet! Ten feet!
"Whau, whau, whau!" I had a perfect shot at the bull's vitals,
which were eye level with the guide! I remember thinking
that the guide could walk under this huge beast and his head
would just scrape the bull's belly!

Now I'm not sure if I froze with fear, shock, or a little of
both. I was ready to dive one way or the other. The guide
stretched out his pre-World War II rifle with his left hand over
the nose of this monster. I thought, "What is he doing?" Is he
going to smack him on the nose with it? BANG! He shot!!
My eyes must have been as huge as baseballs! The end of
the barrel was just past the nostril and about six inches over
the head of the moose. Six inches! Is he crazy? The beast
stood still; his ears had to be ringing worse than mine. Then
he shook his head and massive antlers to clear the ringing.
After a small pause, he cross-stepped slowly to change his
direction. He slowly walked out to about 15 yards.

I was just starting to come out of my state of shock and
amazement when it started all over! "Whau, whau!" His
eyes rolled back and he started posturing again to fight,
swaying his massive antlers back and forth then he started
to circle back at us. At that moment the guide looked at me
and gestured with his hands as if he were taking a picture.
HOLY CRAP! My camera! I grabbed it out of my pocket and
looked down to advance the film. As I did, I heard a "gallop,
gallop, gallop" sound. I looked up and he was gone.

As soon as he got downwind, he disappeared within a
fraction of a second, leaving me without even a picture.

That's when my heart finally dropped out of my throat and back into my chest. I was shaking like a leaf. My skin was cold and clammy; but we were both still alive! I had gone nose to nose with a giant bull moose and lived to tell about it! I didn't get the picture on film but I guarantee you it will be forever etched in my mind! I left that mountain side that day having had the most amazing encounter of my life!

The second most-amazing encounter would happen just three days later when I called up two monster bulls that were ready to fight and, yes, I shot the big one! With a 68-inch spread and scoring 497 6/8 in the Safari Club International (SCI) record book, it became the number one Yakutia moose of all time. Totally massive palms; everything I could ever dream of in a trophy moose. But that's a whole other story in itself. Thanks for a great adventure, Denny!

CHAPTER 21

BEAR CHARGES SNOWMOBILE

ONE OF THE MOST spine-tingling incidents during our two decades in the bush occurred back in the early 90s on one of our spring bear hunts. The bears generally hibernate in the lower elevations of the numerous mountain ranges scattered along the Kamchatka Peninsula. We use snowmobiles on the spring hunts to transport our clients from the camps to the denning areas. Once in the denning area, the guides locate a high vantage point from where they can survey the snow-covered landscape with a spotting scope or binoculars to locate bears traversing the area. Once a bear is spotted, the guide plans a stalk and the hunt is on.

Each guide has his own snowmobile rigged up with a big sled in tow. The guide drives the snowmobile around while the hunter rides along behind on the sled. That's the best way to get around because putting the guide and the hunter together on a snowmobile just wouldn't work.

Most sleds have some sort of seat or chair attached to it, along with a box or crate in which to haul extra gear, lunch, spare snowmobile parts, etc. Quite often, on the way out to the denning areas, the guide and hunter run across bears wandering around searching for food. On this particular hunt, that's exactly what happened. The guide and outfitter have asked me not to use their real names as they think someone might think they were careless or negligent. I don't think that's the case; embarrassing maybe but not negligent. I will respect their wishes. The story is too good not to tell!

The guide, let's call him Yuri, and the hunter, let's call him Bill, were heading through the woods towards the mountains when they rounded a corner on the trail and saw a nice bear walking across a small opening. The bear was struggling in the deep snow, which gave Bill time to rack a shell in the chamber, jump off the sled, and get down on one knee for a shot. Unfortunately, Bill made a bad shot and hit the bear right in the mouth. Obviously, the bear wasn't too happy!

It let out a blood-curdling roar as it shook its head from side to side, spitting blood and teeth into the soft snow. Bears are very intelligent animals and this one quickly put 2 and 2 together. His pain and displeasure had something to do with the two creatures on the loud machine. He immediately charged the men and their machine. Somebody was going to pay for his missing teeth and sore mouth!

Yuri yelled frantically at Bill to get back on the sled so they could get the heck out of dodge. He wanted to put a little more distance between them and the bear before they took another shot. He didn't want anything to do with a charging, wounded bear in this heavy stand of woods. It was too close and too infuriated to try to put down.

Bill jumped back aboard the sled and Yuri hit the throttle and sped away as fast as he could. Just in the nick of time; the bear was almost on the sled. Fortunately, Yuri was able to put some distance between them and the charging blur of brown fury. As the snowmobile and sled sped through the woods, the bear kept his focus on the whirlwind of blowing snow and loud noise that roared along in front of him. Spurred by anger and adrenaline, the bear moved surprising fast through the deep snow and stayed hot on the snowmobile's tail.

Yuri was doing everything he could to shake the bear but was having a hard time negotiating the snowmobile and sled through the thickly-wooded bottomland. Meanwhile, Bill was hanging on for dear life as the sled bucked and kicked like a Brahma bull. Yuri was weaving in and out of the trees, trying not to get the sled hooked up on a root or branch. It wasn't easy! A snowmobile alone would have been no problem but the extra weight and length of the long sled, twice as long as the snowmobile, made it difficult.

Just as he was starting to put a little distance between him and the bear, all hell broke loose! Yuri made a sharp turn to avoid smacking into a snag; the snowmobile missed the snag but the sled didn't! The sled rammed into the snag at 30 miles an hour, turning it sideways and throwing Bill off and into a tree. His rifle smacked the tree so hard, it cracked the stock. Thankfully, Bill only glanced off the tree and didn't break an arm or leg. The momentum from the crash sent Bill rolling down a small hill and into a bush. Thank God for the hill!

As Bill lay in the deep snow, he spotted his banged-up rifle 10 yards way. He knew there was no way he could get to it on time to shoot the bear. He didn't know if it would still even be able to fire a bullet. The bear came barreling around the corner in a cloud of flying snow. He was panting hard but still enraged and determined to put the hurt on the thing that busted up his mouth. Bill froze in terror! It was all over for him. He started imagining how it would all end. He started to make peace with his maker.

Just as he was about to have a heart attack, Bill watched in utter surprise as the bear ran right past him. The enraged bruin was so focused on the fleeing snowmobile and sled that it never noticed Bill had rolled off into a bush. Now flush with adrenaline of his own, Bill scrambled up the hill and retrieved his rifle. The stock was cracked but it should still work. He prepared for the bear to come back for him. It was going to be a fight to the death in this isolated patch of woods in the middle of Siberia.

About this time Yuri looked back to see if Bill was still hanging on to the sled. You can imagine the terror that raced through his mind when he noticed the sled was empty. Bill was gone! But the bear was still right behind him. What in the heck happened? Where's Bill? Why is the bear still chasing him? The guide swung the snowmobile in a big circle and headed for the trail he had just blazed through the woods. Bill had to be lying along the trail somewhere.

With the sled now a whole lot lighter and the bear starting to tire, Yuri was able to put about 125 yards between him and the bear. But the bear wasn't giving up! After what seemed like an eternity, the guide was coming back down the trail into the patch of woods where Bill was crouched in the snow with his rifle. Yuri spotted Bill and sped over to him, yelling for him to get back on the sled. Bill jumped back on the sled and away they went one more time. The bear was still coming!

Yuri drove the snowmobile out into a large field and cut the engine. Bill jumped off, sat down in the snow, and brought his rifle up on one knee. Yuri jumped off right beside him and threw his rifle up to his shoulder. It was going to be Custer's . . . er, Bill's and Yuri's . . . Last Stand! When the bear got to within 80 yards, Yuri and Bill opened fire. The big bruin took a lot of lead and plowed to a stop less than 20 yards way. It let out one last blood-curdling roar and fell limp. It was over.

Yuri and Bill also fell limp. The sheer terror and adrenaline rush left them exhausted. They hugged and congratulated each other for surviving this unbelievable ordeal!

CHAPTER 22

MORE TALES OF BEAR ATTACKS FROM SIBERIA

OVER THE YEARS I have come across dozens of dangerous bear encounter stories while in Russia. You read about some of them in Chapter 4. Here are several more, including not just stories of attacks on people but also tales of attacks on cows, goats, and cadavers! Yes, even cadavers!

One of the weirdest stories came from the Tomsk region of Siberia in 2011. It not only reveals just how dangerous and destructive bears can be when they get hungry but also how cunning they can be. What makes this story so scary is the way the bears were attacking their victims . . . milk cows in small villages. They were getting together and ganging up on the cows much the same way a pack of wolves does when they attack prey. A pack of wolves is dangerous enough . . . but a pack of giant brown bears! That's like something from a science fiction movie. This kind of behavior is very unusual for bears because they are normally solitary predators. While a sow and her cubs may work together, bears not of the same family group working together to coordinate an attack is very strange.

Unfortunately, these kinds of attacks on cattle in the Tomsk area are getting more frequent, according to Konstantin Osadchi, head of the Department of Environmental Protection for the Tomsk region. Bear attacks on cattle in the region jumped from three reported attacks in 2010 to ten in 2011.

"Probably changes took place in the mind of the bears; they are curious or they lost their fear of man," said Osadchi in a statement to the news agency *Interfax*. "Previously cases never happened where bears joined in groups to kill cattle. It is a typical behavior of wolves, not bears."

According to the *Interfax* story, Osadchi said that some of these bears will go right into a barn to attack cows. He states that these attacks are usually made by young bears, about three years old. He speculates that conflicts over food between adults and young animals may be one of the causes of the "pack" behavior of the bears. Osadchi estimates that the bear population in the Tomsk region may be as high as 10,000 bruins. He says the number of bears could increase even more in the next few years due to the huge forest fires that have been occurring nearby. The fires are expected to drive more bears out of the surrounding regions and into the Tomsk region.

According to local authorities, liberalizing the hunting regulations could help to control the burgeoning bruin population but that may not happen because local villagers cannot afford to buy the licenses and tags. "Currently, permission for hunting costs just over $100 and an additional amount more per animal," says Osadchi. "The hunting of bears is very expensive, and therefore unpopular with hunters."

This packing behavior of the bears in remote Russia also occurred in the Olyotorsky region on the Kamchatka Peninsula back in July of 2008. That's when a pack of up to 30 bears surrounded a mining compound and killed and ate two workers. The pack of bears continued to hang around the compound after the attack, looking for more people to eat. Understandably, the workers were so terrified they didn't dare leave their quarters.

Reports coming out of the mining camp said the miners were trapped and so frightened that they refused to go back to work until the bears were dealt with. Government officials in Petropavlovsk ordered a team of snipers to the area to

dispatch the bears after authorizing a special off-season hunt because the regular season was closed at the time.

At about the same time authorities released a statement saying that villagers in nearby Khailino were also afraid to leave their homes after bears were seen rummaging through garbage cans near their homes.

The same kind of thing happened in several villages of the Altai Region in 2010, according to a story Dmitri Sikorski told me a couple of years ago. Sikorski says it got so bad there that local authorities had to issue a curfew in Yailu and Bele, telling residents to be off the streets and in their homes by sunset each night. They warned that anyone who didn't abide by the curfew was at a high risk of being killed and eaten by bears. Both of the villages are located within the Altai Game Reserve, which is where most of the local residents worked. The older residents said they couldn't remember ever seeing so many bears patrolling the towns looking for something— or someone—to eat.

Over 15 brown bears were seen in the two villages within a two-week time span. Local authorities blamed the bruin invasion on a poor berry and pine nut crop. The bears were trying to put on weight for hibernation and were looking for anything they could find. Every night they were breaking into barns, back porches, and garbage cans. One evening they destroyed three chicken houses, killed a milk goat, and a calf.

What made the situation even more dangerous is that the bears were not afraid of the local residents. Several of the residents tried firing warning shots into the air with their shotguns to run the bears off but they still kept coming. The locals wound up having to kill three of most aggressive bears to protect themselves and their livestock, even though killing the bears was forbidden by the law in the reserves.

Members of the regional game department went to the villages to look into the legitimacy of killing bears that present a threat to human lives. While they fussed over whether the local residents had the right to shoot aggressive bears within a nature reserve, the bears were becoming more and more dangerous every day. One bear brazenly walked into the village during the middle of the day and tried to break through the roof of a cattle barn. The farm hands were scared to death. They tried to chase the bear off but it paid no attention to them or their barking dogs. Even firing warning shots into the air and yelling did nothing to dissuade the hungry bear.

Things got so bad in Yaila and Bele that local villagers were finally forced to form a posse to patrol the streets, with orders to shoot and kill any bear that became too aggressive. Besides the two villages, there were also eight remote forest stations located within the sanctuary that were under siege by the bears.

Meanwhile, members of the regional game department were debating amongst themselves on how to handle the situation. They wondered whether maybe they should just feed the bears to keep them away from the villages but some local ecology experts didn't want to start feeding bears as a matter of principle. "The sanctuary is supposed to support Mother Nature's flora and fauna complex in its natural condition, not interfere with the natural processes," a spokesman said. He also added that the present situation, with marauding bears in the region, is not extraordinary. The failure of the berry and pine nut crops or the bears starving is a natural phenomenon, although it usually only happens once in several decades.

One of the most dangerous kinds of bears created by a severe shortage of natural foods is what the locals call a "walker" bear. These are bears that are still hungry in late fall due to the lack of natural foods, so they delay going into hibernation until they can put on enough fat reserves to survive the long Siberian winter. When natural foods are especially scarce, some of these 'walker" bears may not hibernate all winter long. They just keep roaming around looking for something to eat. These bears become especially dangerous when they begin hunting livestock and people because there's nothing else available.

There were so many "walker" bears roaming around on Sakhalin Island during the winter of 2008, looking for livestock and people to eat, that officials dubbed it the Year of the Wild Bear. Local conservation officials said that there were over 200 reported cases of close encounters with bears that winter. Many more close calls went unreported.

A similar situation occurred in the Kurily Isles that same winter where local residents were forced to kill about 40 bears that came into town and got dangerously close to people. One bear was shot in front of the mayor's house!

One of my interpreters told me that this was how they enforce term limits in Siberia! When the mayor's term is up, they send in the bears to eat him! (Sorry, seemed funny at the time!)

Even more bizarre bear behavior was reported in some remote villages of Eastern Siberia recently where bears began raiding cemeteries and hauling dead bodies out of the coffins and eating them. According to the Russian newspaper, *Moskovsky Komsomelets*, two women from Vezhnya Tchova, a small village near the Arctic Circle, were visiting their local cemetery when they came upon a large bear eating a corpse. From a distance it looked like a large man in a fur coat was leaning over the grave of a loved one to pay his respects but when they got closer, they realized it was a bear devouring a corpse!

The shocked women screamed in panic, scaring the bear back into the woods; that's when they discovered the partially-eaten corpse and the dead man's clothes scattered around the scene.

While some bear experts blame this bizarre behavior on a lack of natural foods, others say the bears have plenty of food and they are raiding cemeteries out of laziness, treating the graveyards as big "refrigerators" according to a report in the *Guardian*, a British national newspaper. "In Karelia, one bear learned how to open a coffin," Masha Vorontsova, Director of the International Fund for Animal Welfare

(IFAW), said in an interview with the *Guardian*. "He then taught the others. They are pretty quick learners."

Over the years there have been plenty of bear researchers and biologists who have tried to figure out or explain why bears do what they do. One of them was a guy named Timothy Treadwell, a self-proclaimed researcher who tried living with bears in Alaska's Katmai National Park. Treadwell, a former alcoholic and drug addict, had some strange ideas. He didn't think that bears were inherently dangerous and often tried getting close to them to talk to them . . . and even tried to pet them! He and his girlfriend were killed and partially eaten by a bear back in 2003.

Russia had its own version of Treadwell, Vitaly Nikolayenko, who was also killed and eaten by a bear shortly after Treadwell's death. The 66-year-old Nikolayenko was trying to live with bears on the Kamchatka Peninsula along the Tikhaya River when he was attacked and partially eaten by a bruin. A can of empty pepper spray and the tracks of a medium-sized bear were found next to what was left of his body.

Unlike Treadwell, at least Nikolayenko had a healthy fear of bears. After using a can of pepper spray to defend himself one time, Treadwell said he felt sorry for spraying the bear and he wouldn't ever do it again. This was a decision that may have cost him his life.

Both of these men did, however, prove one thing about bears . . . they are dangerous and unpredictable. Trying to live with them, pet them, talk to them, and give them warm fuzzy names thinking that this will somehow "civilize" them, is not a good idea. Bears are not social creatures with human attributes. They are wild animals and should be left alone.

One person who certainly should have known enough to leave bears alone was a man who lived in the small village of Ozernovsky along the western coast of the Kamchatka Peninsula. Nadya Dolevskaya, a cook and the wife of our head guide, Vacily Dolevskaya, from one of our camps, told me an incredible story about the interaction between this man and a bear in the 1950s. It was a story that actually had me rooting for the bear!

Now 38 years old, Dolevskaya grew up in Ozernovsky and still lives there with her husband and son. Ozernovsky is surrounded by wild, picturesque streams chocked full of salmon and trout. Of course, any time you live near a river full of salmon and trout in Russia, you are going to be living near big, hungry brown bears. And that is exactly the case in Ozernovsky. Many of the residents in this remote village have had close encounters with brown bears.

In the animal kingdom, legend has it that the elephant is endowed with a photographic memory. An elephant never forgets. Well, Dolevskaya would argue that an elephant has nothing over a brown bear in the memory department. The chilling story she told me was about a brown bear that never forgot the man who stole her young, six-month-old cubs.

"I was just a young girl when it happened," says Dolevskaya "The man's first name was Sergey, but I don't remember his last name. But I do remember him as a crazy man who liked to eat bear meat, especially the meat of young bears. He was particularly fond of bears under one year old. He claimed that cub meat was a delicacy. He would go out into the forest and look for young bear cubs. He would run the mother bear off, or kill her if need be, then take the cubs home and eat them.

"One day Sergey came upon a mother bear and her two young cubs. He shot and wounded the mother bear and ran her off. He then killed the two young cubs and took them back to his home in the village where he ate them, as he had done many times before.

"One year later, Sergey was out in the forest again in the same spot looking for something to eat. After a day in the forest, he returned to his home in the village. A few minutes later, people in the village remember seeing a bear enter the town. They were afraid of the bear and fled to their homes. The bear didn't follow them but walked on through the village like it knew where it was going. It walked straight to the home of Sergey, the man who liked to eat young cubs.

"Sergey was working in his garden when the bear came into his yard. The bear attacked and killed him and then went on its way. Later, the people in the village reasoned that the bear had seen the cub-snatcher in the forest and remembered Sergey as the man who took her cubs. She either recognized his face or his scent. Probably both. She then followed Sergey's scent back to the village and right to the man's home. There she attacked and killed him for stealing her cubs.

"None of the villagers were surprised by the attack as they knew that someday the man would be killed by an angry mother bear. They were surprised, however, by the mother bear's great memory. She only attacked and killed the man who had taken her cubs. After she had killed this man, she left the village and did not attack anyone else."

CHAPTER 23

13-YEAR-OLD JUNIOR HIGH STUDENT BAGS RECORD BOOK BEAR

ONE OF THE THINGS I like about my business of taking clients on hunting and fishing trips is watching the excitement on their faces when they bag a nice animal or catch a big fish. I'm just as excited as if I got the critter myself. Many clients have told me that their trip was something that they had dreamed about their entire life, and that I helped make that dream come true. That makes you feel good.

Up until this point, one of the things I was proudest of in my 16 years of taking people on big game hunts to Russia was helping a quadriplegic take a record book brown bear back in 2004. Chris Whitley from Crestview, Florida, was hit by a drunken driver when he was just 17 years old. Relegated to spending the rest of his life in a wheelchair did not dampen his enthusiasm for the great outdoors. He adapted to his disability and continued to pursue his passion for hunting.

When he first called me about doing a brown bear hunt, he told me he was a quadriplegic and wondered if we could help him fulfill his dream of taking a big brown bear, given his limitations. He told me a heartwarming story of a guide who carried him on his back, up the side of a mountain, to shoot a mountain lion. I told him my guides would work just as hard and would figure out a way to help him make his dream come true.

Well they did. I was extremely proud of their efforts. They did such a good job of positioning Whitley along the bank of a salmon stream the bears were traversing that he was even able to pass up several bears before shooting a big brown in the 9-foot class.

And as far as we know, he is the only quadriplegic to ever shoot a big brown bear anywhere in the world!

I've taken many older hunters in their 70s and 80s on these hunts as well. Their last big hurrah, they tell me. And I've also taken a lot of youngsters. These father/son and father/daughter hunts are especially rewarding. Creating a lifetime of memories for a kid and his or her dad is priceless.

While we have had a number of fathers and sons on these hunts, usually the son is in his 20s or older. We even had a 60-year-old son and his 81-year-old father on a hunt! The youngest brown bear hunter to go with us to Russia was 13-year-old Noel Hilty, of Fenton, Michigan. And we took one of the oldest hunters ever, 82-year-old Royce McNeill from Charlotte, North Carolina.

Noel's schoolteacher wanted him to do an independent study on Russia while he was gone for nearly two weeks from class. Earlier, I had suggested to Noel's father, Loren, that his son keep a daily diary on this trip. It's something I had my son, Corey, do when he was 13 and I took him on a fly-in fishing trip to Canada. It's always interesting to see a trip like this through the eyes of a youngster.

Noel did just that. Here are excerpts from Noel's daily journal:

Mom, because I can't send a letter out, I am keeping a journal of everything I did. Thank you and to everyone that made it possible for me to have this experience. Your son, Noel.

1st Day

I am told by the guide that I'm the youngest hunter to book this hunt for brown bear. It gets dark here at 11 P.M., which is later than at home. We had flown here during the past 20 hours from Detroit to Chicago to Frankfurt, Germany and then to Moscow, Russia. Also checked our rifles at customs. We checked into the hotel and on the evening of their Victory Day celebration, we took a walk down the main street of Moscow.

2nd Day

Today another flight took us to Petropavlovsk on the Kamchatka Peninsula on the east side of Russia. A helicopter picked us up and took us to camp. As soon as we got to camp, we asked if we could go hunting and were told yes. Behind the camp, large solid white hares ran from us and we also saw bear tracks within ¼ mile from camp.

About 3 miles behind the camp, the guides spotted 3 bears on a hillside and my dad got a brown bear. Vodka was poured on the bear's head as a sign of respect to the bear and its family. For dinner we had squid salad and pasta with meatballs and pickled garlic greens.

3rd Day

Got up early and headed out. The night before was rainy and softened the snow. Saw one bear but it was small. The early part wasn't bad but by half day we got stuck next to a stream for 1 ½ hours. While following a large bear track, we got stuck two more times and the last time was bad. Tonight my feet swelled and the cook put vodka on them. For dinner we had reindeer, squid, and biscuits with a cabbage center.

4th Day

Got an early start, cold, and conditions were perfect. Bear tracks were every ¼ mile for 15 miles. On a plateau on Andiey (a volcano that's been extinct for millions of years) we came upon my bear. Its size was obvious and I was happy to get it. Also saw a wood grouse, which is on the Red List for extinction. Vodka was poured on my bear's head, same as my dad's.

While heading back to our cabin, we stopped at the guide's trapping cabin and then helped repair a suspension bridge to cross machines on. Harvested bark for tea-making (hard birch sap). Had a late lunch of cold soup containing meat, corn, and garlic. We have two guides, 1 interpreter, 1 cook, and Sergio who lives here 365, 24/7.

5th Day

Rain in morning then turning to sun. The sun was strong and burned our faces. We volunteered to fix bridges today. And the dogs were missing today (Mishka and Tiga). American music and movies are big. One mile from camp, we built a bridge and tore out debris too prevent back up.

6th Day

Day started with rain and heavy winds. Later in the day we were told spring has started. Rivers were starting to swell. We were told that good hunting weather had been given to good people. Helicopter will try to pick us up tomorrow. Some dogs were missing for 2 days. Sergio was really worried because he lost dogs to river ice 2 years ago.

7th Day

Dogs returned overnight. Helicopter won't be able to pick us up because of the fog. Snowmobiles will take us to a utility road. Crossed a river on a cable car. On our way back to Petropavlovsk, we stopped at a small village that their only product is pies (meat, wild berry, potato). The women did not leave their cart unattended. Different shifts kept them open 365, 24/7.

8th Day

We walked downtown and to Abachta Bay where a U.S Coast Guard ship had docked to help celebrate their Victory Day. English is spoken by many and prejudice is so far non-existent. For dinner we had fish soup.

9th Day

Because of fog others in group could not get out of camp. Tomorrow we fly out to Moscow for one day of tourist attractions. Small water and veggies in local diets. *Married With Children* is popular there (popular in U.S. 20 years ago). Found out I got the 2nd biggest bear in group (9 of us total) and only 3 inches shorter. The weather started to clear and we were hoping for them to come (other hunters). Went to dinner in a really nice restaurant. Got a call saying the others in group are coming. (Finally!) Met our interpreter and her son at hotel and went to Avacha Bay (a very great view). Went back to hotel and went to bed.

10th Day

Woke up at 7 A.M. Ate breakfast and proceeded to airport. Will chase sun in flight so after 9- hour flight will land only 1/2 hour after we took off. We almost got younger. Took a taxi to Red Square for sightseeing. Had great dinner at Russia style restaurant with music and great atmosphere.

11th Day

We only flew today. We had breakfast buffet at hotel. (Good food.) I miss my friends and family.

***

So there you have it, the impressions of a 13-year-old on a trip of a lifetime. Noel wrote this journal for a school project to show what it is like in Russia today.

Loren, Noels father, called to tell me that an official scorer for SCI has measured Noel's bear. The skull measured just under 26 inches, which will place it at right around 35th in the world record books. Not too shabby for a 13-year-old kid! The only problem he will have now during the rest of his hunting career . . . is how to top something he did when he was just 13 years old!

Thirteen-year-old Noel Hilty poses with his record book brown bear. Noel is believed to be the youngest American hunter . . . and possible youngest hunter ever . . . to harvest a Russian brown bear. (Loren Hilty photo)

EIGHTY-TWO-YEAR-OLD MAN BAGS BIG BROWN BEAR

Our interpreter Masha and I had just gone back into the cook shack to drink a second cup of coffee when we heard a snowmobile rumbling back into camp. "Somebody must have forgotten something," I said as we got up and walked outside to see what was going on. We had just sent the guys off several minutes earlier after enjoying a hearty, early morning breakfast with them. We watched them load their gear on the sleds, put on their warm hats and jackets, and head down the trail out of camp.

As we stepped outside the cook house we saw 82-year-old Royce McNeill and his guide motor back into camp. "Forget something, Royce?" I shouted over the roar of the noisy snow machine.

"No, I didn't forget anything." McNeill smiled as the guide shut the machine down. "I just shot a bear, about 200 yards from camp! The other guides are skinning it now!"

"What! Are you serious?" I exclaimed. "You shot a bear already? We didn't even hear the shot! Of course it's pretty windy and noisy out today . . . you're not pulling my leg? You shot a bear already?"

"I sure did." McNeill chuckled. "By the way, I have a bone to pick with you, Denny. This is the second hunt I've been on with you and I still haven't even had a chance to be out in the woods more than a couple of hours! What kind of a hunt is this?"

"A pretty darned good one, I'd say!" I laughed as I gave McNeill a big hug. He had become a good friend over the past two years. Actually, my first contact with McNeill happened four years earlier. He had called me to set up a hunt when he was 79 years old. He was all geeked and ready to go, so I was surprised when he didn't show up the airport when we took off for Russia.

When we got to Petropavlovsk, I phoned my wife to see if she had heard anything from McNeill. I knew something bad must have happened. She told me she got a call from his wife to say that McNeill was in the hospital. Apparently on the way to the airport, he had suffered some sort of liver problem and was in pretty bad shape. When we returned from that trip, I called McNeill to see how he was doing. He told me his liver had given out and he was on the transplant list. "But I'm planning on going to Russia with you next spring, Denny," he said in an upbeat voice. "What do we have to do to get ready for next year?"

Over the course of the following year, we talked often and made plans for McNeill's second try for a Russian brown bear. We purchased airline tickets, filled out visa applications, bought bear tags, etc. Then, about a week before the hunt, McNeill called me. "Denny, I have some bad news to tell you," McNeill began. "I won't be able to make the hunt again this spring . . . my wife just passed away. But I'm planning on going next spring!"

"Oh, no! I'm really sorry to hear that, Royce," I said in a state of disbelief. "Don't you worry about this hunt, Royce. I'll get everything I can transferred to next spring."

Wow. Two years in a row McNeill had to cancel due to some serious issues. I was wondering if he would ever make it. He would be 81 by next spring. He had a bad liver and wasn't getting any younger. But we talked a lot and got ready for try number three. This time he made it!

I was really looking forward to meeting McNeill after all the time we had spent on the phone talking and planning. I figured he was a pretty nice guy by how upbeat he was through all this tragedy. He turned out to be an even nicer guy than I could have imagined!

That night at the dinner table, the vodka magically appeared and the toasting began. "Royce has the camp record for the quickest hunt ever," toasted Vasiliy Dolevskiy, head guide at our Kamchatka bear camp. "It took him just 15 minutes and 34 seconds to shoot his bear! He's a master hunter!"

Everyone raised their glasses and saluted the 82-year-old great grandfather from North Carolina. A hunt of this magnitude is quite an accomplishment for any hunter, let alone a hunter of his age. Of course, the 34 seconds was just tacked on to illustrate how quickly McNeill had harvested his big brown. After all, it's not often a big game hunt can be measured in minutes and seconds.

McNeill is one of the oldest, and most successful, hunters we have ever had in Russia during our 16 years of hunting in the Land of the Bear. He is also one of the kindest, most modest, and gentlest human beings I have ever had the pleasure of working with. "Well, Denny, I've hunted bears with you two years in a row now and I still haven't hunted for more than an hour." McNeill chuckled as he referred to the short hunt he experienced last spring as well. "I want to come back again next year and try it again. This time I want to hunt for two hours."

"We'll see what we can do about that." I smiled. "I'll tell the guides to run you around in circles until noon before they take you out to where the bears are!"

Eighty two–year-old Royce McNeill with his record
book brown bear. Royce is believed to be oldest
American hunter to ever harvest a Russian brown bear.
(Denny Geurink photo)

"You know I don't care about the size of the bear, Denny,
or whether I even shoot a bear," responded McNeill. "I just
come on these hunts to be in camp with you and all these
fine people. It's all about the experience; about meeting new
people, eating new foods, and learning new customs. The

older you get, the more you understand it's not about shooing something but about the experience. Shooting something is just a bonus."

Amen, Royce!

McNeill isn't just blowing smoke when he talks like this. He is happy just to be able to still enjoy an exciting big game hunt at his age. While most people his age have either passed on or are living in a rest home, McNeill is still traveling around the world in search of adventure so it's not hard to understand why the experience is all that matters to him. He has come to learn the true meaning of a hunt. Too many people go into a trip like this with binders on, only focusing on shooting something. They miss out on everything that is going on around them.

To tell you the truth, I have noticed over the years that guys like McNeill, who don't really care if they shoot something or not, are always the most successful . . . and shoot the biggest bears! The guy who goes into a hunt all anal, with blinders on, only concerned about shooting the biggest bear in camp, usually has the hardest hunt and winds up with the smallest bear. I think it has something to do with "the bear gods smiling on the people who know that a real hunt is, the experience" as the Eveny people tell me.

"I just hope I can still feed myself when I'm your age," I joked with McNeill, "let alone travel all over the world chasing bears and moose. My hat is off to you. I look forward to sharing another camp with you next spring, my friend."

Author's note: McNeill did come back the following spring and shot the biggest bear of his life, a big bruin that squared over 9 feet and made the record book; but it only took him a half a day to get his bear! So, McNeill wound up taking a total of three Russian brown bears in less than a full day of hunting! God Bless you, Royce! You deserve it!

EPILOGUE

AS A YOUNGSTER GROWING up in rural Michigan I could never have imagined that a big chunk of my life would be defined by what would happen—in of all places—Russia! Whenever I am introduced at a sport show, banquet, or some other function where I am one of the guest speakers, it's always, "Denny was one of the first Americans ever to hunt and fish in Russia." Even when one of my friends introduces me to one of their friends, it's the same; it always comes around to Russia.

Writing this book brought back a lot of memories of my time in the Land of the Bear. I found myself shaking my head a lot as I dug through my old notes. I can't believe I actually hunted with the KGB in the old Soviet Union! I can't believe I hung out with Apollo astronaut, Jim McDivitt, and four-star general and spy plane pilot, Earl O'Loughlin, along the Sea of Okhotsk! I went to the horse races in Moscow with a colonel in the Russian army! I slept in a tent in Siberia surrounded by bears and wolves!

And when I contacted some of my former clients to discuss this project, to make sure I had all my facts in order regarding their expeditions, it would often come down to them shaking their heads as well and saying, "I can't believe I actually went to Russia and did that!"

It's been a wild ride. Witnessing first-hand the transformation of a country from an oppressive, secretive culture to an open, freewheeling society has been fascinating. While a lot has changed in Russia over the past two decades, a lot has remained the same. The biggest changes have occurred in the major cities like Moscow and St Petersburg. They have been transformed from old, run-down islands of decaying civilization to modern, bustling hubs of tourism and culture. The number of restaurants, night clubs, and high-end hotels that have sprung up to meet the demand of foreign visitors is incredible. Here's a country that once closed its doors to the outside world and has now become one of the world's hottest tourist destinations. Where once you couldn't find a restaurant in Moscow, now it seems like there is one on every corner.

When you leave the big cities and get out into the rural areas, the changes are less evident. And when you get out into the really remote areas in Siberia, not much has changed at all. People here are still living in log cabins and scratching out a living from the land. And they're still getting eaten by bears!

There's a lot of ballyhoo in our media about Russia's brand of democracy. To be sure, it is different than ours but it's still in its infancy and is evolving. You have to realize that this is a country that was under the rule of a dictator, czar, or communist boss since its inception. Democracy is as foreign to the Russian people as communism is to us. When they first threw off the yoke of communism, they didn't know how to act. Think of the Russians in the early 90s as teenagers growing up under very strict parents who suddenly turned 21 and were kicked out of the house! It was Katy, bar the door! Like I mentioned earlier, it reminded me of our Wild West in the late 1800s. Nobody knew who was in charge . . . and nobody really cared. They were free!

That's what made our early expeditions so mind blowing. To watch the total rebirth of a country first-hand has been very special to me. While the transformation is still underway, Russia is a whole lot different and a whole lot more stable than it was two decades ago.

Of course, the big attraction for me and the thousand or so clients I have taken with me to Russia during the past two decades is the plethora of wild game animals found in Russia. Besides boasting huge regions of trackless wilderness, the fact that the common, ordinary Russian citizen was not allowed to own a gun under the communist system (they didn't want an armed populace that could overthrow the government . . . which they surely would have!) meant there was very little hunting taking place. This translates into a large, harvestable population of game.

We felt really good about all the money we pumped into the local economy by way of hiring local guides, cooks, interpreters, buying food locally, staying in local hotels, etc., PLUS giving the meat to the villagers, who were starving. There were many years when we pumped over a half a million dollars into the economy!

We are also proud of the fact that we helped reduce poaching and contributed to the sound management of the game populations by making the animals a valuable and renewable resource. Scientists have proven that if managed properly, game animals are an extremely renewable food source just like grain, fruit or vegetable products. We helped demonstrate this.

Like any hunting or fishing trip, the harvesting of game is just the icing on the cake. The experience itself—and the people you enjoy the experience with—are the most important part of the trip. Visiting new places, seeing new sights, meeting new people, eating new food . . . these are all the things that count. And that's what I take away from my many years in the Siberian wilderness. I feel privileged to have been in the right place at the right time on history's timeline.